PEOPLE, STATES, AND WORLD ORDER

PEOPLE, STATES, AND WORLD ORDER

Louis René Beres
Purdue University

 F. E. PEACOCK PUBLISHERS, INC.
401 WEST IRVING PARK RD. / ITASCA, ILLINOIS 60143

For Lisa

"The Very World Rests Upon the Breath of Children."
—*Talmud (Shabbat)*

CREDIT

The author is pleased to acknowledge the help of P. Terrence Hopmann, Director, Quigley Center of International Studies, and Associate Professor, Political Science, University of Minnesota, for suggestions for revisions of the first draft of this manuscript.

Contents

Introduction
THE PLANETARY PREDICAMENT

Planet Earth is in disarray. This is not an entirely new state of affairs. But it is the first time in human history that our fragile network of life support systems could break down irretrievably.

We live in what appears to be the worst of times, an age of death, hate, and brutalization in which the technology of destruction has caught up with our species' most ruinous inclinations. With the transformation of states into military megamachines, humankind has learned to accept the curious logic whereby national security is tied to preparations for nuclear holocaust. As a result, we inhabit a world in which enormously expensive preparations for "overkill" are generally considered effective guarantors of peace.

The world appears to be absurd, a mockery of the human intellect that gave it form and substance.

It appears to be insane, a parody of what might have been.

It appears to be a nightmare in which the ever-widening gap between technical intelligence and reason is now beyond caricature.

It is a world of multiple perils:

- With the continuing spread of nuclear technology, the threat of worldwide nuclear war and nuclear terrorism is growing dramatically.

1

PEOPLE, STATES, AND WORLD ORDER

- The perennial problems of worldwide famine, overpopulation, and inequality are worsening in a system that values military spending more highly than all other human needs combined.
- The specter of uncontrolled international terrorism has been spawned in a world system that remains oblivious to the essential requirements of human rights and global economic reorganization.
- The deterioration of the global environment proceeds unchecked amidst the parallel deterioration of human potentiality. Despite enormous economic possibilities, the number of people unable to attend school, to read or write, to see a doctor, or to have a minimum diet for health continues to increase.

In the absurd theater of modern world politics, these perils point toward an inconceivably mad ending to the drama of planetary life. To reverse the trajectory of our decline, students of international relations and world order must begin to think creatively and systematically about strategies for survival. What this means, in essence, is the combining of an indictment of the present human condition with a satisfactory plan for planetary renewal.

To accomplish this, we must begin to think about the possibilities for a new human community, one that can counteract humankind's growing incapacity for biological and cultural adaptation. We need a reliable ark of revival, a strategy for renaissance that balances the need for regulation and control with the imperatives of autonomy and diversity. Within the boundaries of planetary life and its coming extraterrestrial extensions, survival and dignity must be ensured. We must learn to envision a global habitat that not only arrests the primordial cells of malignant social and political eruptions but that also encourages a new life-affirming ethos. The liberating core of this ethos must be men and women who truly fulfill their own being in the modern world.

THE WORLD ORDER APPROACH TO INTERNATIONAL RELATIONS

The planetary predicament requires a new approach. Such an approach, which I will call *world order*, offers a framework of analysis that is global in orientation and is directed toward the nurturance of such basic values as peace, social justice, economic well-being, and ecological stability. Unlike traditional approaches to international relations, which

2

assume the continuation of war and inequality, the world order approach is founded on the need for transition to an alternative future, one based on nonviolence and justice. Unlike traditional approaches that perpetuate the competitive image of world politics—an image based on cynical assessments of human potentiality and upon Darwinian dynamics of power and domination—the world order approach offers a humane strategy of intervention that challenges the dangerous and exploitative status quo.

As might be expected, the world order approach has yet to replace the dominant orthodoxy of *realpolitik* or power politics. Faced with an uncertain and decentralized world, states continue to act more on the principle of "realism" than on the competing principle of cooperation. In this connection, the following precept of Nicholas J. Spykman, a *realpolitiker* of a previous generation, still directs the customary behavior of states:

> States are always engaged in curbing the force of some other state. The truth of the matter is that states are interested only in a balance which is in their favor. Not an equilibrium, but a generous margin is their objective. There is no real security in being just as strong as a potential enemy; there is security only in being a little stronger. There is no possibility of action if one's strength is fully checked; there is a chance for a positive foreign policy only if there is a margin of force which can be freely used.[1]

It follows, therefore, that

> In a world of international anarchy, foreign policy must aim above all at the improvement or at least the preservation of the relative power position of the state. Power is in the last instance the ability to wage successful war . . . .[2]

This view, that all political life rests in the last instance on power, can be traced at least as far back as Thucydides, who lamented in Book V of *The Peloponnesian War:*

> We both alike know that into the discussion of human affairs the question of justice only enters where the pressure of necessity is equal, and that the powerful exact what they can, and the weak grant what they must.

Such views ignore one overriding fact. *Realpolitik* has never really

3

worked! In a world shaped by nearly six thousand years of organized warfare and other forms of predatory behavior, humankind can hardly take credit for understanding the structures of peace and justice. When this fact is combined with the species' current capacity for nuclear annihilation, the prescriptions of realists appear particularly misconceived.

The time is at hand, therefore, for a new world politics, a system of planetary interaction based upon genuine awareness of the limits of *realpolitik*. Guided by a compassionate struggle for equity and human rights as well as peace, the search for such a system can endow the movement for world order reform with real potency. Recognizing the essential interdependence between domestic and global societies, this search can offer us the last remaining hope for survival.

To define this search for a new world politics, we must first understand the essential aspects and attributes of the world order orientation. Above all else, perhaps, world order represents a transnational perspective on global crisis and transformation from the standpoint of specific values. Moreover, this perspective is prescriptive and policy oriented, not merely descriptive or empirical. To borrow an analogy from medicine, world order involves not only diagnosis but also recommendations for therapy that improve the prognosis. And these recommendations flow from concern for autonomy and dignity of the individual and of peoples, equality and justice in social organization, participation in political and economic decision-making structures, elimination of oppression and coercion in human and international affairs, and harmony among humankind, nature, and technology.[3]

Chart 1 offers a useful summary comparison of traditional and world order approaches to global affairs.[3]

To contend with the global *problematique*, therefore, world order seeks to disenthrall humankind from its self-destructive search for security through power. Challenging the forces that have brought "Spaceship Earth" to the outermost limits of its hazardous journey, world order strives for a system of interdependence that would offer humanitarian global partnerships instead of asymmetrical benefits and burdens. Aware, as we must be, that we are in a time of great transitior to new planetary arrangements, world order directs our attention to th satisfactory conceptualization of alternative world futures.

4

Chart 1

Traditional approaches	*World order approach*
1. Geopolitical focus is the nation-state system.	1. Geopolitical focus is the global community.
2. Problems are seen as discrete issues.	2. Problems are seen as interrelated structural or systemic issues.
3. Analysis is presumed value-free.	3. Analysis is presumed value-oriented.
4. Priority time dimension is the past and present.	4. Priority time dimension is the future, with the past and present as instructive to it.
5. Ultimate analytical objective is description and prediction.	5. Ultimate analytical objective is prediction and prescription.
6. Ultimate operational objective is awareness for problem management.	6. Ultimate operational objective is participation for basic progressive change, with emphasis upon individual involvement.
7. Primary actors are seen as nation-states and governmental elites.	7. Primary actors are seen as ranging from individuals to transnational organizations and supranational institutions.
8. Policy goals are viewed mainly in terms of the maximization of national power and wealth.	8. Policy goals are viewed mainly in terms of the maximization of human well-being and fulfillment.
9. Power is considered primarily with reference to military and economic force.	9. Power is considered primarily with reference to moral suasion and the force of people united in nonviolent action.
10. Large-scale violence is ordinarily deemed an acceptable means to implement policy.	10. Large-scale violence is deemed an unacceptable means to implement policy.
11. Human survival is assumed.	11. Human survival is assumed to be problematic.

SOURCE: This chart is based on Burns H. Weston, "Contending with a Planet in Peril and Change: An Optimal Educational Response," *Alternatives: A Journal of World Policy* V, no. 1 (June 1979): 74-75. Weston based this chart on the work of N. Walbeck and T. Weiss, \ *World Order Framework for Teaching International Politics.*

There are, essentially, two basic paths to such conceptualization: *institutional* and *behavioral*. The first path focuses on improved norms and procedures for global regulation, while the second path emphasizes the transformation of human and state conduct in world affairs. The first path has a long history in the search for a more harmonious configuration of planetary life, either through recommendations for reforming international law within the existing decentralized system of international relations, or through recommendations for the replacement of balance of power world politics with some form of central world government. The second path, which emphasizes the need for alterations of individual and national behavior, has a much shorter history.

With these points in mind, we can now begin the inquiry into the survival of people and states on Planet Earth by exploring the reformist prospects of international law (Chapter 1) and world federal government (Chapter 2). Thereafter, this inquiry may be extended into the new and exciting behavioral realm by considering the reformist potential of human nature (Chapter 3) and of states (Chapter 4). Taken together, the *institutional* (Chapters 1 and 2) and *behavioral* (Chapters 3 and 4) paths to world order reform point to a coherent and compelling array of strategies for a beleaguered planet.

Before turning to these interrelated paths to world order reform, however, I must say a few words about the origins of the *existing* system of global affairs—the system that is the starting point for all considered strategies of improvement. By understanding these origins, by identifying the internal (and perhaps infernal) logic of the system to be transformed, we can better understand the constraints and conditions of future system change. By preparing to answer the question, "Alternative to *what?*" the student of world order reform can begin to make productive use of the "lessons of history."

THE ORIGINS OF MODERN WORLD POLITICS

The death of Aristotle in 322 B.C. marks a convenient watershed in the development of modern world politics. From that date forward there began to emerge the idea of a worldwide humanity that ascribed to all people a common human nature. This was the idea of universality which stemmed from the recognition that the individual, newly awar

6

of a wider political community that had been created by Alexander's extensive empire, was beginning to redefine the lines of authority. (With the invasion of Asia in the spring of 334 B.C., Alexander ushered in the period of world empires.) As a political animal, the individual had begun to relate to a far more comprehensive unit than the city-state, a unit that was soon to circumscribe no less than the whole of the civilized world.

By the Middle Ages, elements of the idea of universality, long since modified by Stoic philosophy and implemented by Rome, had fused with the notion of a *respublica Christiana,* a Christian Commonwealth. Viewed as a unified Christian community, Europe was governed by two divinely appointed authorities, the spiritual and the secular. From this division of earthly authority into two parts, a situation of perfect harmony was cultivated.

The spirit of the Middle Ages also created an extensive hierarchical system extending from lowest to highest, and the earthly division of authority was reunited at the level of God: supreme reality, supreme end, supreme genius. Below that level, the realm of humanity was to be considered as one. Since all the world had been created solely for the purpose of providing the background for the drama of man's salvation, it was to be regarded as a single and unified whole.

This whole universe was tidy, ordered, and neatly arranged. Imagined in childlike and poetic fashion as an immense cathedral, it was so simply conceived that it was represented in its entirety by great painted clocks. At its center lay the earth, the microcosm, at once a mere part of this expanse of creation and yet, at the same time, a single, unified whole unto itself. In the words of Dante:

> . . . . the whole human race is a whole with reference to certain parts, and, with reference to another whole, it is a part. For it is a whole with reference to particular kingdoms and nations, as we have shown; and it is a part with reference to the whole universe, as is manifest without argument.[4]

The idea of an hierarchically ordered world society came to an end after the Thirty Years' War and the Treaty of Westphalia in 1648. Despite the homage paid to the idea of world unity in the Preamble to the Treaty, the Westphalian settlement marks the beginning of a world system in vhich a multiplicity of separate states, all sovereign within their own territory, coexist in a condition of natural liberty or anarchy. While this condition has been tempered by the norms and procedures of international law, it has never been characterized by the presence of global institutions or agencies of world government.

Thus, in May 1618, when a group of Bohemian leaders launched a rebellion against the authority of the Hapsburgs, they initiated a crisis that was to finalize the destruction of the medieval Holy Roman Empire. During the course of the Thirty Years' War, which has traditionally been regarded as the last of the religious wars sparked by the Reformation, the Emperor's power and authority over the many independent German princes and cities was eroded beyond hope for retrieval. But the actual refashioning of world order that followed the cessation of hostilities in 1648 was undertaken not so much on the battlefield as at the conference table. Since the opposing armies had fought each other to an unsteady standstill, the skills of the diplomats were needed to bring order out of the confusion.

The Treaty of Westphalia marked the full emergence of the modern states system, an arrangement for managing world power in which the formal equality of states stands in sharp contrast to actual inequalities of strength. With the shattering of the Holy Roman Empire as a viable political entity, the constituent states now had their own foreign services, their own armies, and their own finances. Instead of the unity of the Christian world, the Peace of Westphalia offered a decentralized international society based upon the interplay of competing states. In this society, conflict was to be managed according to the operation of a balance of power, and the quest for domination or hegemony was to be opposed by threats of deterrence, alliances, and acts of reprisal.

Soon after the Peace of Westphalia, it became unmistakably clear that neither the Spanish nor the Austrian Hapsburgs were going to break down the European state-system and replace it with some haunting new form of the former empire. However, threats to the structure of world order in the second half of the seventeenth century and the first decade of the eighteenth did come from France. While the Treaty of Westphalia had intended to give no state undue preponderance, its enlargement of the dominion of France encouraged a young and ambitious king, Louis XIV (1643-1715), to embark upon a policy of expansion.

The path of Louis' thirst for conquest led finally to a countering of the French threat to the balance of power at Utrecht. In that Dutch city, in

8

1713, the War of the Spanish Succession ended with a typical balance of power settlement. By its terms, no provision was made for the establishment of systemwide institutions of government, and the doctrine of a balance of power was strongly reaffirmed. In the text of the treaty between Great Britain and Spain, one of its foremost objects is stated to be ". . . the establishment of a peace, for Christendom, by a just equilibrium of power."

It should not be a surprise, therefore, that the popularity of alliance remained undimmed after the Treaty of Utrecht. Some of the combinations, however, were quite extraordinary vis-à-vis those that had flourished during the preceding sixty years. Less than six years after the Peace of Utrecht, the Emperor joined with France and Great Britain to oppose Spain, the former ally of France. Alliances, therefore, tended to be fluid, temporary, pragmatic, and non-ideological.

The next major refashioning of world order took place after the defeat of Napoleon at the Congress of Vienna in 1815. There, the principles of a balance of power that had achieved formal recognition at Westphalia and Utrecht were effectively sustained. No iconoclastic reaction to the decentralized character of world politics manifested itself, and no drastic revision of the international system was contemplated. Far from rejecting the idea of separate and competing national units, the Congress of Vienna continued the consecration of equilibrium as the cornerstone of world security. In so doing, it relied heavily upon the formulation of the balance of power offered by Talleyrand as a guiding principle for the Congress:

> It is a combination of the mutual rights and interests of the Powers, by means of which, Europe aims at securing the following objects:
> 1st. That no single Power, nor any union of Powers, shall have the mastery in Europe.
> 2nd. That no single Power, nor union of Powers shall be at liberty to infringe the actual possession and recognized rights of any other Power.
> 3d. That it shall no longer be necessary, in order to maintain the established state of affairs, to live in a state of imminent or actual war, and that the proposed combination shall secure the peace and repose of Europe against the efforts of a disturber, by diminishing his chances of success.[5]

While the resultant Concert System achieved some success in establishing the principle of joint consultation and in normalizing the

9

expectation of collective diplomatic treatment of major international issues, it did not produce a transnational institution politically superior to the system's constituent state units. Not unlike the Concert System, the later Hague System also pointed toward changes within the multistate system rather than a drastic transformation of the system itself.

After World War I, the feeling was widespread that the balance of power had failed as an arrangement for the management of power. Understandably, a cry went up for a "community of power" to replace the "balance of power." The Covenant of the League of Nations became the institutionalized form of this community of power. Nevertheless, the sovereignty-centered idea of consent that had served as the basis of authority in the world system since the Peace of Westphalia in 1648 continued to operate, and the management of power was still an operation to be undertaken by individual states acting alone or in groups. Although the League Secretariat appears to have conceived of the new organization as a move towards a somewhat more centralized distribution of sovereigh authority in the world system, the global sphere had not yet lost its distinctive character.

According to the so-called British theory, the origins of World War I lay only in the breakdown of the European Concert. This being the case, all that was now needed was a regular mechanism suitable for convening a European conference when crisis demanded one. The fact that sovereign authority was still to reside separately and exclusively with state actors in the postwar world system was not regarded as too serious a weakness. Since the good will of state actors was assumed, proponents of this theory were confident that a permanent forum such as the one offered by the League would adequately serve the cause of international security and world peace. According to Richard Rosecrance:

> The cause of World War I, on this reasoning, was misunderstanding. No striking renovation of the international system was, therefore, necessary to prevent conflict. The mere provision of an institutional format for the old international Concert would be sufficient. The British apparently did not believe that others could be malicious; they believed only that they could be misinformed. Effective means of communication, then, would deter war. The League Council was thus to be the permanent Concert.[6]

The League, therefore, did not become a repository of sovereign authoritative prerogatives supported by force, and power in the worl

10

system was still managed by the maintenance of credible deterrence postures, viable alliances, and threatened acts of reciprocity. As Hajo Holborn has put it, "The League of Nations of 1919 was not what its English name said it was, a closely united group of states ready for immediate concerted action. The French name *Societe des Nations* described the nature of the organization more aptly."[7] In short, any hoped-for subordination of the state to the larger world system was not realized. Unlike proponents of the British Theory, those individuals who actively sought a League of Nations that would fundamentally transform the assumptions of the state system were understandably disappointed.

After the total collapse of world peace that arrived in the wake of World War II, diplomats once again resolved to achieve an improved system for managing power. To this end a revised version of the League was established. Like the League, the establishment of the United Nations represented a new effort to manage power through international organization.

Although the effective distribution of force and sovereign authority, and with it the framework of the state system originally bequeathed at the Peace of Westphalia, was left unchanged, in principle at least, the United Nations Charter goes much further than its major predecessor in calling for centralized determination and application of sanctions. While the League procedures regarding the application of enforcement measures were fully decentralized, the Charter has centralized the process for determining whether there exists a threat to the peace or an act of aggression and the process for determining the application of the appropriate enforcement measure. This greater centralization, however, has in no way equipped the United Nations with sanctions as they are understood in domestic law. And while it might be argued that the immunity of the five major powers that comprise the permanent members of the Security Council does not really affect the legal system of the Charter, and that if—at the very worst—all five would be lawbreakers, the system would continue to exist validly for the rest of the international community, such a view would demonstrate a fundamental misperception of international political reality. Says Volfgang Friedmann:

11

Such a view must accept that, in terms of enforceability, there are two international legal orders, one for the five major powers, comprising some 500 million people and an overwhelming proportion of the military and industrial power of the earth, and another for the rest. Politically, the maintenance of peace in such conditions depends not on legal sanctions, but on the balance of power between the major states. This is, in effect, the contemporary position.[8]

Like the League, the United Nations has left the basic contours of the global system unimpaired. Individual states remain in possession of force, and the management of power continues to rest upon foundations of "deadly logic." Most important for our present concern, however, is the fact that, *in principle at least,* there is evidence of an increasing commitment to the sharing of sovereign-authoritative prerogatives with centralized, systemwide institutions, a commitment stemming from the conviction that such sharing is the key to effective power management and a better world order. It is with an understanding of this commitment that we now turn to Chapter 1 and the reformist strategy of international law within the present global setting.

NOTES

1. Nicholas J. Spykman, *America's Strategy in World Politics: The United States and the Balance of Power,* (New York: Harcourt, Brace and Company, 1942), p. 21.
2. Spykman, *America's Stragegy in World Politics,* p. 41.
3. These values are adapted from the "aims and scope" of a prominent new journal in the field of world order studies, *Alternatives: A Journal of World Policy,* published for the Centre For The Study of Developing Societies (India) and The Institute for World Order (United States).
4. See *De Monarchia,* translated by F.C. Church; written in 1310, Book I, Sec. VII; London, 1878, p. 189.
5. From James W. Gerard, *The Peace of Utrecht: A Historical Review of the Great Treaty of 1713-14, And of the Principal Events of the War of the Spanish Succession* (New York and London, 1885), Appendix to Chapter 1, p. 393.
6. Richard N. Rosecrance, *Action and Reaction in World Politics* (Boston: Little, Brown & Co., 1963), p. 182.
7. Hajo Holborn, *The Political Collapse of Europe* (New York: Knopf, 1965), p. 102.
8. Wolfgang Friedmann, "National Sovereignty, International Cooperation, and the Reality of International Law," *The Strategy of World Order,* vol. III (New York: World Law Fund, 1966), p. 512.

CHAPTER 1

World Order Reform Through Institutional Change

INTERNATIONAL LAW

Through the years international law has been widely viewed as a static body of formal rules designed to regulate the conduct of states. From the world order point of view, this concept has been replaced with one that recognizes international law as a dynamic *process* that can be used for the implementation of essential global values among different kinds of global actors. In short, international law is examined from a world order orientation as a strategy for survival on an endangered planet.[1]

Within the decentralized system of world politics that has been with us since the Peace of Westphalia in 1648, international law has always had a distinctive character. Unlike systems of national or municipal law, which exist within political systems that have government, international law exists within an anarchic system of states. This is not to suggest that states coexist in an entirely "Darwinian" situation (i.e., a thoroughly no-holds-barred "struggle for existence"), but merely to say that they exist together without the "cementing" institutions and agents of government. Hence, modern international law has always been regarded as *distinctive,* as *horizontal* rather than *vertical,* as law of *coordination* rather than one of subordination and superordination.

This distinctive quality of international law is expressed along each of the four basic dimensions that characterize any legal order: (1) sources

13

of legal norms, (2) determination of delinquent behavior, (3) determination of sanctions, and (4) application of sanctions.

According to Article 38 of the Statute of the International Court of Justice, international law derives from international conventions or treaties; international custom; the general principles of law recognized by civilized nations; and, subject to the provisions of Article 59 of the Statute, which states that the decision of the Court has no binding force except between parties and in respect of that particular case, judicial decisions and the teachings of the most highly qualified publicists.

The determination of delinquent behavior in national legal systems is centralized in specific officials and institutions, namely police and courts. In the international legal order, however, such determinations are effectively decentralized. That is, they are left up to the individual states.

The determination of what punishment ought to be applied is typically centralized in courts under domestic law. In the international legal order, however, such decisions are essentially left up to individual states.

Finally, the application of sanctions or punishments in national systems is left to courts and penal institutions while in the international legal order it is effectively left to the states themselves. Just as in primitive domestic legal systems, the execution of sanctions is ordinarily undertaken by the offended state or its allies rather than by agents of specially established central institutions.

In redirecting the focus of international law, a world order approach encourages an orientation that is *normative, systemic, futuristic,* and *multidisciplinary.* Taken together, these overlapping and interdependent features define an approach that may significantly enhance the reformist objectives of international law. The following discussion is organized according to these four features and characterizes the basic elements of a world order approach in their present form.

NORMATIVITY

A world order approach to international law is avowedly normative in that it begins with a particular set of preferences or values to be maximized. While individual scholars, of course, disagree about

14

emphasis, major contours of world order inquiry identified in the introduction to this book are widely accepted. According to Richard A. Falk and Saul H. Mendlovitz:

> World order is used here to designate that study of international relations and world affairs that focuses primarily on the questions: how can the likelihood of international violence be reduced significantly? And how can tolerable conditions of worldwide economic welfare, social justice, and ecological stability be created?[2]

Historically, of course, this normative orientation to international law is not entirely without precedent. A great many theorists and publicists have demonstrated concern for avoidance of war,[3] and their recommendations have typically been cast in terms of more centralized distributions of force and sovereign authority in the world system. In short, they have advocated the implementation of more centralized or "vertical" systems of international law as a means of coping with a preeminent source of international danger. In this connection Chapter 2 will describe the many peace plans that have been proposed through the ages, from Pierre Dubois' *The Recovery of the Holy Land* in 1306 to Clark and Sohn's *World Peace Through World Law* in 1966 and Richard Falk's *A Study of Future Worlds* in 1975.

But while a concern for the avoidance of war is not entirely novel in international legal studies, there are still several persuasive reasons why a world order approach is normatively unique. First, a careful analysis of prior peace plans reveals that a great many of them were motivated by narrow political concerns. These were conceived primarily for the accomplishment of some objective other than peace. For example, a look at Georg Podebrad's plan to protect Christianity from the Turks (1464), Pope Leo's proposal for conquest of the Holy Land (1518), Francois de la Noue's *Discours politiques et militaires (Political and Military Discourse* (1587), and *The Grand Design of Henry IV* (1638) reveals peace more as a "by-product" than as an overarching value in its own right.[4]

Second, the concern for avoiding war in earlier writings on international law was not manifest in terms of a general interest in human welfare. There is no hint in these proposals of a genuinely multidimensional concern for human improvement. Matters pertaining to quality of life are clearly regarded as extraneous.

Third, in emphasizing the processive character of international law, a world order approach signals a positive orientation. Drawing upon the idea that views law not merely as an instrument of restraint but as a positive force for directing man to his proper goals (an idea that is derived from Aristotle's conception of the natural development of the state from man's social impulses), world order scholars have resurrected the tradition of law as an affirmative instrument rather than as a purely negative force.

SYSTEMS ANALYSIS

A world order approach to international law is systemic in that the scope of its investigations is coextensive with the dimensions of our endangered earth. Obviously in disagreement with the Leibnizian idea that this is the "best of all possible worlds," world order theorists recognize the global interrelatedness of certain problems that must be solved. It follows that a holistic or world-system perspective is needed, a perspective that disavows ethnocentrism and that is equal to the multitude of crises to which we must respond.

This systemic orientation to international law is not, however, entirely unique to a world order approach. While the particular methods and modes of system theory *are* quite distinctive, the vision of human oneness or cosmopolis played a notable role in the early stages of the development of an international legal order. Ideas of a global society ruled by natural law—ideas which strongly influenced the later development of international law—date back to Greece and Rome. The work of the Spanish cleric Suarez and the Italian jurist Gentili took the singularity of mankind as a starting point and ultimately exerted considerable influence on the writing of Hugo Grotius. Gentili, for example, in *The Law of War* (1598), asserts that "All this universe which you see, in which things divine and human are included, is one, and we are members of a great body. And, in truth, the world is one body."

Grotius's *The Law of War and Peace* (1625) reaffirms that all men are subject to the law of nature, which in turn forms the basis of the *jus gentium* or the law of nations. Having a single basic nature and

16

capacity to reason in common, all men are bound by the claims of international law as well as of natural law. Thus, the idea of human oneness, an intrinsically "systemic" notion, lies at the heart of the developing law of nations.

But while a systemic orientation to international legal studies is not entirely unique to a world order approach, the representatives of this approach are in the forefront of those scholars who depend upon the concept "system" to organize their inquiries. Building upon the foundation work of Kaplan and Katzenbach, McDougal, De Visscher, and John Herz,[5] Richard Falk and Saul Mendlovitz have continually emphasized the importance of systemic context to the efficacy of law in world politics.[6] Presently, for example, international law functions within a system that lacks government. Hence, there exists no hierarchy of institutions and officials to apply rules in a relationship of subordination and superordination.[7] From a world order standpoint, this fact is necessarily the starting point for any assessment of international law today.[8]

At the same time, world order legal theorists have resisted identification with the attitudes of the most cynical brand of realism. While they have understood law to be a relatively dependent explanatory factor in examining the requirements of peace and certain other values, they have not gone on to conclude that law is totally unimportant. And while they seem to imply that the increasing importance and effectiveness of the legal factor would most likely parallel the increasing centralization of global power and authority, this has not led them to disparage this factor in the extant, decentralized world system. Even in a world system that lacks government, it is argued, international law plays a special role in the implementation and sustenance of world order values.

FUTURISM

A world order approach to international law is futuristic in that it directs attention to alternative systems of world legal order. Unlike more traditional approaches to the subject, a world order orientation does not require scholars to tie their inquiries to what exists today or to their historically tutored conceptions of international law. It thereby encourages scholars to range widely, freely, and imaginatively in their studies. It does so, however, without encouraging abandonment of a concern for feasibility.

This developing perspective on international law is as important for theorists who are satisfied with the present pattern of world legal relationships as it is for those who are utterly disenchanted. After all, the character of global relations is constantly in flux (whether we like it or not) and, thus, signifies a parallel change in the contextual background of international law. It is essential to be able to understand the character of such change and to render it subject to purposeful control. A world order approach to international law encourages such an understanding.

Thus, even satisfaction with the current status of world law is not cause for complacency. The present configuration of world politics represents only one of a variety of possible configurations, and world order orientations to international law encourage scholars to explore the implications of system change for a number of basic values. This involves the imaginative conceptualization of alternative world systems that can be examined from the standpoint of international law and the attainment of peace, social justice, economic welfare, and ecological stability.

MULTIDISCIPLINARY FOCUS

A world order approach to international law is multidisciplinary in that it takes into account many insights from a variety of fields, such as economics, psychology, sociology, history, philosophy, and political science. This multidisciplinary orientation derives from the recognition that the various dimensions used to characterize the world legal order as a system include factors that are "borrowed" from a significantly broad range of human studies.

A world order approach to international law is also multidisciplinary because of the particular kinds of values with which it is concerned. In this sense, the multidisciplinary orientation derives from the normative character of the approach. Since the maximization of preferences must be described in broadly political, historical, economic, psychological, sociological, and philosophic terms, these kinds of dependent variables must be considered beyond the bounds of narrowly legal factors. A world order approach broadens the realm of concern of international law to include certain factors previously thought to be extraneous.

Closely related to the two bases of multidisciplinary orientation just mentioned is the futuristic component of the world order approach. Since this sort of approach expresses an explicit concern for *future systems* of world legal order from the *normative* standpoint of maximizing a particular set of values, it must be multidisciplinary. Taken together, the first three characteristic features of a world order approach—normativity, systems analysis, and futurism—yield an indissolubly multidisciplinary compound.

INTERNATIONAL LAW AND WORLD PEACE

According to long-standing international law, war must always be evaluated along two distinct, logically independent dimensions: (1) the reason for fighting, and (2) the means used in the fighting. Medieval writers described this division by distinguishing *jus ad bellum* (justice of war) from *jus in bello* (justice in war). Not until this century, however, did violations of the first dimension become a genuine crime under international law. And this crime is defined not according to the absence of just cause, but rather according to the presence of aggression.

Justice of War

After World War I, there were many charges and countercharges concerning the moral outrage that had occurred within the world legal order. Yet, war still was not considered a crime under international law. Indeed, a fifteen-member Commission on Responsibilities that was charged with investigating violations of the laws of war (the issues surrounding *jus in bello*) reported to the Paris Peace Conference: "A war of aggression may not be considered as an act directly contrary to positive law, or one which can be successfully brought before a tribunal." The criminal provisions of the Versailles Treaty were thus confined to violations of the laws of war and did not concern the issue of the war's legality or illegality.

Although the Commission on Responsibilities seemed to sense the inadequacy of this situation in recommending that "for the future, penal sanctions should be provided for such gross outrages," the Covenant of the League of Nations contained no statement defining aggressive war as criminal. At the same time, however, it did establish a procedure for the international resolution of disputes among its members and for the application of international force against any state that resorted to war in defiance of this procedure. It could be inferred from this development that an offending government was guilty of a crime under international law.

Between the world wars, a major treaty was enacted to abolish war: the International Treaty for the Renunciation of War as an Instrument of National Policy. Commonly known as the Pact of Paris or the Kellogg-Briand Pact (after the French foreign minister and the American secretary of state), the treaty was signed in August 1928 and was eventually accepted by forty-two nations in addition to France and the United States. According to its two substantive articles:

Article 1. The High Contracting Parties solemnly declare . . . that they condemn recourse to war for the solution of international controversies, and renounce it as an instrument of national policy in their relations with one another.

Article 2. The High Contracting Parties agree that the settlement or solution of all disputes or conflicts, of whatever nature or whatever origin they may be, which may arise among them, shall never be sought except by pacific means.

After World War II, the Nuremberg Trials (August 1945 - June 1949) sought to prove that aggressive warfare is a crime under international law and that those responsible for such war may be punished. This was a novel effort, since the act of initiating aggressive warfare—"crimes against peace"—had never before been the basis of a formal charge or proceeding under international law. The tribunal drew its authority from the London Charter of the International Military Tribunal, which was signed on August 8, 1945, and specified as "crimes against peace" the "planning, preparation, initiation, or waging of a war of aggression, or a war in violation of international treaties, agreements, or assurances." Its ultimate judgments, affirming that waging a war of aggression is an international crime, were based as well upon the Hague Agreements of 1899 and 1907, the Versailles Treaty, the Locarno Pacts of 1925, the

Kellogg-Briand Pact of 1928, and a number of Non-Aggression Agreements.

On December 11, 1946, the General Assembly of the United Nations adopted a resolution affirming "the principles of international law recognized by the Charter of the Nuremberg Tribunal and the judgment of the Tribunal." And on November 21, 1947, the General Assembly directed the International Law Commission to undertake a study of the principles in question and to prepare a draft code "of offenses against the peace and security of mankind."[9]

In 1974, the UN General Assembly reached a consensus definition of aggression. This definition serves as a guide that, it is hoped, will ultimately become a binding norm of international law. Although the definition has no independent legal force, it may be considered binding upon the world community as an authoritative interpretation of the Charter of the United Nations, which, as the premier law-making multilateral treaty, is the basic source of modern international law. In this connection, the pertinent elements of the Charter are contained in paragraphs 3 and 4 of Article 2, the provisions of Articles 33 and 37 concerning the peaceful settlement of disputes, and the Article 51 reservation of the right to self-defense.[10]

TEXT OF DRAFT—DEFINITION OF AGGRESSION[11]

The General Assembly,

Basing itself, on the fact that one of the fundamental purposes of the United Nations is to maintain international peace and security and to take effective collective measures for the prevention and removal of threats to the peace, and for the suppression of acts of aggression or other breaches of the peace,

Recalling that the Security Council, in accordance with Article 39 of the Charter of the United Nations, shall determine the existence of any threat to the peace, breach of the peace or act of aggression and shall make recommendations, or decide what measures shall be taken in accordance with Articles 41 and 42, to maintain or restore international peace and security,

Recalling also the duty of States under the Charter to settle their international disputes by peaceful means in order not to endanger international peace, security and justice,

Bearing in mind that nothing in this definition shall be interpreted as in any way affecting the scope of the provisions of the Charter with respect to the functions and powers of the organs of the United Nations,

Considering also that since aggression is the most serious and dangerous form of the illegal use of force, being fraught, in the conditions created by the existence of all types of weapons of mass destruction, with the possible threat of a world conflict and all its catastrophic consequences, aggression should be defined at the present stage,

Reaffirming the duty of States not to used armed force to deprive peoples of their right to self-determination, freedom and independence, or to disrupt territorial integrity,

Reaffirming also that the territory of a State shall not be violated by being the object, even temporarily, of military occupation or of other measures of force taken by another State in contravention of the Charter, and that it shall not be the subject of acquisition by another State resulting from such measures or the threat thereof.

Reaffirming also the provisions of the Declaration on Principles of International Law concerning Friendly Relations and Co-operation among States in accordance with the Charter of the United Nations,

Convinced that the adoption of a definition of aggression ought to have the effect of deterring a potential aggressor, would simplify the determination of acts of aggression and the implementation of measures to suppress them and would also facilitate the protection of the rights and lawful interests of, and the rendering of assistance to, the victim,

Believing that, although the question whether an act of aggression has been committed must be considered in the light of all the circumstances of each particular case, it is, nevertheless, desirable to formulate basic principles as guidance for such determination.

Adopts the following definition:

Article 1

Aggression is the use of armed force by a State against the sovereignty, territorial integrity or political independence of another State or in any other manner inconsistent with the Charter of the United Nations, as set out in this definition. [Explanatory note: In this definition the term *State* (a) is used without prejudice to questions of recognition or to whether a State is a Member of the United Nations, and (b) includes the concept of a "group of States" where appropriate.]

Article 2

The first use of armed force by a State in contravention of the Charter shall constitute *prima facie* evidence of an act of aggression although the Security Council may in conformity with the Charter conclude that a determination that an act of aggression has been committed would not be justified in the light of other relevant circumstances including the fact that the acts concerned or their consequences are not of sufficient gravity.

Article 3

Any of the following acts, regardless of a declaration of war, shall, subject to and in accordance with the provisions of article 2, qualify as an act of aggression:

(a) The invasion or attack by the armed forces of a State of the territory of another State, or any military occupation, however temporary, resulting from such invasion or attack, or any annexation by the use of force of the territory of another State or part thereof;

(b) Bombardment by the armed forces of a State against the territory of another State or the use of any weapons by a State against the territory of another State;

(c) The blockade of the ports or coasts of a State by the armed forces of another State;

(d) An attack by the armed forces of a State on the land, sea or air forces, marine and air fleets of another State;

(e) The use of armed forces of one State, which are within the territory of another State with the agreement of the receiving State, in contravention of the conditions provided for in the agreement or any extension of their presence in such territory beyond the termination of the agreement;

(f) The action of a State in allowing its territory, which it has placed at the disposal of another State, to be used by that other State for perpetrating an act of aggression against a third State;

(g) The sending by or on behalf of a State of armed bands, groups, irregulars or mercenaries, which carry out acts of armed force against another State of such gravity as to amount to the acts listed above, or its substantial involvement therein.

Article 4

The acts enumerated above are not exhaustive and the Security Council may determine that other acts constitute aggression under the provisions of the Charter.

Article 5

No consideration of whatever nature, whether political, economic, military or otherwise, may serve as a justification for aggression.

A war of aggression is a crime against international peace. Aggression gives rise to international responsibility.

No territorial acquisition or special advantage resulting from aggression are or shall be recognized as lawful.

[On the recommendation of its working group, the committee agreed on Apr. 12 to include in its report to the General Assembly the following explanatory notes on articles 3 and 5:

1. With reference to article 3, paragraph (b), the Special Committee agreed that the expression "any weapons" is used without making a distinction between conventional weapons, weapons of mass destruction and any other kind of weapon.

2. With reference to article 5, paragraph 1, the committee had in mind, in particular, the principle contained in the Declaration on Principles of International Law concerning Friendly Relations and Cooperation among States in accordance with the Charter of the United Nations, according to which "No State or group of States has the right to intervene, directly or indirectly, for any reason whatever, in the internal or external affairs of any other State."

3. With reference to article 5, paragraph 2, the words *international responsibility* are used without prejudice to the scope of this term.

4. With reference to article 5, paragraph 3, the committee states that this paragraph should not be construed so as to prejudice the established principles of international law relating to the inadmissibility of territorial acquisition resulting from the threat or use of force.]

Article 6
Nothing in this definition shall be construed as in any way enlarging or diminishing the scope of the Charter, including its provisions concerning cases in which the use of force is lawful.

Article 7
Nothing in this definition, and in particular article 3, could in any way prejudice the right to self-determination, freedom and independence, as derived from the Charter, of peoples forcibly deprived of that right and referred to in the Declaration on Principles of International Law concerning Friendly Relations and Cooperation among States in accordance with the Charter of the United Nations, particularly peoples under colonial and racist regimes or other forms of alien domination; nor the right of these peoples to struggle to that end and to seek and receive support, in accordance with the principles of the Charter and in conformity with the above-mentioned Declaration.

Article 8
In their interpretation and application the above provisions are interrelated and each provision should be construed in the context of the other provisions.

Although the Definition of Aggression was a historic achievement by any standard, a number of major problems continue to exist and cannot be overlooked. Of these, the most important seem to concern the absence of any reference to the *threat* of force, the continuing deference to the protection of sovereignty, the omission of any reference to economic aggression, the implication that first use of force may be legitimate where it is not "in contravention of the Charter," and the placing of the use of force for purposes of "self-determination, freedom, and independence . . ." outside the bounds of prohibited acts.

Equally important, the Definition of Aggression fails to characterize the precise scope of the right of self-defense under the law of the Charter (Article 51). Since the classification of each act involving the use of force is the responsibility of the Security Council (or, under special circumstances, the General Assembly), ultimate judgments concerning aggression are based less on objective fact-finding than upon traditional considerations of power and national interest. Without explicit and unambiguous means to distinguish between aggressor and aggrieved, the broad prohibition against the use of force contained in Article 2(4) is unlikely to withstand self-serving assults from appeals to Article 51.

As in the case of earlier efforts to distinguish between *bellum justum* (the just war) and *bellum injustum* (the unjust war), the latest attempt to regulate recourse to war through international law is flawed by the absence of authoritative decision making by disinterested parties. An even more basic problem, however, lies in the continuing failure of all states in the system to identify their paramount national interests with a strict interpretation of the norms contained in Articles 2(4) and 51. As long as individual states, especially the most powerful, continue to base their evaluations of the use of force on short-term political judgments, the idea of self-defense will continue to shield the practice of aggression.

International Law and Terrorism

The Definition of Aggression also occasions special difficulties in the international legal effort to counter terrorism. Although the exemption from the Definition of the use of force in pursuit of self-determination is, in part, intended to uphold the reasonableness of certain forms of insurgency, it has the same effect as earlier distinctions between just and unjust wars. That is, the exemption offers a legal justification for virtually any act of violence that can be couched in appropriate terminology.

The legal systems embodied in the constitutions of individual states are part of the international legal order and are therefore an interest that all states must defend against attack. In this connection, Hersch Lauterpacht, a highly regarded authority on international law, offers the following rule concerning the scope of state responsibility for preventing private acts of insurgency against foreign states:

> International law imposes upon the state the duty of restraining persons within its territory from engaging in such revolutionary activities against friendly states as amount to organized acts of force in the form of hostile expeditions against the territory of those states. It also obliges the states to repress and discourage activities in which attempts against the life of political opponents are regarded as a proper means of revolutionary action.[12]

Lauterpacht's rule reaffirms the Resolution on the Rights and Duties of Foreign Powers as regards the Established and Recognized Governments in case of Insurrection adopted by the Institute of International Law in 1900. However, his rule still stops short of the prescription offered by the eighteenth-century Swiss scholar Emerich de Vattel. According to Book 2 of Vattel's *The Law of Nations*, states that support insurgency directed at other states become the lawful prey of the world community:

> If there should be found a restless and unprincipled nation, ever ready to do harm to others, to thwart their purposes, and to stir up civil strife among their citizens, there is no doubt that all others would have the right to unite together to subdue such a nation, to discipline it, and even to disable it from doing further harm.

The central problem, of course, is to allow international law sufficient leverage in counterterrorist strategies without placing it in the position of supporting the status quo at any cost. In serving the interests of an improved world order, international law must promote the interests of international stability and peace without impairing the legitimate objectives of international justice. But how can the proper balance be determined? And how can the Security Council, which must discharge its institutional responsibilities on such matters, be guided in distinguishing between legitimate claims of self-determination and illegitimate acts of terror?

26

According to existing international law, the answer would seem to lie in a continuing concern for *discrimination* and *proportionality* in the use of force. Once force is applied without regard to the distinction between combatants and noncombatants, terrorism is apparent. And once force is applied to the fullest possible extent, terrorism is taking place. In the words of the Report of the UN General Assembly's Ad Hoc Committee on International Terrorism in 1973, "Even when the use of force is legally and morally justified, there are some means, as in every form of human conflict, which must not be used; the legitimacy of a cause does not in itself legitimize the use of certain forms of violence, especially against the innocent." These words bring us to the second dimension for evaluating war under international law, the means used in the fighting.

Justice in War

The laws of war of international law that concern *jus in bello* are of ancient origin. They flow from the principle, perhaps as old as the history of organized warfare, that the ravages of war ought to be mitigated as much as possible. While the laws of war remained essentially unwritten (and were therefore part of customary international law) until the middle of the nineteenth century, they began to be systematized and codified during the American Civil War. In 1863, President Lincoln approved the promulgation by the War Department of "Instructions for the Government of Armies of the United States in the Field." These instructions, comprising 159 articles, covered such subjects as "military necessity," "punishment of crimes against the inhabitants of hostile countries," "prisoners of war," and "spies."

During the last quarter of the nineteenth century, there arose in Europe and the United States a tide of sentiment for wider codification of the laws of war. The principal fruits of that sentiment were the series of treaties known today as the Hague and Geneva Conventions, specifically the Hague Conventions of 1899 and 1907 and, later, the Geneva Prisoner of War, Red Cross, and Protection of Civilians Conventions of 1929 and 1949. The four major conventions drafted by the Geneva Diplomatic Conference of 1949 (Treatment of Prisoners of War; Amelioration of the Condition of the Wounded and Sick in Armed Forces in the Field; Amelioration of the Condition of Wounded, Sick, and Shipwrecked Members of Armed Forces at Seas; and Protection of

27

Civilian Persons in Time of War) built largely upon the Nuremberg Principles of 1946. These principles formally became part of the body of the laws of war of international law on December 11, 1946, when the U.N. General Assembly adopted a resolution affirming "the principles of international law recognized by the Charter of the Nuremberg Tribunal and the judgment of the Tribunal." According to the Nuremberg Principles, war crimes include, but are not limited to: "murder, ill-treatment, deportation to slave labor of civilians in occupied territory; murder or ill-treatment of prisoners of war; killing hostages, wanton destruction of cities, towns, or villages; or devastation not justified by military necessity."

In all of these treaties and principles, the laws of war are stated as general norms of conduct, and neither the specific means of enforcement nor the specific penalties for violations are indicated. However, the substance of these norms has been incorporated into the municipal laws of individual states and has been set forth in general orders, manuals of instruction, and other official documents. In the United States, for example, the rules first proposed in 1863 were replaced by a U.S. Army field manual in 1914, which—updated in 1956—are still in force. In this manual, it is made clear that the laws of war are an integral part of the laws of the United States and that they must be enforced against both soldiers and civilians, including enemy personnel, by general courts-martial, military commissions, or other military or international tribunals. The well-known case of Lieutenant William Calley during the Vietnam war was an example of punishment under the Uniform Code of Military Justice for "grave breaches" of the Geneva Conventions of 1949 and the customary norms of the laws of war from which these conventions derive.

It should also be understood that the plea of "superior orders" is not a valid defense against the charge of war crimes. Since the birth of the United States, American law has held that soldiers must obey *lawful* orders but that they must, under almost all circumstances, *disobey* unlawful orders. In 1804, Chief Justice Marshall declared that superior orders will justify a subordinate's conduct only "if not to perform a prohibited act." Similar decisions were handed down in 1809 and 1813.

Although English law rested for a long time on the opposite doctrine of unconditional obedience and absolute nonliability for violations of international law when under superior orders, the War Office took a complete about-face in April 1944:

> The fact that a rule of warfare has been violated in pursuance of an order of the belligerent Government or of an individual belligerent commander does not deprive the act in question of its character as a war crime; . . . members of the armed forces are bound to obey lawful orders only and . . . cannot therefore escape liability if, in obedience to a command, they commit acts which both violate unchallenged rules of warfare and outrage the general sentiment of humanity.

Although this about-face had been foreshadowed in the sixth edition of Oppenheim's *International Law* (1940), it was more directly a self-serving step in preparation for the coming Nuremberg Trials. Ironically, the about-face was tantamount to adoption of German law, which had rejected the plea of superior orders from the very beginning. The Military Penal Code adopted by the Reichstag in 1872 specified that if a penal law was violated through the execution of a superior order, ". . . the obeying subordinate shall be punished as an accomplice (1) if he went beyond the order given to him, or (2) if he knew that the order of the superior concerned an act which aimed at a civil or military crime or offense."

Do the laws of war "work"? Is there any justification for applying the restraints of law to the most patently lawless human institution? Can there be any defensible purpose in stipulating crimes of war for which there exist no centralized means of determination and punishment? From what we know of the erratic and capricious enforcement of the laws of war, are they really worth preserving? An answer is offered by Telford Taylor, U.S. Chief Counsel at Nuremberg and now Professor of Law at Columbia University:

> Violated or ignored as they often are, enough of the rules are observed enough of the time so that mankind is very much better off with them than without them. The rules for the treatment of civilian populations in occupied countries are not as susceptible to technological changes as rules regarding the use of weapons in combat. If it were not regarded as wrong to bomb military hospitals, they would be bombed all of the time instead of some of the time.[13]

Crimes of War[14]

1. Making use of poisoned or otherwise forbidden arms or munitions;

2. Treachery in asking for quarter or simulating sickness or wounds;

3. Maltreatment of corpses;

4. Firing on localities that are undefended and without military significance;

5. Abuse of or firing on a flag of truce;

6. Misuse of the Red Cross or similar emblems;

7. Wearing of civilian clothes by troops to conceal their identity during the commission of combat acts;

8. Improper utilization of privileged (exempt, immune) buildings for military purposes;

9. Poisoning of streams or wells;

10. Pillage;

11. Purposeless destruction;

12. Compelling prisoners of war to engage in prohibited types of labor;

13. Forcing civilians to perform prohibited labor;

14. Violation of surrender terms;

15. Killing or wounding military personnel who have laid down arms, surrendered, or are disabled by wounds or sickness;

16. Assassination, and the hiring of assassins;

17. Ill-treatment of prisoners of war, or of the wounded and sick— including despoiling them of possessions not classifiable as public property;

18. Killing or attacking harmless civilians;

19. Compelling the inhabitants of occupied enemy territory to furnish information about the armed forces of the enemy or his means of defense;

20. Appropriation or destruction of the contents of privileged buildings;

21. Bombardment from the air for the exclusive purpose of terrorizing or attacking civilian populations;

22. Attack on enemy vessels that have indicated their surrender by lowering their flag;

30

23. Attack or seizure of hospitals and all other violations of the Hague Convention for the Adaptation to Maritime Warfare of the Principles of the Geneva Convention;

24. Unjustified destruction of enemy prizes;

25. Use of enemy uniforms during combat and use of the enemy flag during attack by a belligerent vessel;

26. Attack on individuals supplied with safe-conducts, and other violations of special safeguards provided;

27. Breach of parole;

28. Grave breaches of Article 50 of the Geneva Convention for the Amelioration of the Condition of the Wounded and Sick in Armed Forces in the Field of 1949 and Article 51 of the Geneva Convention of 1949 Applicable to Armed Forces at Sea: "wilful killing, torture or inhuman treatment, including biological experiments, wilfully causing great suffering or serious injury to body or health, and extensive destruction and appropriation of property not justified by military necessity and carried out unlawfully and wantonly";

29. Grave breaches of the Geneva Convention Relative to the Treatment of Prisoners of War, of 1949, as listed in Article 130: "wilful killing, torture or inhuman treatment, including biological experiments, wilfully causing great suffering or serious injury to body or health, compelling a prisoner of war to serve in the forces of the hostile Power, or wilfully depriving a prisoner of war of the rights of fair and regular prescribed" in the Convention;

30. Grave breaches of the Fourth Geneva Convention of 1949, as detailed in Article 147: "wilful killing, torture or inhuman treatment, including biological experiments, wilfully causing greater suffering or serious injury to body or health, unlawful deportation or transfer or unlawful confinement of a protected person, compelling a protected person to serve in the forces of a hostile Power, or wilfully depriving a protected person of the rights of fair and regular trial prescribed in the present Convention, taking of hostages and extensive destruction and appropriation of property, not justified by military necessity and carried out unlawfully and wantonly." In addition, conspiracy, direct incitement, and attempts to commit, as well as complicity in the commission of, crimes against the laws of war are punishable.

INTERNATIONAL LAW AND THE PREVENTION OF NUCLEAR WAR

International law serves to prevent nuclear war through a series of bilateral and multilateral agreements, statutes, and safeguards. This series, which constitutes the so-called nonproliferation regime, is highlighted by the Atomic Energy Act of 1954; the Statute of the International Atomic Energy Agency, which came into force in 1957; the Nuclear Test Ban Treaty, which entered into force on October 10, 1963; the Outer Space Treaty, which entered into force on October 10, 1967; the Treaty Prohibiting Nuclear Weapons in Latin America, which entered into force on April 22, 1968; and the Seabeds Arms Control Treaty, which entered into force on May 18, 1972. However, the *most* important element of the nonproliferation regime is still the Treaty on the Non-Proliferation of Nuclear Weapons, which entered into force on March 5, 1970.

The following is a brief discussion of the essential features of the most important treaties.

The Nuclear Test Ban Treaty (1963), also known as the Limited Test Ban Treaty, bans nuclear weapon tests in the atmosphere, in outer space, and under water. Under the terms of the treaty an underground nuclear explosion is also prohibited "if such explosion causes radioactive debris to be present outside the territorial limits of the state under whose jurisdiction or control such explosion is conducted." But underground testing has continued to take place, making it possible for the nuclear weapon parties to the treaty to create new generations of highly destructive weapons.

The Outer Space Treaty (1967) prohibits the placing of nuclear or other weapons of mass destruction in orbit around the earth and stipulates that celestial bodies are to be used only for peaceful purposes. But outer space remains open for ballistic missiles carrying nuclear weapons, and the deployment in outer space of weapons not capable of mass destruction is still unrestricted. In this connection, special note should be taken of threats posed by superpower satellites and antisatellite systems. In the absence of an adequately verifiable ban on antisatellite (ASAT) systems, a space weapons race appears unavoidable.

The Treaty of Tlatelolco (1968) prohibits nuclear weapons in Latin America. It establishes, therefore, the first internationally recognized nuclear weapon-free zone in a populated section of the planet. Regrettably, Argentina and Brazil, the two states in the region with the greatest potential for nuclear weapon status, are still not parties to the agreement. In addition to the agreement among the states of Latin America, there are two additional protocols dealing with matters of concern to non-Latin American states. Under the terms of Protocol I, non-Latin American states must keep their territories within the zone free of nuclear weapons. Under the terms of Protocol II, nuclear powers pledge not to use or threaten to use nuclear weapons against states within the zone.

The Sea-Bed Treaty (1972) prohibits the placement of nuclear weapons on the sea bed beyond a twelve-mile zone. It thus bans nuclear weapons and other weapons of mass destruction from nearly 70 percent of the earth's surface. However, the treaty permits the use of the sea bed for facilities that service free-swimming nuclear weapon systems and offers no obstacle to a nuclear arms race in the whole of the marine environment.

The Nonproliferation Treaty (1970) prohibits the transfer of nuclear weapons by nuclear states and the acquisition of such weapons by nonnuclear weapon states. The latter are subject to international safeguards to prevent diversion of nuclear energy from peaceful uses to the production of nuclear explosive devices. Created with a view to control the destabilizing spread of nuclear weapons, the treaty is currently facing difficulties because of the failure of states possessing nuclear weapons to fulfill their disarmament/arms control obligations and because of the inconsistent policies of those states that supply nuclear materials or technology to other states.

In its broadest outline, the treaty is designed to:

- prevent the spread of nuclear weapons.
- provide assurance, through international safeguards, that the peaceful nuclear activities of states that haven't developed nuclear weapons will not be diverted to making such weapons.
- promote the peaceful uses of nuclear energy through full cooperation.
- express the determination of the parties that the treaty should lead to further progress in comprehensive arms control and nuclear disarmament measures.

Moreover, since the problem of the spread of nuclear weapons is linked to the strategic arms race between the superpowers, the arms control agreements between the Soviet Union and the United States must also be included. Beginning with the Limited Test Ban Treaty of 1963 and continuing through the ABM Treaty and the Interim Agreement on Strategic Offensive Arms in 1972 (SALT I), the superpowers, on June 18, 1979, signed the Treaty Between the United States of America and the Union of Soviet Socialist Republics on the Limitation of Strategic Offensive Arms (SALT II). These agreements, together with a number of others, are intended to ensure the stability of the nuclear relationship between the superpowers and thereby the stability of the nuclear nonproliferation regime as a whole.

Table 1-1
Bilateral Arms Control Agreements between the
United States and the Soviet Union as of February 1978

	Signed	Entered Into Force
"Hot Line" Agreement	6/20/63	6/20/63
Improved "Hot Line" Agreement	9/30/71	9/30/71
Nuclear Accidents Agreements	9/30/71	9/30/71
ABM Treaty	5/26/72	10/3/72
Interim Agreement on Offensive Strategic Arms	5/26/72	10/3/72
Standing Consultative Commission for SALT	12/21/72	12/21/72
Basic Principles of Negotiations on the Further Limitation of Strategic Offensive Arms	6/21/73	6/21/73
Threshold Test Ban Treaty with Protocol	7/3/74	
Protocol to the ABM Treaty	7/3/74	5/24/76
Treaty on the Limitation of Underground Explosions for Peaceful Purposes	5/28/76	
Convention on the Prohibition of Military or Any Other Hostile Use of Environmental Modification Techniques	5/18/77	

SOURCE: Taken from Appendix 1, *Seventeenth Annual Report of the U.S. Arms Control and Disarmament Agency* (Washington D.C.: U.S. Government Printing Office, May 1978), p. 48.

As of late 1980, the outlook for Senate ratification of the SALT II

34

REFORM: INTERNATIONAL LAW

Agreement was very unfavorable. Nevertheless, as the last remaining serious hope for limiting the threat of nuclear war, we may hope that the superpowers will soon begin to reaffirm the mutuality of their strategic interests and the interdependence of their fates. With this in mind, the basic features of the Treaty, which would be in force until the end of 1985, will be considered briefly. The Treaty is comprised of the following parts: Treaty text with its agreed statements and common understandings; the Protocol to the Treaty with its agreed statements and common understandings; the Memorandum of Understanding Regarding the Establishment of a Data Base on the Numbers of Strategic Offensive Arms; the Joint Statement of Principles and Basic Guidelines for Subsequent Negotiations on the Limitation of Strategic Arms; and the Soviet Backfire Statement. The parts are summarized below:

- An equal aggregate limit on the number of strategic nuclear delivery vehicles—ICBM launchers, SLBM launchers, heavy bombers, and air-to-surface ballistic missles (ASBM's) with ranges over 600 km. Initially, this ceiling is 2,400, but it will be lowered to 2,250 by the end of 1981.
- An equal aggregate limit of 1,320 on the total number of MIRV'ed ballistic missile launchers and heavy bombers equipped for launching cruise missiles with ranges over 600 km.
- An equal limit of 1,200 on the total number of MIRV'ed ballistic missile launchers and a limit of 820 on the number of launchers of MIRV'ed ICBM's.
- Ceilings on the throw-weight and launch-weight (i.e., total missile weight) of light and heavy ICBM's.
- A ban on the testing and deployment of new types of ICBM's with one exemption for each side (including a definition of a new type of ICBM based on missile parameters).
- A freeze on the number of RV's on current types of ICBM's, a limit of 10 RV's on the one exempted ICBM for each side, a limit of 14 RV's on SLBM's, and a limit of 10 RV's on ASBM's.
- A limit of 28 on the average number of ALCM's with ranges over 600 km deployed on heavy bombers.
- A ban on the testing and deployment of ALCMs with ranges over 600 km on aircraft other than those counted as heavy bombers.

- A ban on construction of additional fixed ICBM launchers and on any increase in the number of fixed heavy ICBM launchers.
- A ban on heavy mobile ICBM's, heavy SLBM's, and heavy ASBM's.
- A ban on certain types of strategic offensive systems not yet employed by either side, such as ballistic missiles with ranges over 600 km on surface ships.
- An agreement to exchange data on a regular basis on the numbers deployed for weapons systems constrained in the agreement.
- Advance notification of certain ICBM test launches.

The Protocol, which is an integral part of the Treaty, sets forth short-term limitations (until December 31, 1981) on certain systems. Consisting of a preamble and four Articles, the Protocol provides for the following temporary limitations:

- A ban on the flight testing of ICBMs from mobile launchers and on the deployment of Mobile ICBM launchers. Since the MX missile will not be ready for flight testing prior to the expiration of the Protocol, this limitation will not affect the development of an American mobile-based MX missile.
- A ban on the testing and deployment of air-to-surface ballistic missiles (ASBMs).
- A ban on the deployment of ground-launched cruise missiles (GLCMs) and sea-launched cruise missiles (SLCMs) having ranges greater than 600 kilometers.

The Memorandum of Understanding, signed by Ambassadors Earle and Karpov (respectively, chiefs of the United States and Soviet SALT delegations) on June 18, 1979, fulfills paragraph 3 of Article XVII of the Treaty, under which the parties are required to maintain an agreed data base consisting of the numbers of strategic offensive arms of each Party by specific categories. The Memorandum of Understanding establishes this data base and stipulates that the Parties have, for the purposes of the Treaty, agreed on the number of arms in each category for each Party as of November 1, 1978.

The Joint Statement of Principles, also signed on June 18, 1979, sets forth the intent of the Parties concerning subsequent negotiations on strategic arms limitations. In its three-paragraph preamble and four sections, the Joint Statement commits the Parties to continue to negotiate limitations on destabilizing strategic arms; to subject further limitations and reductions of strategic arms to adequate verification by national technical means; to perfect the operation of the Standing Consultative Commission in order to promote assurance of compliance with Treaty obligations; to pursue significant and substantial reductions in the numbers of strategic offensive arms; and to consider other steps to enhance strategic stability, to ensure the equality and equal security of the Parties, and to implement the aforementioned principles and objectives.

The Soviet Backfire Statement stems from the following written statement handed to former President Carter by President Brezhnev on June 16, 1979:

> The Soviet side informs the U.S. side that the Soviet "Tu-22M" airplane, called "Backfire" in the U.S.A., is a medium-range bomber, and that it does not intend to give this airplane the capability of operating at intercontinental distances. In this connection, the Soviet side states that it will not increase the radius of action of this airplane in such a way as to enable it to strike targets on the territory of the U.S.A. Nor does it intend to give it such a capability in any other manner, including by in-flight refueling. At the same time, the Soviet side states that it will not increase the production rate of this airplane as compared to the present rate.

President Brezhnev confirmed that the Soviet Backfire production rate would not exceed 30 per year. Former President Carter stated that the United States would enter into the SALT II Agreement on the basis of the commitments contained in the Brezhnev statement and that it would consider the carrying out of these commitments to be essential treaty obligations.

As indicated, the benefits of a SALT II agreement between the superpowers would extend to the more general goal of nonproliferation. In fact, SALT was initially conceived largely as a necessary incentive to nonnuclear powers to accept the Nuclear Nonproliferation Treaty. According to Article VI of the NPT:

> Each of the Parties to the Treaty undertakes to pursue negotiations in good faith on effective measures relating to cessation of the nuclear arms race at

an early date and to nuclear disarmament, and on a treaty on general and complete disarmament under strict and effective international control.

In the absence of Soviet-American compliance with this element of the NPT, it is difficult to imagine that states not possessing nuclear weapons will continue in their restricted condition. If the superpowers fail to reach a binding SALT II agreement, the resultant spread of nuclear weapons would create new opportunities for a Soviet-American nuclear war. In a world as interdependent as ours, where arms control efforts in one sector have implications for other sectors, a superpower arms race and "horizontal" proliferation are a seamless web. Within this web, the United States and the Soviet Union must learn to set an appropriate example in the worldwide search for denuclearization.

There are, moreover, additional steps that need to be taken to improve the contribution of international law to the avoidance of nuclear war. These steps can be identified in a series of five specific and interrelated proposals.

First, the United States and the Soviet Union must return to the relative sanity of strategies based on "minimum deterrence," i.e., strategies based upon the ability to inflict an unacceptable degree of damage upon the aggressor after absorbing a nuclear first strike. It is widely understood by experts in the field that each side has this ability right now and that each can continue to have such an ability without further deployment of nuclear weapons and with substantial reductions in the existing arsenals.

Since the survival of even the smallest fraction of American or Russian ICBMs, bombers, and submarines could assure the destruction of the other, we now have fantastic levels of "overkill." No conceivable breakthrough in military technology can upset either side's minimum deterrence capability. Even if 90 percent of all American nuclear forces were destroyed by a Soviet first strike, the remaining 10 percent could wipe out the 219 major Soviet cities four times over.

These facts notwithstanding, both the United States and the Soviet Union continue to forge ahead with strategic weapons programs that go beyond the requirements of "assured destruction" or "minimum deterrence." In the United States, these programs feature new mobile missiles known as the MX, which will have the capacity to destroy much of the Soviet ICBM force in a first strike; the Minuteman Mark 12A nuclear warhead, which will equip American Minuteman III missiles with ultraprecise and provocative guidance systems; and the Trident I and cruise missiles, which will also increase American ability to destroy Soviet ICBMs and other hardened targets.

For its part, the Soviet Union, in its continuing "modernization" of strategic forces, has focused great effort on increasing the power, flexibility, accuracy, and survivability of its intercontinental missiles. It has developed a whole new generation of ICBMs and is augmenting these offensive capabilities with an improved air defense system that will provide early warning of missile attack and with an enlarged civil defense network.

Taken together, these programs are expected to provide the ability to fight a nuclear war or—in appropriate military parlance—a "counterforce" capability. Moreover, both countries are hard at work on new technologies for the destruction of incoming missiles. No longer satisfied with simple nuclear deterrence, both are not only "thinking about the unthinkable," but busily preparing for it. As a result, each side now exists in fear that the other will strike first, a fear that naturally provides each with a considerable incentive to strike first itself.

Second, the time is at hand for a banning of all nuclear weapons testing, i.e., a comprehensive test ban (CTB). Notwithstanding the 1963 Partial Test Ban Treaty, the 1974 Treaty on the Limitation of Underground Nuclear Weapon Tests, the 1976 Treaty on Underground Nuclear Explosions for Peaceful Purposes, and the SALT II provisions dealing with flight testing of ICBMs, new types of ballistic missiles, and certain kinds of cruise missiles, only a comprehensive test ban can substantially inhibit further nuclear weapons innovations. To be genuinely promising, CTB would also have to include a moratorium on peaceful nuclear tests because such tests are indistinguishable from nuclear weapons tests.

Presently, both superpowers are on record in favor of a comprehensive test ban. On March 17, 1977, and again on October 4, 1977, former President Carter told the U.N. General Assembly: "The time has come to end all explosions of nuclear devices, no matter what their claimed justification, peaceful or military."

Third, the United States and the Soviet Union must renounce first use of nuclear weapons. Unfortunately, although a no-first-use pledge would be an important first step in the process of "delegitimizing" nuclear weapons, offering even the fulcrum of more ambitious and universal efforts at denuclearization, the United States continues to oppose such a measure. This opposition stems from NATO strategy of deterring Soviet conventional attack with American nuclear weapons.

It is clear, from existing policy, that a no-first-use pledge would be contrary to the most basic elements of American nuclear deterrence strategy. To permit a renunciation of the first-use option, which has its origins at a point when the U.S. had a nuclear monopoly, the United States would have to calculate that the prospective benefits of such renunciation in superpower stability and arms control would outweigh the prospective costs in NATO instability and vulnerability. To allow such a calculation, which would entail redeployment of its theatre nuclear forces away from frontiers and, ultimately, removal of these forces altogether, the U.S. would have to undertake enormous efforts to strengthen its conventional forces. These efforts would be necessary in order to preserve a sufficiently high nuclear threshold.

Fourth, the world's states must seriously seek an effective arrangement for nuclear weapon-free zones. Although the ultimate objectives of such an arrangement would be consistent with former Indian Prime Minister Desai's plea to the U.N. General Assembly's Special Session on Disarmament—that the "whole world should be declared a nuclear-free zone"—a more intermediate objective would be limited to particular regions. The incremental effect of such a strategy might very well be worldwide denuclearization.

As has already been noted, the concept of nuclear weapon-free zones has received international legal expression in the Treaty for the Prohibition of Nuclear Weapons in Latin America (the Treaty of Tlatelolco) and its two protocols. Unlike two earlier treaties that sought to limit the spread of nuclear weapons into areas yet to be contaminated—the Antarctic Treaty of 1961 and the Outer Space Treaty of 1967—the Latin American treaty concerns a populated area. It contains measures to prevent the type of deployment of nuclear weapons that led to the Cuban missile crisis, methods of verification by both the parties themselves and by their own regional organization, and International Atomic Energy Agency (IAEA) safeguards on all nuclear materials and facilities under the jurisdiction of the parties.

40

In the coming years, it would surely be helpful if the Treaty of Tlatelolco were taken seriously by all states in the region, especially Brazil and Argentina, who have yet to sign. In the absence of far-reaching respect for commitments to the Nonproliferation Teaty, nuclear weapon-free zones offer a promising means of reducing the number of opportunities for superpower confrontation and conflict. A majority of states already supports the idea of nuclear weapon-free zones, and proposals for regional programs have been advanced for Scandinavia, the Balkans, the Mediterranean, Africa, South Asia, and the South Pacific.

All in all, from the standpoint of preventing nuclear war, the idea of nuclear-free zones is a good one. By avoiding certain features of the NPT that are objectionable to certain states, such zones could become a promising security alternative for countries that are not parties to the agreement. This does not mean that nuclear-free zones would interfere with the NPT; rather, it means that they could reinforce the Treaty's essential objective of promoting an effective nonproliferation regime. Moreover, by obtaining pledges from the superpowers to abstain from nuclear engagement in stipulated regions of the world, nuclear-free zones could limit the number of possible confrontation sites.

Fifth, international agreements can contribute to the effectiveness of the nonproliferation regime by affecting nuclear export policy. Since access to nuclear weapons technology now depends largely on the policies of a small group of supplier states, such policies constitute a vital element of nonproliferation efforts. In the years ahead, those states that sell nuclear technology and materials will have to improve and coordinate their export policies.

The heart of the problem, of course, is the fact that nuclear exports—while they contribute to the spread of nuclear weapons—are a lucrative market for supplier states. Recognizing the conflict in objectives between nonproliferation and a nuclear export market, the International Atomic Energy Agency, Euratom, and the Treaty on the Nonproliferation of Nuclear Weapons (NPT) impose obligations on nuclear exports concerning the development of nuclear explosives. Article I of the NPT pledges the signatories "not in any way to assist, encourage, or induce any nonnuclear weapon State to manufacture or otherwise acquire nuclear weapons or other nuclear explosive devices." At the same time, Article IV of the NPT ensures that "All parties to the Treaty undertake to facilitate, and have the right to participate in, the fullest possible exchange of equipment, materials, and scientific and technological information for the peaceful uses of nuclear energy."

In the management of nuclear exports, sanctions can also play an important role in affecting the decisions of recipient states. In this connection, the threat of such sanctions is already a part of the U.S. Agreements for Nuclear Cooperation with many countries, the IAEA Statute, and the Foreign Assistance Act as amended by the International Assistance and Arms Export Control Act of 1976. Specific sanctions for noncompliance in these cases include suspension of agreements and the return of transferred materials, curtailment or suspension of assistance provided by the IAEA, suspension from membership in IAEA, and ineligibility for economic, military, or security assistance.[15]

INTERNATIONAL LAW AND HUMAN RIGHTS

Since the advent of the Carter administration, human rights have assumed an increasingly prominent place on the agenda for world order reform. While this development reflects an encouraging departure from the usual primacy of *realpolitik*, it should not be assumed to be a recent innovation as far as international law is concerned. Indeed, since the end of World War II, the protection of human rights has been coequal with the avoidance of war as the dominant objective of international legal reform. In the words of the Preamble to the United Nations Charter and Articles 55 and 56:[16]

Preamble
WE THE PEOPLES OF THE UNITED NATIONS DETERMINED

to save succeeding generations from the scourge of war, which twice in our lifetime has brought untold sorrow to mankind, and

to reaffirm faith in fundamental human rights, in the dignity and worth of the human person, in the equal rights of men and women and of nations large and small . . .

HAVE RESOLVED TO COMBINE OUR EFFORTS TO ACCOMPLISH THESE AIMS . . .:

Article 55
With a view to the creation of conditions of stability and well-being which are necessary for peaceful and friendly relations among nations

based on respect for the principle of equal rights and self-determination of peoples, the United Nations shall promote:

a. high standards of living, full employment, and conditions of economic and social progress and development;

b. solutions of international economic, social, health, and related problems; and international cultural and educational cooperation; and

c. universal respect for, and observance of, human rights and fundamental freedoms for all without distinctions as to race, sex, language, or religion.

Article 56

All Members pledge themselves to take joint and separate action in cooperation with the Organization for the achievement of the purposes set forth in Article 55.

In continuing pursuit of universal respect for, and observance of, human rights and fundamental freedoms for all without distinction as to race, sex, language or religion, the Universal Declaration of Human Rights was adopted by the U.N. General Assembly without a dissenting vote, on December 10, 1948.

UNIVERSAL DECLARATION OF HUMAN RIGHTS
TEXT
Preamble

Whereas recognition of the inherent dignity and of the equal and inalienable rights of all members of the human family is the foundation of freedom, justice and peace in the world,

Whereas disregard and contempt for human rights have resulted in barbarous acts which have outraged the conscience of mankind, and the advent of a world in which human beings shall enjoy freedom of speech and belief and freedom from fear and want has been proclaimed as the highest aspiration of the common people,

Whereas it is essential, if man is not to be compelled to have recourse, as a last resort, to rebellion against tyranny and oppression, that human rights should be protected by the rule of law,

Whereas it is essential to promote the development of friendly relations between nations,

Whereas the peoples of the United Nations have in the Charter reaffirmed their faith in fundamental human rights, in the dignity and worth of the human person and in the equal rights of men and women and have determined to promote social progress and better standards of life in larger freedom,

Whereas Member States have pledged themselves to achieve, in cooperation with the United Nations, the promotion of universal respect for and observance of human rights and fundamental freedoms,

Whereas a common understanding of these rights and freedoms is of the greatest importance for the full realization of this pledge.

Now, Therefore,

THE GENERAL ASSEMBLY

proclaims

This universal declaration of human rights as a common standard of achievement for all peoples and all nations, to the end that every individual and every organ of society, keeping this Declaration constantly in mind, shall strive by teaching and education to promote respect for their rights and freedoms and by progressive measures, national and international, to secure their universal and effective recognition and observance, both among the peoples of Member States themselves and among the peoples of territories under their jurisdiction.

Article 1

All human beings are born free and equal in dignity and rights. They are endowed with reason and conscience and should act towards one another in a spirit of brotherhood.

Article 2

Everyone is entitled to all the rights and freedoms set forth in this Declaration, without distinction of any kind, such as race, colour, sex, language, religion, political or other opinion, national or social origin, property, birth or other status.

Furthermore, no distinction shall be made on the basis of the political, jurisdictional or international status of the country or territory to which a person belongs, whether it be independent, trust, non-self-governing, or under any other limitation of sovereignty.

Article 3

Everyone has the right to life, liberty and security of person.

Article 4

No one shall be held in slavery or servitude; slavery and the slave trade shall be prohibited in all their forms.

Article 5

No one shall be subjected to torture or to cruel, inhuman or degrading treatment or punishment.

Article 6

Everyone has the right to recognition everywhere as a person before the law.

44

Article 7

All are equal before the law and are entitled without any discrimination to equal protection of the law. All are entitled to equal protection against any discrimination in violation of this Declaration and against any incitement to such discrimination.

Article 8

Everyone has the right to an effective remedy by the competent national tribunals for acts violating the fundamental rights granted him by the constitution or by law.

Article 9

No one shall be subjected to arbitrary arrest, detention or exile.

Article 10

Everyone is entitled in full equality to a fair and public hearing by an independent and impartial tribunal, in the determination of his rights and obligations and of any criminal charge against him.

Article 11

1. Everyone charged with a penal offence has the right to be presumed innocent until proved guilty according to law in a public trial at which he has had all the guarantees necessary for his defence.

2. No one shall be held guilty of any penal offence on account of any act or omission which did not constitute a penal offence, under national or international law, at the time when it was committed. Nor shall a heavier penalty be imposed than the one that was applicable at the time the penal offence was committed.

Article 12

No one shall be subjected to arbitrary interference with his privacy, family, home or correspondence, nor to attacks upon his honour and reputation. Everyone has the right to the protection of the law against such interference or attacks.

Article 13

1. Everyone has the right to freedom of movement and residence within the borders of each state.

2. Everyone has the right to leave any country, including his own, and to return to his country.

Article 14

1. Everyone has the right to seek and to enjoy in other countries asylum from persecution.

2. This may not be invoked in the case of prosecutions genuinely arising from non-political crimes or from acts contrary to the purposes and principles of the United Nations.

Article 15

1. Everyone has the right to a nationality.

2. No one shall be arbitrarily deprived of his nationality nor denied the right to change his nationality.

Article 16

1. Men and women of full age, without any limitation due to race, nationality or religion, have the right to marry and to found a family. They are entitled to equal rights as to marriage, during marriage and at its dissolution.

2. Marriage shall be entered into only with the free and full consent of the intending spouses.

3. The family is the natural and fundamental group unit of society and is entitled to protection by society and the State.

Article 17

1. Everyone has the right to own property alone as well as in association with others.

2. No one shall be arbitrarily deprived of his property.

Article 18

Everyone has the right to freedom of thought, conscience and religions; this right includes freedom to change his religion or belief, and freedom, either alone or in community with others and in public or private, to manifest his religion or belief in teaching, practice, worship and observance.

Article 19

Everyone has the right to freedom of opinion and expression; this right includes freedom to hold opinions without interference and to seek, receive and impart information and ideas through any media and regardless of frontiers.

Article 20

1. Everyone has the right to freedom of peaceful assembly and association.

2. No one may be compelled to belong to an association.

Article 21

1. Everyone has the right to take part in the government of his country, directly or through freely chosen representatives.

2. Everyone has the right of equal access to public service in his country.

3. The will of the people shall be the basis of the authority of government; this will shall be expressed in periodic and genuine elections which shall be by universal and equal suffrage and shall be held by secret vote or by equivalent free voting procedures.

Article 22

Everyone, as a member of society, has the right to social security and is entitled to realization, through national effort and international co-operation and in accordance with the organization and resources of each State, of the economic, social and cultural rights indispensable for his dignity and the free development of his personality.

Article 23

1. Everyone has the right to work, to free choice of employment, to just and favourable conditions of work and to protection against unemployment.

2. Everyone, without any discrimination, has the right to equal pay for equal work.

3. Everyone who works has the right to just and favourable remuneration ensuring for himself and his family an existence worthy of human dignity, and supplemented, if necessary, by other means of social protection.

4. Everyone has the right to form and to join trade unions for the protection of his interests.

Article 24

Everyone has the right to rest and leisure, including reasonable limitation of working hours and periodic holidays with pay.

Article 25

1. Everyone has the right to a standard of living adequate for the health and well-being of himself and of his family, including food, clothing, housing and medical care and necessary social services, and the right to security in the event of unemployment, sickness, disability, widowhood, old age or other lack of livelihood in circumstances beyond his control.

2. Motherhood and childhood are entitled to special care and assistance. All children, whether born in or out of wedlock, shall enjoy the same social protection.

Article 26

1. Everyone has the right to education. Education shall be free, at least in the elementary and fundamental stages. Elementary education shall be compulsory. Technical and professional education shall be made generally available and higher education shall be equally accessible to all on the basis of merit.

2. Education shall be directed to the full development of the human personality and to the strengthening of respect for human rights and fundamental freedoms. It shall promote understanding, tolerance and friendship among all nations, racial or religious groups, and shall further the activities of the United Nations for the maintenance of peace.

3. Parents have a prior right to choose the kind of education that shall be given to their children.

Article 27

1. Everyone has the right freely to participate in the cultural life of the community, to enjoy the arts and to share in scientific advancement and its benefits.

2. Everyone has the right to the protection of the moral and material

interests resulting from any scientific, literary or artistic production of which he is the author.

Article 28

Everyone is entitled to a social and international order in which the rights and freedoms set forth in this Declaration can be fully realized.

Article 29

1. Everyone has duties to the community in which alone the free and full development of his personality is possible.

2. In the exercise of his rights and freedoms, everyone shall be subject only to such limitations as are determined by law solely for the purpose of securing due recognition and respect for the rights and freedoms of others and of meeting the just requirements of morality, public order and the general welfare in a democratic society.

3. These rights and freedoms may in no case be exercised contrary to the purposes and principles of the United Nations.

Article 30

Nothing in this Declaration may be interpreted as implying for any State, group or person any right to engage in any activity or to perform any act aimed at the destruction of any of the rights and freedoms set forth herein.

Although the Universal Declaration of Human Rights is not a legally binding instrument per se, its provisions articulate many of the "general principles of law recognized by civilized nations," a proper source of international law under Article 38 of the Statute of the International Court of Justice. Moreover, it serves as an authoritative guide to the interpretation of the U.N. Charter, which—as a multilateral treaty of unique importance—is the premier source of modern international law.

Eighteen years later, in an attempt to further buttress the legal quality of the Declaration, the U.N. General Assembly adopted and opened for signature, ratification, and accession the following international agreements: (1) the International Covenant on Economic, Social and Cultural Rights, (2) the International Covenant on Civil and Political Rights, and (3) the Optional Protocol to the International Covenant on Civil and Political Rights. All of these agreements have gone into effect.

The overarching impetus for an expanded international legal order on human rights came in response to the unparalleled German barbarism of 1933-45. At the close of the war, it became apparent that the concept of sovereignty could no longer include absolute state control over citizens. This idea was expressed by the Charter of the International Tribunal at

Nuremberg, which identified a "new" category of crimes under international law—Crimes Against Humanity. The offenses constituting Crimes Against Humanity include "murder, extermination, enslavement, deportation, and other inhumane acts committed against any civilian population in time of war and before a war." They also include "persecution on political, racial, or religious grounds in execution of or in connection with any crime within the jurisdiction of the Tribunal, whether or not in violation of the domestic law of the country where perpetrated."

On December 11, 1946, the U.N. General Assembly, in its resolution "reaffirming the principles of international law" recognized by the Charter of the Nuremberg Tribunal and the judgment of the Tribunal, removed any doubts about the status of Crimes Against Humanity as crimes under international law. Moreover, on December 13, 1946, the General Assembly unanimously adopted a resolution condemning genocide as a particular kind of crime against humanity committed with intent to destroy, in whole or in part, a national, ethnic, racial, or religious group. These efforts reached their fullest expression on December 9, 1948, when the General Assembly adopted a Convention on the Prevention and Punishment of the Crime of Genocide. This Genocide Convention came into force on January 12, 1950. The United States has still not ratified the Convention, allegedly because it requires compulsory adjudication by the International Court of Justice.

These examples of the growing international law of human rights signal a major expansion in the world order responsibilities of international law. While it would be considerably naive to expect such principles to have any effect independent of the self-interested behavior of states, it is no longer contrary to the law of nations that a state shall intervene in the territorial sphere of validity of another state to uphold basic standards of human rights. Under earlier customary international law, no rule was more widely recognized than that a state's treatment of its own nationals is a matter entirely within the domestic jurisdiction of that state.[17]

Today's international legal order on human rights also rests upon a number of regional foundations. The European Convention for the Protection of Human Rights and Fundamental Freedoms went into force in 1953. In this connection, a European Commission on Human

Rights has been empowered to receive and investigate complaints. In 1969 in Latin America an American Convention on Human Rights grew out of the Inter-American Specialized Conference on Human Rights. As in the European case, the convention provides a Commission on Human Rights.

The United Nations Commission on Human Rights was established in 1946 to carry out studies and to draft treaties concerning human rights provisions of the Charter. To date, however, the Commission has made little use of its limited powers. Regrettably, Article 2(7) of the Charter, which denies authority to the United Nations "to intervene in matters which are essentially within the domestic jurisdiction of any state . . .," still mitigates against effective implementation of the international legal order on human rights.

Relations between East and West have also been affected by the developing international law of human rights. In this connection, the Final Act of the Conference on Security and Cooperation in Europe (CSCE), the so-called Helsinki Agreement of 1975, is most significant. Although attempts by dissidents in the Soviet Union and Eastern Europe to urge their governments to comply with the Helsinki Agreement have often produced unsatisfactory outcomes, and although the successor conference in Belgrade in 1977 was essentially a failure, there have been some noteworthy improvements. In the Soviet Union, for example, the very fact that dissenters and human rights groups have been formed to monitor implementation of the Helsinki Agreement reflects fundamental changes in Soviet society.

At the same time, the Soviet Union continues to maintain that the CSCE provisions against intervention in the internal affairs of states normally take precedence over the provisions on human rights. While Principle Seven of the Final Act calls for the participating states to "respect human rights and fundamental freedoms, including the freedom of thought, conscience, religion or belief, for all without distinction as to race, sex, language, or religion," Principle Six calls for nonintervention in internal affairs. According to Principle Six: "The participating States will refrain from any intervention, direct or indirect, individual or collective, in the internal or external affairs falling within the domestic jurisdiction of another participating State, regardless of their mutual relations." It follows that before international law can offer a fuller contribution to human rights, the divergence of East-West viewpoints on CSCE principles will have to be narrowed in favor of Principle Seven.

In this connection, the Soviet position on the Helsinki Agreement stands in ironic contrast to the Brezhnev Doctrine. The Doctrine subordinates the prerogatives of sovereignty and territorial independence to the requirements of socialist revolution and affirms the right of the Soviet Union to intervene in the affairs of Communist countries when it deems these requirements to be endangered. As defined in an article in *Pravda* in September 1968, "The sovereignty of each Socialist country cannot be opposed to the interests of the world of Socialism, of the world revolutionary movement." It is, of course, the Soviet Union which determines when such opposition appears. And it is the Soviet Union that decides which countries are sufficiently within the Communist camp to warrant "protective intervention" along the lines of the move into Afghanistan in late 1979.

In the United States, former President Carter underscored the importance of U.S. domestic CSCE implementation efforts by issuing a memorandum on December 6, 1978, to key government departments and agencies whose activities are affected by the Helsinki Agreement. Moreover, U.S. efforts to strengthen U.N. mechanisms that deal with human rights issues include making the Commission on Human Rights more effective and creating a new organ centered on a High Commissioner for Human Rights. Yet the credibility of the American commitment to human rights continues to be impaired by the failure of the U.S. Senate to ratify key U.N. human rights conventions. Despite urging by former President Carter, the Senate has yet to ratify the International Convention on the Elimination of All Forms of Racial Discrimination; the International Covenant on Economic, Social, and Cultural Rights; the International Covenant on Civil and Political Rights; the American Convention on Human Rights; and the Convention on the Prevention and Punishment of the Crime of Genocide.

At the same time, the United States has taken a potentially productive approach to the international law of human rights by tying its foreign assistance policy to human rights practices. In accordance with the terms of the Foreign Assistance Act of 1961, as amended, the Department of State prepares an annual country-by-country Report on

Human Rights Practices. Submitted to the House Committee on Foreign Affairs and the Senate Committee on Foreign Relations, this report is designed to strengthen global support of human rights through a unilateral American policy of sanctions. To the extent that such a policy reflects genuine understanding of the requirements of the international law of human rights in a decentralized legal order, it provides a suitable model for worldwide imitation.

Nevertheless, American interests in human rights and national security do not always harmonize, and certain countries whose human rights practices are censured are still beneficiaries of this country's foreign assistance program. While it would be naive to argue that security concerns must never take precedence over the pursuit of human rights, it must also be understood that, over the longer term, American support of human rights would be a markedly realistic policy. Indeed, there is a fundamental compatibility between American support for human rights and American national security. In the words of former Secretary of State Cyrus Vance before the Senate Committee on Foreign Relations on March 27, 1980, ". . . we pursue our human rights objectives, not only because they are right but because we have a stake in the stability that comes when people can express their hopes and find their futures freely. Our ideals and our interests coincide."

In the final analysis, it is clear that international law has become an increasingly important part of the ongoing struggle for human rights and world order reform, but that much still remains to be done. Although the appropriate norms have now been explicitly stipulated and codified through numerous treaties, charters, conventions, covenants, declarations, judicial decisions, and final acts, their effective implementation is still inhibited by political cleavages and highly subjective and self-serving patterns of interpretation. Most governments continue to cling stubbornly to the full prerogatives of unlimited sovereignty, reluctant to extend the status of the subject of international law to individual persons. No state is on record in favor of allowing every citizen of this endangered planet access to international courts for claims concerning human rights.

STRATEGIES FOR WORLD ORDER

Even if the norms of the international legal order on human rights

52

become incorporated into the municipal legal systems of the global community, their world order objective may not be assured. After all, the widespread incorporation of the laws of war of international law has been only modestly paralleled by acts of national compliance. For international law to become genuinely productive of human rights, the extant forms of competitive international relations will have to be replaced by a new world politics of cooperation and interdependence. We require a new world order regime, a planetary network of obligations stressing global interests over adversary relationships. The centerpiece of this new world order must be the cosmopolitan understanding that all states and all peoples form one essential body and one true community.

The task, then, is to make the separate states conscious of their vital planetary identity. With such a redefinition of national interests, states can progress from the dying forms of *realpolitik* to the primordial power of unity and interdependence. Since all things contain their own contradiction, the international legal order based upon competitive nationalism can be transformed into an organic world society.

But how can such a society come into being? How, exactly, can a system based on competition and conflict be transformed into a cooperative world order regime? What particular transition strategies need to be adopted?

Richard A. Falk has described a series of overlapping and interlinked stages to meet the challenge of transition.[18]

Stage I: Consensus Formation

According to Falk the first stage in the transition is the shaping of "a new political consciousness by building widespread public acceptance of world order values and spreading enthusiasm for constructive prospects of global reform."[19] This suggests that before any substantial progress can be made in global institutions, humankind must face up to the full urgency of planetary crisis. Fear and reality go hand in hand. Until general publics throughout the world develop a far-reaching awareness of the "endangered planet" hypothesis, the prospects for global system transformation must remain severely limited.

Stage II: Transnational Mobilization

53

Once there is worldwide consensus, groups must be mobilized "to act in concerted fashion on behalf of world order values."[20] To encourage transnational awareness it may be necessary to bypass the clogged conduits of national power in favor of a worldwide political movement. Such a movement would reject the cynicism of "triage" and "lifeboat ethics" now in fashion and would strive for effective positions of political power. Perhaps, as Falk suggests, a world party must be formed to advocate a suitably transformed world. Or perhaps labor unions, trade associations, and religious institutions must establish transnational pressure groups to promote world order values.[21] In any event, a new coalition would be needed and—as Rajni Kothari, a distinguished Indian scholar, suggests—this coalition would need to comprise hitherto submerged political and economic interests. According to Professor Kothari:

> The real danger to the world arises less from diffusion of power, at which Western strategists seem to be worried, than from its immense concentration . . . . As the diffusion spreads along economic, technological and social dimensions, and finds its moorings in a widely shared set of values, it should pave the way for greater confidence at all levels and, on that basis, a greater and more genuine sense of common destiny.[22]

Stage III: Global Transformation

In this stage, the global system would experience "the effective transfer of the new consensus into prevailing modes of conduct and organization."[23] While Falk feels that the resultant institutional arrangements would most likely be formed along functional lines (i.e., lines directed toward specific problem areas such as disarmament, environmental protection, ocean resources, etc.), they could be formed differently. There are many ways of identifying alternative systems of world politics (see Chapter 4).

Central to the success of any such multistage strategy of transition is an appropriate system of global education. To respond to the requirements of an improved world legal order, civic education everywhere must be: "(1) global and holistic in perspective, (2) structural in analysis, (3) informed by humanistic values, (4) geared especially to the future, and

(5) committed unambiguously to participation in, and for, fundamental progressive change."[24] Moreover, these guidelines must be understood within a specific methodology that fosters the systematic examination of alternative hypotheses about world order. Above all else, perhaps, students of international relations must be prepared to stipulate imaginative connections between world order values and those factors that are presumed to be value-maximizing. In so doing, they can fulfill the most basic requirements of the challenge of transition.

INTERNATIONAL LAW AND OTHER WORLD ORDER VALUES

If international law is to be a really meaningful strategy for survival on this endangered planet, it must promote not only peace, justice, and human rights, but also economic welfare and ecological stability. Recognizing this imperative, the United Nations sponsored during the 1970s a series of major conferences concerning myriad human needs. It is widely hoped that these conferences will prove to have been the starting point for an expanded system of international legal norms that reflects a truly comprehensive world order regime.

During the decade of the seventies, there were the following U.N. conferences: Conference on the Human Environment, Stockholm, 1972; Conference on Population Policy, Bucharest, 1974; Conference on Food Policy, Rome, 1974; Conference on the Law of the Sea, Caracas, Geneva, New York, 1974-75; General Assembly Special Sessions on Raw Materials and Economic Development, New York, 1974-75; and the Women's Year World Conference, Mexico City, 1975. These major efforts have produced the establishment of a World Environmental Secretariat, the creation of a World Food Council, and a Charter of Economic Rights and Duties of States. However, a great deal remains to be done for international law to embrace a world order focus.

International law must be structured to meet the challenges of inequality and interdependence. In the light of a deepening division between the rich nations and the poor nations, it must be used to create and support norms that supplant self-centered national efforts with coordinated, global actions. Confronted with severe recession and inflation on a worldwide scale, it must be a guide for the pricing decisions of essential commodities, most notably petroleum, with a view to equitable sharing of both benefits and burdens. In spite of divergent and competitive strategies in pursuit of economic growth, it must be relied upon to harmonize the interests of separate states in a manner that is collectively rational.

International law must be based on the understanding that world order objectives are inextricably interrelated. Industrial states have known for a long time that economic development and profits are often at odds with health and well-being. Population control is often regarded by citizens of the poorer half of the world as a means by which the richer half can "keep them down." The enforcement of international standards to preserve the integrity of the global environment is often seen by the developing world as a basic threat to its rapid industrialization and economic survival. The militarization of the world economy occasions the governments of the developing countries to devote as much public revenue to military programs as to education and health care combined. In a world of extraordinary economic and social potential, the number of people whose circumstances do not meet the most minimum standards of existence is large and continually growing larger.

Even the superpowers, while first in military strength, are not spared the ravages of a world GNP that fails to keep pace with the needs of a rising population. With investment in capital and human resources lagging, the United States and Soviet Union now rank lower than many other states in terms of certain leading indicators of social well-being. For example, in a ranking of 140 nations in terms of certain military and social indicators by the distinguished economist, Ruth Leger Sivard, the United States and the Soviet Union received respective rankings of sixth and twentieth for economic-social standing. This indicator is defined as an average of ranks for GNP per capita, education, and health. The United States stands high in education, reasonably high in per capita income, but relatively low in health indicators. The Soviet Union offers a mediocre showing in all three, but especially the economic, elements of the ranking system.[25]

The following are some specific indicators. The United States ranks sixteenth in public expenditures per capita for health, thirty-first in population per hospital bed, seventeenth in infant mortality rate (deaths under one year per 1,000 live births), seventh in life expectancy (expectation of life at birth), and eighth in percent of population with safe water. For the first four of these same indicators, the Soviet Union ranks twenty-eighth, seventh, thirty-fourth, and twenty-ninth, respectively. There is no available data on safe water in the Soviet Union.[26]

To a significant extent, superpower deficiencies in economic-social standing are a direct result of high-level military expenditures. Contrary to the conventional wisdom that such spending is a boon to the economy, stimulating investment and producing jobs, its overall effect is to retard economic-social well-being through inflation, diversion of investment, diversion of scarce materials, and misuse of human capital. For the superpowers to improve their standings along the critical dimensions of human need fulfillment, their military expenditures will need to give way to such competing priorities as education and health care.

The same "message" holds true for all other states in world politics. An exceptionally rapid rise in military expenditures in the developing world has been a major trend in recent years. Since 1960, such expenditures of developing states have risen four-fold, while those in developed states have risen a more modest 44 percent.[27]

Since 1960, the world has spent more than $4 trillion on military programs. At today's prices, this outlay would be valued at almost $7 trillion. For the developing world's three billion people this sum exceeds the value of the product of three years' labor.[29]

On a global basis, society now invests $16,000 a year per soldier but $260 a year in the education of a school-age child. Developing nations carry three times as much insurance against military attack as against all the health problems that strike people on a regular basis.

On a global basis, the support of national military forces costs $92 a year per person; support of the United Nations and all its programs in food, health, labor, etc. costs 57¢ a year, while international peace-keeping operations cost 5¢ a year.[29]

What these points suggest, of course, is a compelling need for a new international legal order of security, equity, economic welfare, and ecological stability. A profound expansion of world legal norms and procedures is in order. To accomplish such an expansion, the states of the world will have to give meaningful content to their rhetorical expressions of commitment to global community and human survival.

NOTES

1. In terms of its modern intellectual history, world order perspectives on international law derive from the work of Harold Lasswell and Myres McDougal at the Yale Law School, Grenville Clark and Louis Sohn's *World Peace Through World Law*, (Cambridge, Harvard University Press, 1966) and the large body of writings by Richard A. Falk of Princeton University and Saul H. Mendlovitz of Rutgers University. Some specific works are as follows: McDougal and Associates, *Studies in World Public Order* (New Haven, Yale University Press, 1960); McDougal and Florentino P. Feliciano, *Law and Minimum World Public Order* (New Haven, Yale University Press, 1962); Clark and Sohn, *World Peace through World Law* (Cambridge, Harvard University Press, 1966); and Falk and Mendlovitz, eds., *The Strategy of World Order*, four volumes (New York, World Law Fund, 1966), especially Volume 2, *International Law*. Today, the most ambitious expression of a world order approach is the Institute for World Order's (formerly World Law Fund) World Order Models Project, a transnational effort of scholars underway since 1967. Notwithstanding its law-related origins, world order seems to have become more widely adopted by scholars of general international relations than by international law specialists. This is reflected by the fact that virtually all developing world order studies programs are located in academic departments other than law schools and by the fact that their directors and faculty are not typically professors of international law.

2. Richard A. Falk and Saul H. Mendlovitz, eds., *Regional Politics and World Order* (San Francisco, W.H. Freeman, 1973), p. 6.

3. Some theorists, however, have approached the war problem from the standpoint of *mitigation* rather than avoidance. For example, in the third book of his masterwork, *The Law of War and Peace* (1625), Grotius articulates certain *temperamenta* designed to make war more humane. This idea—that the dictates of international law can be used to "humanize" warfare—is heartily ridiculed by Voltaire in his classic tale, *Candide*.

4. Some exceptions are: Emeric Crucé's *New Cyneas* (1623); William Penn's *Essay Towards the Present and Future Peace of Europe by the Establishment of an European Diet, Parliament, or Estates* (1693); John Bellers' *Some Reasons for a European State* (1710); Rousseau's *A Lasting Peace Through the Federation of Europe* (1761); and Immanuel Kant's *Perpetual Peace* (1795). In our own century we may note H.G. Wells' *The Common Sense of World Peace* (1929); Clarence Streit's *Union Now* (1949); and Emery Reves' *Anatomy of Peace* (1945). All of these works *do* reflect a primary commitment to peace.

5. See Morton A. Kaplan and Nicholas deB. Katzenbach, *The Political Foundations of International Law* (New York, Wiley, 1961); Myres S. McDougal and Associates, *Studies in World Public Order* (New Haven, Yale University Press, 1960); Charles De Visscher, *Theory and Reality in Public International*

Law (Princeton, Princeton University Press, 1957); and John H. Herz, *International Politics in the Atomic Age* (New York, Columbia University Press, 1959).

6. See for example Falk's comment that "law is an integral aspect of a functioning social system. It is not an autonomous force able to overlook the dominant expectations that guide action in the relevant community" *(Legal Order in a Violent World* (Princeton, Princeton University Press, 1968), p. 39. This same idea is articulated by Falk in "The Relevance of Political Context to the Nature and Functioning of International Law: An Intermediate View," Karl Deutsch and Stanley Hoffmann, eds., *The Relevance of International Law* (New York, Anchor, 1971), pp. 177-202. See also the Falk and Hanrieder introduction to their co-edited work, *International Law and Organization* (New York, Lippincott, 1968).

7. It is characteristic of world order orientations that international law can be studied as a property of systems that are anarchic as well as of systems that maintain a hierarchy of relationships for subordination and superordination. Although this signifies a *broad* realm of concern, breadth of conception is not unique to a world order approach. Indeed, Grotius adopted a broad understanding of international law in *The Law of War and Peace* in 1625, and even J.L. Brierly defines the subject "as the body of rules and principles of action which are binding upon civilized states in their relations with one another" *(The Law of Nations,* Sixth Edition, New York, Oxford University Press, 1963, p. 1).

8. While use of the term *system* is new, the idea of emphasizing the contextual background of world law is not. In most traditional writings, this background is cast in the language of an "international society." Brierly, for example, states that "the character of the law of nations is necessarily determined by that of the society within which it operates . . ."*(The Law of Nations, op. cit.,* p. 41).

9. Article 13 of the U.N. Charter instructs the General Assembly to "initiate studies and make recommendations for the purpose of . . . encouraging the progressive development of international law and its codification." Acting under this Article, the General Assembly created the International Law Commission as its principal subsidiary organ to assist in this task.

10. According to Article 2(3): "All Members shall settle their international disputes by peaceful means in such a manner that international peace and security, and justice, are not endangered."

According to Article 2(4): "All Members shall refrain in their international relations from the threat or use of force against the territorial integrity or political independence of any state, or in any other manner inconsistent with the Purposes of the United Nations."

According to Article 33: "(1) The parties to any dispute, the continuance of which is likely to endanger the maintenance of international peace and security, shall, first of all, seek a solution by negotiation, enquiry, mediation, conciliation, arbitration, judicial settlement, resort to regional agencies or arrangements, or other peaceful means of their own choice. (2) The Security Council shall, when it deems necessary, call upon the parties to settle their dispute by such means."

According to Article 37: "(1) Should the parties to a dispute of the nature referred to in Article 33 fail to settle it by the means indicated in that Article, they shall refer it to the Security Council. (2) If the Security Council deems that the continuance of the dispute is in fact likely to endanger the maintenance of international peace and security, it shall decide whether to take action under Article 36 or recommend such terms of settlement as it may consider appropriate."

According to Article 51: "Nothing in the present Charter shall impair the inherent right of individual or collective self-defence if an armed attack occurs against a Member of the United Nations, until the Security Council has taken measures necessary to maintain international peace and security. Measures taken by Members in the exercise of this right of self-defence shall be immediately reported to the Security Council and shall not in any way affect the authority and responsibility of the Security Council under the present Charter to take at any time such action as it deems necessary in order to maintain or restore international peace and security."

11. From *Department of State Bulletin* 70 (May 6, 1974), pp. 501-502.

12. See Hersch Lauterpacht, *International Law*, vol. 3, *The Law of Peace*, parts 2-6, (Cambridge, Cambridge University Press, 1977), p. 274.

13. Telford Taylor, *Nuremberg and Vietnam: An American Tragedy* (New York, Bantam Books, 1970), p. 40.

14. Gerhard von Glahn, *Law Among Nations* 3rd edition (New York, Macmillan, 1976), pp. 693-695.

15. See Lewis A. Dunn, "The Role of Sanctions in Non-Proliferation Strategy," Final Report of the Hudson Institute, prepared for the Office of Technology Assessment, U.S. Congress, February 2, 1977, pp. 1-2.

16. Human Rights are also mentioned in Articles 1, 13, 62, 68, and 76.

17. See J.L. Brierly, *The Law of Nations*, 6th edition, New York and Oxford, Oxford University Press, 1963), p. 291.

18. See Richard A. Falk, *Future Worlds* (New York: The Foreign Policy Association, No. 229, Headline Series, February 1976).

19. Falk, *Future Worlds*, p. 47.

20. Falk, Future Worlds, p. 50.

21. Falk, *Future Worlds*, p. 51.

22. See Rajni Kothari, "Towards A Just World," *Macroscope, An Occasional Newsletter of the Transnational Academic Program of the Institute for World Order*, no. 7. (Spring 1980), p. 8.

23. See Falk, *Future Worlds*, p. 51.

24. See Burns H. Weston, "Contending With a Planet in Peril and Change: An Optimal Educational Response," *Alternatives*, Vol. V, No. 1, June 1979, p. 60.

25. See Ruth Leger Sivard, *World Military and Social Expenditures, 1979*

(Leesburg, Virginia, 1979), p. 17. This annual study is sponsored by The Arms Control Association; The Institute for World Order; Peace Through Law Education Fund; The Rockefeller Foundation; The Stanley Foundation; The Peace Research Institute (Dundas); and The British Council of Churches.

26. Sivard, *World Military and Social Expenditures, 1979*, pp. 28-29.
27. Sivard, *World Military and Social Expenditures, 1979*, p. 7.
28. Sivard, *World Military and Social Expenditures, 1979*, p. 6.
29. Sivard, *World Military and Social Expenditures, 1979*, p. 16.

CHAPTER **2**

World Order Reform Through Institutional Change
WORLD FEDERAL GOVERNMENT

Through the centuries the idea has persisted that international law cannot provide world order reform and that a meaningful institutional strategy requires nothing less than the replacement of balance of power world politics with world federal government. The basic rationale of this idea is that the relations of states can never be harmonized in the midst of anarchy. It follows that, in contrast to the views considered in Chapter 1, institutional orientations to world order reform must aim for much more than a network of treaties, conventions, customs, resolutions, and general principles of international civility. Instead, say the advocates of global federalism, institutions must aim at a fundamental alteration of the existing distribution of military force and sovereign authority.

How promising are these orientations? Does world federal government offer a more promising institutional strategy of world order reform than existing international law? Can there be any realistic hope for replacing longstanding dynamics of balance of power relationships with those of centralized world politics?

This chapter will address these questions. In so doing, it will offer a way in which the world federalism idea may be suitably and systematically investigated. This investigation will provide a basis for comparing the advantages and disadvantages of two distinct institutional strategies of world order reform. Chapters 3 and 4 will analyze a variety of *behavioral* strategies.

Before proceeding to this investigation of world federal government, however, the background of the world federalism idea in the literature of political thought will be considered. No attempt will be made to account for all relevant proposals. Only the most widely known cases in the history of Western thought will be selected for discussion.[1] These have been chosen not only for their general fame, but also for their broadly representative character and for the range and continuity of thought that they reflect.

World federalism proposals will be explained and compared in terms of several critical dimensions. These include the precise character of the proposed federal scheme, the suggested means of achieving the desired arrangement (coercive or voluntary), the degree of universality implied (Europe or the entire world), the historical background of the proposal, the underlying purpose of the proposal, the composition of the proposed membership, and the prospective role of the Great Powers. Here, too, it will be noticed that, until very recently, world federalism has aimed narrowly at the avoidance of war rather than at a broad range of world order values.

THE CHARACTER OF WORLD FEDERAL GOVERNMENT

Understanding the following proposals can be aided by a brief consideration of the distinctive character of global federation. Although there are significant differences in detail among individual conceptions, the basic features of world federal government are generally described in terms of a more centralized distribution of sovereign authority—the ultimate right to make decisions and enforce obedience in world politics. In the world federal system, therefore, sovereign authority is shared by states with an especially established global center. Hence, the ultimate right to determine when military force may be used between states is vested in the global center, while force resides (1) both within the appropriate institutions of the center and within all of the states or (2) within the states only.

Moreover, *federation* must be distinguished from *confederation*. The latter arrangement is merely an alliance of governments, what in German is called a *staatenbund* as distinguished from a *bundesstaat* or in French a *confederation d'etats* rather than an *etat federal*. With respect to the locus of sovereign authority and military force, the difference is crucial. Unlike the federal configuration of forces, confederation leaves the anarchic condition of world politics unaffected. The state of nations remains in the state of nature.

With the onset of world federal government, states would be deprived of the ultimate right to decide when military force may be used. It follows that a critical question in the examination of world federalism proposals concerns the precise distribution of force. Depending upon the particular distribution of force between the states and the separate federal center, the alternative system of world order will be more or less effective.

Exactly how much military force, if any, must be possessed by the federal center? The World Federalists, USA specify only "an adequate armed peace force." Does this mean a *preponderant* share? Or does it mean only enough force to appear able to deliver unacceptably destructive sanctions upon recalcitrant states? And what about the ability to *appear willing* to unleash such sanctions? Does *perceived willingness* necessarily accompany the federal center's possession of a certain measure of force? These are the kinds of questions that must be raised in considering the proposals for world federal government.

There are also other sets of questions that must be used to evaluate the world federalism proposals. What, exactly, is the relationship of sovereign authority to military force? According to the seventeenth-century English philosopher, Thomas Hobbes, sovereign authority derives from the assurance of protection. And since such assurance requires force, sovereign authority and force go hand in hand. "The obligation of subjects to the sovereign," says Hobbes in Chapter XXI of *Leviathan*, "is understood to last as long, and no longer, than the power lasteth by which he is able to protect them." Similarly, Bodin, a sixteenth-century French political theorist, argues that sovereign-authoritative prerogatives stem entirely from the capacity to provide safety. In *De la République,* he comments:

The word of protection in generall extendeth unto all subjects which are under the obeysance of one soveraigne prince. . . . As we have said, that the prince is bound by force of armes, and of his lawes, to maintaine his subjects in suretie of their persons, their goods, and families: for which the subjects by a reciprocall obligation owe unto their prince faith, subjection, obeysance, and succour.

Alternatively, several notable political thinkers have felt that sovereign authority need not require military force. In this regard, the distinction between *auctoritas* (authority) and *potestas* (power) was already laid down by Cicero in the first century B.C., while Plato's concept of all authority was founded upon the absence of compulsion. Indeed, it has even been argued that force *cannot* be the basis of authority. In this view, not only *can* sovereign authority emanate from sources unsupported by force, it *must* secure obedience without the threat or use of force.

For example, Hannah Arendt, the distinguished twentieth-century political theorist, suggests that the authoritarian relation between those who command and those who obey rests upon "the hierarchy itself, whose rightness and legitimacy both recognize and where both have their predetermined stable place."[2] Similarly, the contemporary French scholar, Bertrand De Jouvenel, emphasizes the volitional core of authority relations: "Authority is the faculty of inducing assent. To follow an authority is a voluntary act. Authority ends where voluntary assent ends."[3] It follows from these views that the margin of obedience that is won only through force demonstrates the failure of authority.

Understood in terms of questions to use when considering the following proposals for world federal government, these arguments raise the issue of creating an effective world authority without the threat of force. Isn't it plain, after all, that a world order that depends on force as its *ultima ratio* must be a permanent source of struggle rather than stability? Didn't Grotius, the seventeenth-century writer on international law, make it clear that authority in the world system necessarily derives from the claims of morality on the minds of people?

But what "forceless" principles of obligation might be appropriate to world federal government? Plato may provide some guidance. In the analogies that occur again and again in the great political dialogues, the appropriate basis of authority is *special knowledge* or *expertise*. In the relations between the captain of a ship and the passengers or between the physician and the patient, for example, special knowledge or expertise provides the basis for compliance. Force is unnecessary. The obligation inheres in the relationship itself.

What does this suggest about the prospects for a "forceless" world federal government? Could the federal center of sovereign-authoritative decision secure the compliance of states on the basis of some special claim to knowledge or expertise, or would the basis of authority here be something other than expertise, namely, some *commonly felt need for centralized management?* And if such need must be the compelling element in the relationship between states and the federal center, how might national leaders be encouraged to value it highly? These questions, too, must be raised in the course of examining the following proposals for world federal government.

Finally, in considering these proposals for world order reform through institutional change, the following questions must be asked: What is the relevance of world federal government for world order reform in our own time? How might the form of these various proposals be adapted to the requirements for transformation at the end of the current millenium? What are the essential differences between the strategies of world order reform through international law and world order reform through world federal government?

MEDIEVAL/CLASSICAL PROPOSALS

Pierre Dubois's Federation of Christian States

Perhaps the earliest proposal of the medieval period linking the effectiveness of war prevention to a federal distribution of force and sovereign authority is that of Pierre Dubois, the French jurist and politician. In 1306, Dubois wrote *De Recuperatione Terra Sancta (The Recovery of the Holy Land)*, a tract proposing the organization of Christian states for the maintenance of peace in Europe. Peace, Dubois asserted, was the highest attainable good, and as such, it had to be secured among all Christians so that a strongly united and indivisible community of states could be brought into existence. The Christian Commonwealth, argued Dubois, needed ample institutional backbone.

Dubois's favored conception was a federation of Christian states. To

67

implement this federation, an appropriate General Council would be convened by the Pope, whereupon it would be made clear to all that Christians will no longer be permitted to bear arms against other Christians, thereby spilling "baptized" blood. Those who enjoy combat were advised to do battle against the enemies of Christian belief. All disputes between states would be adjudicated by an international court of arbitration composed of judges elected by the Council. In the event of disagreement with the award of the tribunal, appeals would be taken directly to the Pope. Failure to submit to binding arbitration or to the final determinations of such a process would be punishable by Papal excommunication.

As he was one of the first to propose an international court of arbitration endowed with obligatory jurisdiction over member states, Dubois was a pioneer in the advocacy of more centralized arrangements for world order reform. Moreover, he also urged that the Council and its members institute a boycott against a state making war and even advocated concerted military action against offending states. To obtain the necessary force, member states would contribute their armies to the General Council when called upon to do so. In this sense, Dubois may be regarded as an intellectual precursor of the two great international organizations of our own century, although he certainly envisioned a far greater degree of centralization than was ever realized or even contemplated by the League of Nations or the United Nations.

What was the author's actual purpose in putting forth his proposal for peace? Above all, it must be kept in mind that Dubois was more the practical politician than the contemplative academic philosopher. While the primary concern reflected by *The Recovery of the Holy Land* is for the establishment of a federation of states to keep the peace, his overarching concern was for the establishment of French supremacy and for the undertaking of an effective crusade against the "infidels" in possession of the Holy Land. In conformity with the prevailing conception of universality, his dream was for a worldwide Christian commonwealth. Not to be ignored, however, was the extent to which he tied this conception to the leadership of his country. The General Council was to convene on French soil by a Pope who was, in effect, entirely under French influence. In the manuscript of 1306, Dubois speaks frankly and clearly about the enlargement of France at the expense of Germany, Spain, and the Pope, offering his king rather straightforward advice on the establishment of French supremacy in Europe. An examination of his later writings also reveals this primary purpose—expanding the power of France. The principal implication that can be drawn from this underlying motive is that the author's proposal in no way represents the product of a carefully reasoned, coherent, and, above all, dispassionate examination of the world federalism idea.

Podebrad's Federation of Christian Princes

The next major proposal linking the effectiveness of war prevention to a federal arrangement for world order reform is that of Georg Podebrad, King of Bohemia, and Antonius Marini of Grenoble, his counsel and ambassador. Dated 1464, this plan calls for a federation of Christian princes from France, Italy, Germany, and Spain to preserve peace among themselves and to protect Christianity against the Turks. This coalition was to function through an assembly *(Congregatio)* of princes' representatives meeting in turn in various different cities; a court *(Judicium)* to adjudicate differences between the princes, a member prince and a nonmember, and between nonmembers; and a *Syndic* or *Fiscal Procurator* to receive contributions from the member princes. This plan was actually presented in treaty form to several governments by Marini on behalf of his king. Despite regal sponsorship, however, all that was eventually realized were friendship pacts with Hungary and France, and the project of Podebrad remained, like the others, a mere proposal.

The text of the plan begins with a plea to restore the Christian Commonwealth to its earlier state of glory. Since the appearance of Mohammed, says Podebrad, the Commonwealth has been fragmented. The Turks have stolen Greece and stormed Constantinople. It is essential, therefore, that the unity of the Christian world be restored. Accordingly, there is nothing better for one's piety, nothing more suitable for one's virtue, and nothing more glorious for one's honor than to take pains to see to it that a real, pure, and lasting peace is achieved under the aegis of Christian unity and that the Christian faith is protected against the "terrible Turks."

To secure such a peace, a Christian federation must be established within which the use of arms is to be absolutely and forever proscribed. The independent right to wage war is denied. Only the federation itself is to be endowed with this right. In the event that conflict arises between a member state and a non-member state, pacific means of settlement are to be applied. If, however, such means prove futile, the entire federation is to enter into the matter on the side of its common ally. If neither of the conflicting parties belongs to their organization, the member states are expected to intervene, with or without resort to arms, as the particular situation requires.

The Pope and the Emperor in the proposed federation are not to be accorded their usual special place in the Christian world. The Emperor is to be consigned to the same position as that of the other German princes, while the Pope—who is not even permitted to become a member of the federation—is expected to cooperate with it in certain matters. Even Dubois, it may be recalled, who strongly defends the rights of France vis-à-vis the Church, is of the opinion that it is the Pope who should convene the General Council. In this respect, therefore, Podebrad's proposal is rather unique.

The chief organ of the federation, the assembly, is to be organized on a nationalistic basis. Each nationality is to be accorded one vote, and the various political divisions are not to be granted separate votes. Thus, all princes of a given nationality are obliged to reach agreement before voting in the assembly. The plan of Podebrad and Marini clearly links the effectiveness of war avoidance to a federal distribution of sovereign authoritative prerogatives supported by force. Like its predecessors, however, no coherent, well-reasoned examination of this link is ever undertaken. It is assumed to be self-evidently true.

Pope Leo's Proposal

Another important proposal of world federalism was made by Pope Leo X. This proposal, dated 1518, represents a last major attempt on the part of the Catholic Church to organize the entire Christian world for the accomplishment of that time-honored ideal—the conquest of the Holy Land. Leo negotiated a Treaty of Universal Peace for the purpose of securing a five-year truce among the European Princes and a defensive alliance against the Turks. Members of the alliance were to be the Pope,

70

the Emperor, the Kings of France, England, Spain, and their confederates. Additional princes were to be granted admission within eight months, and armed forces were to be contributed by each member. While this treaty was ultimately ratified by the Emperor, the Pope, and the King of Spain, the outbreak of hostilities between France and Spain rendered it ineffective.

Francois de la Noue's Organization of States

Writing in 1587, Francois de la Noue, a Protestant aristocrat, advanced the similar idea of an organization of European states to undertake a crusade against the Turks. In connection with this organization, or *union générale* between the princes, de la Noue suggests a general international conference to be convened in Augsburg for the purpose of discussing and solving major European problems.

Emeric Crucé's Appeal for Universality

The first truly *universal* peace arrangement was *The New Cyneas* of Emeric Crucé. Written in 1623, the project called for a worldwide organization that would embrace both Christian and non-Christian states. As such, it was the first perceptible departure from the narrower ideal of a Christian Commonwealth. Denouncing religious differences as grounds for war, Crucé exhorted Christians not to look upon Moslems or Jews as their natural enemies; all religions, he argued, must be recognized as being fundamentally alike in their common purpose of acknowledging and worshipping God. Such a spirit of tolerance was especially remarkable and daring at a time when the idea of concerted action against the Turks still reigned supreme.

To implement his plan for world peace, Crucé suggested a permanent council of ambassadors to settle all differences by a majority vote. Meeting in a neutral city, "where all sovereigns should have perpetually their ambassadors," these representatives of all monarchs and sovereign republics (including the Pope, the Emperor of the Turks, the Jews, the Kings of Persia and China, the Grand Duke of Muscovy, and monarchs from India and Africa) would be "trustees and hostages of the public peace." The decisions of the assembly, determined by majority vote, would be regarded as "inviolable law," and those who opposed it would

71

be pursued and forced into submission by force of arms in the event that "gentle means" proved unsatisfactory. A universal police force, "useful equally to all nations and acceptable to those which [had] some light of reason and sentiment of humanity," would be created to enforce the assembly's decisions.

Yet, while he admitted the necessity of securing submission to the decrees of the Council through armed force when necessary, Crucé placed a greater emphasis on the power of moral compulsion than did Dubois. In this conviction, *The New Cyneas* reflected the sentiments of Rabelais, who urged that all means of peaceful settlement be attempted before resorting to war. Moreover, like later attempts at collective security that recognized a special place for the most powerful, Crucé suggested that in order to give more authority to the appropriate judgments,

> one would take advice of the big republics, who would have likewise their agents in this same place. I say great Republics, like those of the Venetians and the Swiss, and not those small lordships that cannot maintain themselves, and depend upon the protection of another. That if anyone rebelled against the decree of so notable a company, he would receive the disgrace of all other princes, who would find means to bring him to reason.[1]

In contrast to other proposals, Crucé sought no special advantages for his own country. He was not at all anxious to offer France dictatorial power in the proposed union. Rather, he wished to see his country as merely one of the many members of the organization. Like Montaigne, who claimed that man's duties to mankind ought to prevail over those to individual states, Crucé recognized only one logical claim to his allegiance—the world itself: "What a pleasure it would be to see men go here and there freely, and mix together without any hindrance of country, ceremonies, or other such differences, as if the earth were, as it really is, a city common to all."[5] Indeed, in the breadth of his vision and the magnanimity of his spirit, Crucé reflected the cosmopolitan spirit of liberal internationalism.

Thus, unlike other proposals, *The New Cyneas* may be regarded as free of inspiration by either patriotic or religious motives. The greater glory of France and the Church was subordinated to universal peace for its own sake. Nevertheless, Crucé's appeal for a global federation reflects no significant strides forward in the direction of science. While his appeal rested on world organization for its own sake, it did not make a perceptible shift toward well-reasoned analysis of the basic hypothesis. The link between the effectiveness of war prevention and global federalism must be subjected to further scrutiny.

The Grand Design

Crucé's work served as the basic model for the later peace proposal of Maximillian of Bethune, Duke of Sully. Appearing some fifteen years after the publication of *The New Cyneas*, Sully's proposal is perhaps the most celebrated of all major peace plans, serving in turn as model for its principal successors. There is little doubt that William Penn *(An Essay Toward the Present and Future Peace of Europe)*, John Bellers *(Some Reasons for a European State Proposed to the Powers of Europe)*, the Abbé de Saint-Pierre *(Project for Perpetual Peace)* and Rousseau *(A Lasting Peace Through the Federation of Europe)* all looked to *The Grand Design* as the starting point of their own schemes for the establishment and maintenance of world peace. In the words of James Brown Scott, *The Grand Design*

> is without question the most famous of the many projects advocating a federation of States in order to secure and to maintain peace between nations. The project is in very truth the classical project of international organization, and it has been both the inspiration and the foundation upon which well-wishers of their kind have, consciously or unconsciously, raised their humbler structures.[6]

As to the origin of this proposal, Sully, minister of finance, confidant, and friend to Henry IV, claimed that the plan was his monarch's own conception. While considerable disagreement exists on this point, most scholars attribute *The Grand Design* to Sully directly. From the perspective of the present study, however, it matters little whether Sully or Henry actually conceived of the plan.

The main purport of *The Grand Design* was to encourage the states of Europe to unite in a great federation of hereditary monarchies, elective monarchies (to include the Empire and the Papacy), and republics, thereby dividing Europe "equally among a certain number of powers and in such a manner that none of them might have cause either of envy or fear from the possessions of power of the others." In accomplishing this objective, the number of states would be reduced to fifteen, and laws and ordinances appropriate to "cementing a union" between them would be implemented "to maintain that harmony which should be once established." Nothing worse than "trifling difficulties" were envisaged.

Whatever "trifling difficulties" did arise would be resolved within the framework of a General Council representing the different states. Based upon the model of the ancient *Amphictyons* of Greece, the Council was to consist of a certain number of commissaries, ministers, or plenipotentiaries from "all the governments of the Christian Republic." Constantly assembled as a senate, these representatives would "deliberate on any affairs which might occur; to discuss the different interests, pacify the quarrels, clear up and determine all the civil, political, and religious affairs of Europe, whether within itself or with its neighbors."[7] While subsidiary local assemblies were also envisaged, only the decisions of the Council would be regarded as final and irrevocable.

For military support of the Council's decision, the plan provided for a composite army, i.e., armed forces contributed by the princes in proportion to their capabilities. Using such forces, the princes would undertake missions of conquest in Asia and on the coast of Africa. Thus, the foundation of European peace was to be war.

Unlike Crucé, therefore, but in much the same vein as Dubois, Sully's principal underlying purpose was the maximization of French power rather than the implementation of a more effective arrangement for the management of power. As in *The Recovery of the Holy Land,* considerations of an imperialistic character move into the foreground of this proposal.

Whether or not this accounts for the absence of a coherent and sustained examination of the world federalism idea, the closer resemblance to Dubois than to Crucé is borne out further by Sully's primary concern with Christian Europe. Unlike *The New Cyneas, The Grand Design* did not seek the establishment of a universal union. And like its predecessors in this regard, the resultant exclusion of large areas of the world from the proposed federation may be regarded as extremely debilitating. Finally, it must be mentioned that while Crucé emphasized the need for moral force to supplement his proposal for a more effective arrangement of power management, Sully disregarded this factor altogether.

William Penn Recommends a European Parliament

Influenced by Sully's *Grand Design,* William Penn advanced the next noteworthy proposal for world peace based on global federation. As its name implies, *An Essay Towards the Present and Future Peace of Europe by the Establishment of an European Diet, Parliament, or Estates* reflects a continental rather than universal area of concern. First published anonymously in London in 1693, this tract—uninspired by designs of narrow political maneuver—suggests the creation of a European parliamentary assembly to which all disputes between states not settled by directed negotiation would be submitted for binding decision. Such decision would be taken by a three-fourths vote with no abstentions or neutral positions permitted, and failure to comply with its dictates would provoke the concerted military might of the member states.

Penn does not subscribe to a doctrine of equality among states. The number of deputies to be sent by each state was to be in proportion to its power, revenues, exports, and imports. The viability of this new power management arrangement was linked, therefore, to the extent to which its specified allocation of sovereign authoritative prerogatives in the Diet conformed to the actual capabilities of member states. Somewhat like Crucé before him, Penn accorded a special place to the major actors in the world sytem.

John Bellers's Proposal

Seventeen years after the publication of Penn's proposal, John Bellers conceived of *Some Reasons for a European State Proposed to the Powers of Europe.* Essentially a reproduction of the famous Quaker's own scheme, it included an analysis of Sully's *Grand Design* and proposed the following action:

> That at the next General Peace, there should be Settled an Universal Guarantee and an Annual Congress, Senate, Dyet, or Parliament, by all the Princes and States of Europe; as well Enemies, as Neuters, joyned as one

State, with a renouncing of all Claims upon each other, with such other Articles of Agreement as may be needful for a standing *European* Law; the more Amicably to Debate, and the better to Explain any obscure Articles in the Peace, and to prevent any Dispute that might otherwise raise a New War in this Age or the Ages to come; by which every Prince and State will have all the strength of Europe to protect them in the possession of what they shall Enjoy by the next Peace.[8]

The assumption that sovereign princes and states could unite to enforce a general peace and yet continue to maintain their sovereign authoritative prerogatives at home was supported by reference to the success of methods used by the German Diets, the Union of the Provinces of Holland, and the Cantons of Switzerland. Europe would be divided into at least one hundred equal cantons or provinces, so that every sovereign state could send a minimum of one member to the Senate and a contribution of men, ships, or money to the joint armed forces of the federation. And like Penn before him, Bellers proposed that representation in the Senate reflect the relative capabilities of its members; thus, a state would be privileged to send one representative for every thousand troops it furnished:

And for every Thousand Men, etc., that each Kingdom or State is to raise, such Kingdom or State shall have a Right to send so many Members to this *European* Senate; whose Powers and Rules should be first formed by an Original Contract among their Principals.[9]

It is interesting to note that Bellers's proposal closely reflected the assumptions of an age characterized by the increasingly widespread deification of reason:

Because that Assembly must go by Argument grounded upon Reason and Justice, and the Major Part of the Senate not being interested in the Dispute will be the more inclined to that Side which hath most Reason with it; Whilst the Greatest Monarchs in time of Peace own themselves and Subjects to the Sovereignty of Reason.[10]

There was, then, no apparent reason to express concern over the determinations of the proposed Senate. Their essential rightfulness and success were effectively mandated by the ubiquity of Reason.

Saint-Pierre's Proposed Union

Following his involvement with the French delegation to the peace conferences at Utrecht, C. I. Castel de Saint-Pierre, Abbot of Tiron, published his own proposal for general and everlasting peace. Far more detailed than the earlier plans of Penn and Bellers, the *Project for Perpetual Peace* further elaborated some of the ideas that the Abbé had already begun to sketch out as early as 1707 and that were first published in Cologne in 1712. Founded upon the earlier ideas contained in Sully's *Grand Design*, the debt is frequently made explicit by Saint-Pierre. According to the Abbé:

> It falls out happily for this Project, that I am not the Author of it; 'twas Henry the Great was the first Inventor of it; 'twas that *European Solon* whom God first of all inspired with the means to make the Sovereigns of Europe desirous to establish among them an equitable Polity . . . I have by dint of Thought, hit upon a Plan in the main like that of that excellent Prince, my having hit upon it too, does not in any wise diminish the Glory of Invention due to him . . . .

Why was Saint-Pierre so generous in ascribing the credit for his project to another? Perhaps the most likely answer is that, like Sully before him, the Abbé credited Henry IV so as to obtain a wider audience for his proposal.

Unlike *The Grand Design*, however, Saint-Pierre's proposed union did not seek to alter the map of Europe by force. Rather, it was to be established by a treaty of alliance signed by the sovereigns of Europe. Yet, while Saint-Pierre more closely resembles Crucé than Sully in this renunciation of forceful conquest, the resemblance reverses itself with respect to the desired comprehensiveness of the new order. Like Sully and unlike Crucé, Saint-Pierre had a European rather than universal perspective in the elaboration of his favored arrangement for the federal management of power.

The plan itself consisted of five fundamental articles. The first of these suggested the formation of a Grand Alliance or European Union to secure a permanent peace between the Christian states of Europe as defined by the frontiers assigned by the Treaty of Utrecht. The second concerned the collection of revenues necessary to sustain the proposed union. But it is the third fundamental article which is in many ways the most important. This article involved the renunciation on the part of the Grand Allies of the resort to force:

> The grand Allies have renounced and renounce for ever, for themselves and for their successors, resort to arms in order to terminate their differences present and future, and agree henceforth always to adopt the method of conciliation by mediation of the rest of the grand Allies in the place of general assembly, or, in case this mediation should not be successful, they agree to abide by the judgement which shall be rendered by the Plenipotentiaries of the other Allies permanently assembled, provisionally by a plurality of voices, definitively by three-quarters of the votes, five years after the provisional award.[11]

Thus, in the event of a dispute between states, the interested parties first were to attempt to reconcile their differences through the obligatory mediation of the several members of the Grand Alliance. If such efforts at mediation were unsuccessful, arbitration would be necessary.

Article IV dealt with the refusal of a member to accept either the general rules or particular judgments of the alliance:

> If any one among the Allies refuses to execute the judgments or the regulations of the grand alliance, negotiate treaties countrary thereto, or make preparations for war, the grand alliance will arm, and will proceed against him until he shall execute the said judgments or rules, or give security to make good the harm caused by his hostilities, and to repay the cost of the war according to the estimate of the Commissioners of the grand alliance.[12]

In short, those sovereign-authoritative prerogatives invested in the federation itself would be supported by appropriate force.

Finally, the fifth article was concerned with the implementation of future laws and agreements by the plenipotentiaries:

> The Allies agree that the Plenipotentiaries shall regulate finally, by a plurality of voices in their permanent assembly, all articles which may be necessary and important to procure by the grand alliance more coherence, more security, and all other possible advantages. Provided that nothing in these five fundamental articles is very changed without the unanimous consent of all the Allies.[13]

78

These were the five fundamental articles which Saint-Pierre considered necessary to attain lasting and perpetual peace.

Rousseau Comments on Federation

The work of the Abbé de Saint-Pierre was revived by Jean Jacques Rousseau in 1761 as the first part of his essay, *A Lasting Peace Through the Federation of Europe.* In this work, Rousseau compared the behavior of states in the world system to that of people in the state of nature and concluded that the powers of Europe were standing opposite each other in a continuing state of war. All existing treaties that bound states represented the fabric of temporary truce, not of genuine peace. The anarchy of interstate relations stood in sharp contrast to the presumed order of the civil state.

What alteration was required to remove the anarchic element? The remedy could be found "only in such a form of federal government as [would] unite nations by bonds similar to those which already unite their individual members, and place the one no less than the other under the authority of the law."[14] According to Rousseau, the "free and voluntary association which now unites the States of Europe" could be converted into an authentic federation capable of limiting interstate violence.

> the Federation must embrace all the important Powers in its membership; it must have a Legislative Body, with powers to pass laws and ordinances binding upon all its members; it must have a coercive force capable of compelling every State to obey its common resolves whether in the way of command or of prohibition; finally, it must be strong and firm enough to make it impossible for any member to withdraw at his own pleasure the moment he conceives his private interest to clash with that of the whole body.[15]

Rousseau subscribed wholeheartedly to the proposition that links war to the decentralized character of world politics. Recognizing the absence of a common superior over the world's constituent state units as the cause for war, his analysis led to a federal solution. But did it really? The previous comments are found in Part I of the essay, which is described as merely a statement of Saint-Pierre's project and may not accurately reflect his own views as well.

Part II of the essay, which is devoted to criticism of Saint-Pierre's project, shows Rousseau's ambivalence toward the Abbé's principal assumptions. Most importantly, perhaps, Rousseau expressed little faith in the assumption that federation could be accomplished peacefully. Thus it was as likely as not that the process of federating Europe would bring about the very forms of violent conflict it seeks to prevent:

> No Federation could ever be established except by a revolution. That being so, which of us would dare to say whether the League of Europe is a thing more to be desired or feared? It would perhaps do more harm in a moment than it would guard against for ages.[16]

Moreover, if we are to assume consistency between the ideas expressed in *A Lasting Peace* and those of *The Social Contract*, additional doubt is cast on Rousseau's advocacy of federation. According to Rousseau, sovereign authority, being no more than the exercise of the general will, is necessarily indivisible:

> But our political thinkers, not being able to divide sovereignty in principle, have divided it in its object: into force and will; legislative power and executive power; the rights of levying taxes, of administering justice, and making war; the internal government and the power of treating with foreigners. But by sometimes confounding all these parts, and sometimes separating them, they make of the sovereign power a fantastical being composed of related pieces; as if man were composed of several bodies, one with eyes, another with arms, another with feet, but none with anything more.[17]

This conception of sovereign authority as indivisible logically precluded a proposal for federation which, by definition, involves a division of sovereign-authoritative prerogatives. The character of federation necessarily conflicts with the character of sovereignty as defined in *The Social Contract*. For these reasons, it is by no means self-evident that Rousseau seeks the sharing of State power with specially established, European-wide institutions.

Jeremy Bentham's Faith in Public Opinion

The next major peace proposal appropriate to a discussion of world federalism is that of Jeremy Bentham. Written sometime between 1786 and 1789, his *Plan for an Universal and Perpetual Peace* was not revealed to the world in published form until 1843. At its basis were the following two prerequisites:

1. The reduction and fixation of the force of the several nations that compose the European system.
2. The emancipation of the distant dependencies of each state.[18]

The first of these propositions suggests that disarmament rather than a transfer of force to federal institutions represents a part of the desired way to peace. While Bentham's conception of the means necessary to sustain an effective arrangement for the management of power includes the sharing of sovereign-authoritative prerogatives with newly created, systemwide institutions, no provision is made to support the dictates of these institutions with proper force. A Common Court of Judicature is proposed "for the decision of differences between the several nations,"[19] but it is not to be equipped with any instruments of coercive power. Once established, assumes Bentham, a common international tribunal itself makes war unnecessary: "Just or unjust, the decision of the arbiters will save the credit, the honour of the contending party."[20] The proposal, therefore, links the effectiveness of power management to shared sovereign authority but denies that such authority necessarily requires the support of force.

Bentham favors not only the implementation of a Common Court of Judicature, but the creation of a Common Legislature between states as well. Such a Congress or Diet is to be properly constituted when each power has sent two emissaries to an assigned place of meeting; one emissary would be the principal representative, and the other would be his deputy or replacement. The proceedings of the Congress would be made public, and its power would consist of "reporting its opinion" and "in causing that opinion to be circulated in the dominions of each State."[21] Moreover, it would be empowered to place refractory states under the "ban of Europe."[22] Thus, the instrument for the sanction of resolutions is not to be force, but public opinion.

The View From Königsberg

Immanuel Kant's philosophical essay, *Perpetual Peace*, emerged from Königsberg, Germany, in 1795. Having shunned actual political

81

participation throughout his lifetime, Kant created his scheme without reference to any narrow political purpose. While Bentham had certainly been concerned with the abolition of colonial dependencies in his advocacy of continental institutions endowed with sovereign-authoritative prerogatives, Kant issued his proposal without serious concern for the current problems of Europe. At best, he related to the everyday stuff of politics by looking to the revolution in France as an indication that the world was beginning to progress towards the ideal. Such concerns notwithstanding, however, his essay on perpetual peace remains on the level of a philosophical sketch. It was not intended as a practical guide for the statesmen of his own time.

Resembling Saint-Pierre's project in the manner of setting forth views in the form of articles, Kant's proposal for the realization of perpetual peace rests on the creation of republican constitutions in every state as its first definitive article. Upon what form of reasoning does this claim for republican constitutions rest? According to Kant, since republican constitutions structure the exercise of sovereign authority according to well-defined laws promulgated with the consent of the citizenry, their implementation makes the initiation of hostilities exceedingly difficult. True to that spirit of Enlightenment that rests upon the freedom to make use of one's reason in all matters, Kant freely assumes that by letting individuals decide for themselves whether or not they wish to make war (a definitional requirement of republicanism), all such conflict will necessarily cease. Newly empowered to make use of their reason, *citizens* will certainly and immediately recognize the avoidance of war to be in their own interests. The implied requirement of homogeneity as to republicanism contained in Kant's first definitive article is explicitly embodied in Article IV, Section 4 of the Constitution of the United States: "The United States shall guarantee to every state in this Union a republican form of government. . . ." A similar clause was contained in the Covenant of the League of Nations, but to no meaningful effect.

Kant's second definitive article for perpetual peace specifies that the law of nations must rest on a federation of free (i.e., republican) states. Recognizing that states often pursue their objectives by war rather than by litigation, Kant proposes a league of a special sort—a league of peace. Such a league would differ from a peace pact in that the latter seeks only the end of an ongoing war, while the former seeks the end of all wars. Yet, unlike men who must submit to the constraints of a newly constituted public force upon leaving the state of nature, states would be able to partake of this league or association without becoming subject to public law. The liberty of each independent state would be respected and protected.

The proposal, therefore, is for the expedient of a civic federation of states. This expedient of "free federalism" is dictated by reason and must be introduced into the law of nations. While Kant recognizes that the "tribunal" of reason's initial dictate is for the establishment of a World State—an arrangement by which states would, like individuals, renounce their anarchic liberty in order to submit themselves to compulsory public laws—the prevailing conception of the law of nations compels states to repudiate this dictate. They reject in practice what they certainly must accept in principle, and the positive ideal of a universal world republic must be sacrificed to the negative expedient of an ever-extending federation. Federation is thus conceptualized as an admittedly second-best measure for the prevention of war and is to exist always with the continuing risk of proving ineffective.

In the second article Kant demonstrates an *in principle* preference for a comprehensive and true world union over federation. However, he regards such union as visionary in light of existing ideas of public law, and he puts forth his proposal for a league or federation with the full understanding that it is no better than a halfway measure because it is the best attainable alternative to the unrealizable ideal.

But must Kant's assertion that reason *prefers* the separate coexistence of states within a federation to their union under one *superior* power be regarded as a contradiction of his in-principle advocacy of world republic? The answer to this question is certainly negative, for Kant's notion of a world state does not refer to an arrangement that may be implemented by fusing the existing separate state entitles into union with one power superior to the rest. The process by which such a society might be achieved is necessarily based on the freely given consent of each constituent state unit to incorporate itself into a *new unit* superior to itself. Fusion into one overgrown power may only result in universal *monarchy* and ultimately anarchy.

SUMMARY

With the possible exception of Rousseau's *A Lasting Peace,* the foregoing proposals recommend the creation of federal institutions at the global level. However, none of these proposals is founded upon appropriately examined hypotheses. Even though several of the most notable appear to be products of well-reasoned inquiry, none of them is developed in accordance with the basic canons of scientific investigation. Indeed, none of the would-be creators of world federal government have undertaken a genuinely systematic analysis of their favored configuration. And none of them has expressed a normative concern for a broad spectrum of world order value preferences.

TWENTIETH-CENTURY PROPOSALS

The first well-known modern plan for world federal government was put forth by H.G. Wells after World War I.[23] In his *The Outline of History* and in a later work, *The Common Sense of World Peace*, Wells displays uncommon solicitude for the idea of a worldwide nationality and "the nascent federal world state to which human necessities point."[24] According to Wells, "the sovereign independence of states represents the cardinal difficulty before us." Only by "pooling sovereignty," Wells felt, can a viable structure of world peace be established.[25] As in the case of his intellectual forerunners, Wells was inclined to look upon the need for increased global centralization as obvious and the world federal arrangement as the institutional consequence of a seemingly faultless logical process.

Ten years after the appearance of Wells's *The Common Sense of World Peace*, a plan appeared that was destined to become the world federalist classic: Clarence K. Streit's *For Union Now: A Proposal for a Federal Union of the Democracies*.[26] This pamphlet, later to become the first chapter of the author's more complete work on the subject, *Union Now: A Proposal for an Atlantic Union of the Free* (1949), proposes a union of the world's democracies into a comprehensive world federal republic. Several years after its publication, however, it was criticized as unambiguously elitist. In particular, Philip Curtis Nash characterized Streit's conception of world federation as "a group of 'ins' against the 'outs'" and his avowed intent to leave out Russia from his prospective world organization as unpardonable.[27]

There were other calls for world federal government advocacy in 1939. In addition to Streit's *For Union Now*, W.B. Curry wrote *The Case*

84

for a Federal Union[28] (a plan explicitly informed by the Streit proposal) and Nicholas Murray Butler made several widely discussed public statements on behalf of the federal principle in world political relationships. Both Curry and Butler identify the root cause of international conflict as international anarchy and the remedy as world federal government. As Butler put the matter, "We have now come to the point where the only path left is the application, in terms of the twentieth-century world, of the federal principle." To buttress the feasibility of his position, the then-president of Columbia University and of the American Academy of Arts and Letters (not to mention the Carnegie Endowment for International Peace), reminds his audience that the various states at the time of the Federal Convention must be regarded as the true correlatives of nations in world politics.[29]

It was also in 1939 that Grenville Clark issued his first call for global federation, albeit one with strictly limited purposes and with highly restricted powers.[30] These built-in limitations derive more from Clark's concern for a "practical" chance of acceptance than from the assumption that they were the most desirable means of avoiding war. According to Clark, the organs of the proposed federation should be a Congress and a Supreme Court, although he did not provide for the creation of a separate executive department. Rather, the Congress would establish quasi-executive agencies as the need arose.

As to the use of military force, considerable authority would be delegated to the Congress. In Clark's own terms, this authority represents the "stiffest dilution of sovereignty" contained in the entire proposal and reflects his belief that any effective centralized arrangement for the management of global power must be supported by effective sanctions. The military measures which could be authorized by Clark's congress include the right to maintain air and naval forces, to fix the contributions of member countries, and to name and remove the commanders-in-chief. Clark's world federation would have preeminent military power, and a notable feature of his proposal is the qualification that the new world federation ought not to be implemented at all unless its military strength was predominant over any other combination that might arise. Since predominance is not a necessary condition for successful deterrence, the military power of Clark's world federation would be so great that it would be capable not only of deterrence, but also of victory.

85

The ideas of Duncan and Elizabeth Wilson are also an integral part of the world federalism literature of 1939. In their *Federation and World Order,* they claim (six years before the dawn of the atomic age) that the advent of very powerful weapons has made indulgence in war especially costly. What is needed? The answer, they contend, lies only in some form of world organization that may partially supersede the state:

> This is the germ of the idea which has come to be known as Federal Union. Can we not, we have asked ourselves, set up a common Federal Parliament for mankind which will be directly representative not of States, but of individual men and women, leaving to the Nation-State the administration of those purely national affairs whose conduct does not threaten, because it does not affect, the nations of other States?[31]

Searching for a model on which to shape their design, the Wilsons suggest the existing federal parliaments that have a long record of success behind them, namely Switzerland and the United States. They regard international federation as the most promising arrangement for world order reform because it is the logical "halfway house" between international anarchy, which may or may not be tempered by alliances and leagues, and the kind of super state that would completely eliminate the existing multiplicity of separate sovereignties.

One year after the appearance of the Streit, Curry, Butler, Clark, and Wilson proposals, William C. Brewer advanced his case for world federal government under the heading of a "World Alliance" with a constitution patterned after the Constitution of the United States.[32] During that same year David Hoadley Munroe's *Hang Together: The Union Now Primer* joined the growing collection of tracts arguing for the establishment of specially constituted world federal agencies and institutions. *Hang Together* represents an attempt to condense, explain, and examine Streit's *For Union Now.* Citing adherence to an absolute conception of national sovereignty as the principal source of international contention and conflict, Munroe proposes the extension of the American system of federal union to the whole world. A government comprised of an executive, a legislative, and a judicial branch would, he feels, provide an institutionalized *cordon sanitaire* around the spreading "pathology" of war.[33]

In 1942, Oscar Newfang advanced the case for world federal government.[34] Newfang argued that what is true for individual state systems is true for the entire world system as well.[35] Whatever the scope of the system involved, central institutions endowed with certain sovereign-authoritative prerogatives must be the repository of force. Once implemented, such institutions would eliminate the conflict-ridden state of world affairs.

Although it falls short of an actual recommendation for global federation, P.E. Corbett's *Post War Worlds*,[36] which appeared in the same year as Newfang's *World Government,* favored world federation in principle. Sounding very much like his predecessor from the Age of Enlightenment, Immanuel Kant, Corbett argues that although it would certainly be nice to have states willingly transfer some of their sovereign-authoritative prerogatives to some specially constituted global center, the obstacles are simply too great. These obstacles are the "revolutionary" character that any abdication of national prerogatives would necessarily reflect and the incremental character of the establishment process itself (an assertion that suggests that people will have to be satisfied for a very long while with "quasi-federal machinery"). In short, argues Corbett, "we shall have to content ourselves with something far short of universal federation."[37] What this "something" turns out to be is less than a federation but more than simply a league or an alliance that "combines the beginnings of a World Commonwealth with other, limited, groupings of states around regional or other special interests."[38]

In 1943, Ely Culbertson's plan for world federation was made public,[39] but it was the proposal of Emery Reves two years later that received the lion's share of attention. In 1945, Emery Reves succeeded Clarence Streit as the principal figure in the movement for world federation. The crux of Reves's argument may be summed up in two principal "observations" that can be made concerning war:

1. Wars between groups of men forming social units always take place when these units—tribes, dynasties, churches, cities, nations—exercise unrestricted sovereign power.

2. Wars between these social units cease the moment sovereign power is transferred from them to a larger or higher unit.[40]

On the base of these "observations," says Reves, "we can deduce a social law with the characteristics of an axiom that applies to and explains each and every war in the history of all time":

> War takes place whenever and wherever nonintegrated units of equal
> sovereignty come into contact.

One need not be a logician to recognize that this proposition is not
necessarily implied by the above premises. Moreover, unless "contact"
is tied definitionally to the use of force, in which case the statement is
tautological, the proposition is clearly untrue.

In the following year, Albert Einstein revealed the following salient
observation in an interview with *The New York Times:* "In the light of
new knowledge, a world authority and an eventual world state are not
just *desirable* in the name of brotherhood, they are *necessary* for
survival."[41] During that same year, 1946, the World Movement for
World Federal Government was founded in Luxembourg. The United
World Federalists of the United States was formed in February 1947 by
bringing together various existing organizations: Americans United for
World Government, World Federalists (U.S.A.), Student Federalists,
Massachusetts Committee for World Federation, and World Citizens of
Georgia. The plan for world federal government drawn up by the
United World Federalists is presented in the books of Cord Meyer.[42]

In 1949, Robert Maynard Hutchins, Chairman of the Committee to
Frame a World Constitution, continued to "carry the ball" for world
federal government. According to Hutchins, "such an authority must
have a monopoly of atomic bombs, which means that every nation
would be at its mercy, and it must have the right to enter, inspect, and
destroy atomic installations anywhere in the world. No nation could call
itself sovereign in any usual sense under such conditions."[43] Moreover,
Hutchins argues, with somewhat questionable logic, that the feasibility
of world government derives from its compelling need: "The slogan of
our faith today must be, world government is necessary, and therefore
possible."[44]

The appearance in 1949 of Clarence Streit's larger work, *Union Now:
A Proposal for an Atlantic Federal Union of the Free,* overshadowed all
contemporary efforts.[45] Expanding upon the ideas presented earlier in
For Union Now, Streit makes his contention manifestly clear that
universality must be the goal of any plan for world federal government,
but that the plan must begin with democratic states. What is needed is a
"nucleus," and this nucleus must be the world's democracies.

In cooperation with Justice Owen J. Roberts and John F. Schmidt,

88

Streit continued to advance the case for world federal government with publication of *The New Federalist*.[46] Not surprisingly, this book draws its inspiration from *The Federalist*, attempting to apply between states in world politics the same federal principles which Madison, Hamilton, and Jay applied to the thirteen states.[47] In the same year, 1950, Grenville Clark's *A Plan for Peace* appeared.[48] Clark argues that "disarmament is the crux of the problem of world order" and that only world federal government can superintend the process of disarmament successfully. Moreover, the best strategy for implementing the desired federal constellation of power and authority is a basic revision of the United Nations Charter—a recommendation that foreshadows his later and much more influential work.[49]

A unique event in the history of world federal proposals is the London Parliamentary Conference for World Government, which took place in September 1951. Attended by members of parliaments from all over the world, its organizers assumed that world order reform requires the surrender of national sovereignty to the greater sovereignty of a world federal government. The parliamentarians who gathered for the conference began the creation of world government groups throughout the world and hailed their meeting as a demonstration to governments and to peoples that despite widespread cynicism there exists competent opinion that recognizes the solution as possible.

Seven years after this conference, Linus Pauling, the Nobel laureate, produced *No More War*. In his work, dedicated to the proposition that good scholarship is necessarily prior to the conditions of peace, Pauling argues on behalf of greater efforts in the "research for peace." More concretely, he proposes the establishment of a research organization, the World Peace Research Organization, within the structure of the United Nations.[50]

Bertrand Russell represents still another intellectual star in the world government firmament of our own century. Writing in 1961, Russell asserts:

> The present anarchic national freedoms are likely to result in freedom only for corpses. . . . It seems indubitable that scientific man cannot long survive unless all the major weapons of war, and all the means of mass destruction, are in the hands of a single Authority, which, in consequence of its monopoly, would have irresistible power and, if challenged to war,

89

could wipe out any rebellion within a few days without much damage except to the rebels. This, it seems plain, is an absolutely indispensable condition of the continued existence of a world possessed of scientific skill.[51]

Not unexpectedly, however, Russell—in the manner of both his predecessors and successors—avoids the postulation of a specific solution to the problems of disarmament: How can individual states be made to believe that their own willingness to disarm will be generally enough reciprocated to make such action gainful? Machiavelli, in his essay *On Fortune*, makes good use of metaphor in pinpointing the crux of the general problem of ensuring an adequate supply of collective goods (the problem of which disarmament is one particular instance): "The world is a stupendous machine, composed of innumerable parts, each of which being a free agent, has a volition and action of its own; and on this ground arises the difficulty of assuring success in any enterprise depending on the volition of numerous agents. We may set the machine in motion, and dispose every wheel to one certain end; but when it depends on the volition of any one wheel, and the correspondent actions of every wheel, the result is uncertain."

In the decade of the '60s just past, we may count Grenville Clark and Louis Sohn's latest effort among the most prominent of those associated with the idea of world federal government.[52] Their joint proposal has been so widely read that almost all subsequent works on the subject use it as a convenient starting-point. In brief, *World Peace Through World Law* recommends the creation of a "world authority" that would forbid violence or the threat of violence as a means of settling differences between states. This world authority would be capable of supporting its dictates with appropriate force. Specifically, the authors envision the creation of a "permanent world police force" for the purpose of forestalling or suppressing the use of force by states.

This plan does not recommend the transfer of *all* sovereign-authoritative prerogatives to the specially created global authority. Only the right to use force is to be transferred to the new agency. There is, then, no suggestion of transforming the system of separate states into a genuinely single-state world.

Strongly influenced by the formulations and efforts of Clark and Sohn, Betty Reardon and Saul H. Mendlovitz of the Institute for World

Order in New York City reflect the most current sort of world government advocacy. After reflecting upon a number of alternative systems of world order from the standpoint of both desirability and feasibility, they come out in favor of a system

> . . . that requires the establishment of a world authority equipped with legislative bodies for making laws against international violence, and, in addition, agencies to enforce these laws, keep the peace, and resolve conflicts. 'World Law' is a shorthand term describing such an authority and related institutions; and hence this model of world order is termed the 'world law model.'[53]

And further on:

> The world law model is admittedly utopian. But is it any less utopian than hoping to achieve world order through a series of evolutionary, small-term incremental kinds of agreements, one-step advances, or accommodations when in the meanwhile man is likely to blow himself up along the way?[54]

NEW FEDERAL PATHS TO WORLD ORDER REFORM: THE WORLD ORDER MODELS PROJECT AND RICHARD A. FALK'S *A STUDY OF FUTURE WORLDS*

In February 1968, a meeting that was to set into motion a uniquely ambitious, transnational research activity, The World Order Models Project (WOMP), took place in New Delhi. Under the direction of the Institute for World Order in New York City, WOMP was conceived with a view toward generating the sort of global reform that could bring about peace, social justice, economic well-being, and ecological stability.

To accomplish this objective, eight research groups were ultimately established and charged with the production of "preferred world" models for the 1990s. The work of these groups has culminated in a series of books (under the general editorship of WOMP director, Saul H. Mendlovitz) entitled *Preferred Worlds for the 1990s. A Study of Future Worlds*, by Richard A. Falk, the research director of the United States WOMP "team," is one of these books.[55]

In view of its theme, *A Study of Future Worlds* must be considered within the context of past federal reformist strategies. At the same time,

Falk's book is markedly different from its forerunners.

First, *A Study of Future Worlds* enlarges the locus of world order concern from war to a whole panoply of economic, social, and environmental hazards. Second, Falk offers a framework for the study of world order reform that combines a multidimensional concern with a systemic, futuristic, and interdisciplinary orientation. Third, *A Study of Future Worlds* is informed by a concern for feasibility as well as desirability. While its thinking is surely utopian, its outline for a "world order system responsive to global humanism" has been advanced with sensitivity to the problems of transition. Fourth, *A Study of Future Worlds* represents the product of a long-term collaborative undertaking (WOMP) that has placed methodological awareness at the center of its concerns.

Fifth, *A Study of Future Worlds*, as a principal outcome of the WOMP experience, represents not only a major theoretical work in its own right, but also the contemporary intellectual beginnings of a genuine world order "movement."

While there are substantial differences—both substantive and methodological—between the orientations of the WOMP research groups, there is substantial agreement on at least one overarching point: World order studies must continue to develop as both a disciplined field of inquiry and as the proper source of practicable strategies for global transformation. In the opinion of Falk, the resultant union of thought and action is an essential prerequisite to the creation of a tolerable future for us all.

To progress toward such a union, Falk explores particular ways of speculating about alternative world futures and advances a set of proposals for achieving world order reform by the year 2000. Beginning with the understanding that a state system comprised of sovereign and conflictual actors can never satisfy the requirements of an improved global society, Falk identifies four specific and explicit value preferences:

1. The minimization of large-scale collective violence.
2. The maximization of social and economic well-being.
3. The realization of fundamental human rights and conditions of political justice.

92

4. The rehabilitation and maintenance of environmental quality, including the conservation of resources.[56]

A considerable array of additional values is also offered to inform the design of a more propitious future, although the realization of these values is not conceived as a primary world order task.

The model of a preferred system of world order that emerges from the search for realization of the four basic WOMP/U.S.A. values stems from the presumed need for "central guidance" in world affairs. Unlike the traditional world federal government configuration in terms of its mode of achievement, this model relies on a prescribed buildup of functional agencies at regional and world levels rather than on a transference of power and authority from states to a specially constituted global actor. The proposed central guidance capability, referred to as "The World Polity Association," is comprised of an intricate and elaborate bureaucratic structure. Admittedly "cumbersome," this structure is offered to the reader in order to underscore the extraordinary complexity of future world politics and the changes in institutions, roles, and capabilities that will be necessary to make such politics broadly acceptable.

After he sets forth the principal elements of institutional reorganization, Falk considers the transition process. He places special emphasis on efforts that involve appropriate changes in the prevailing orientations of national elites. Hence, a truly critical arena of world order reform is alleged to be *within* states, while the activities of various transnational elites and specialized international institutions are taken to circumscribe other, somewhat less critical, arenas.

These different arenas are related to specific time intervals by Falk in his "Prospectus for Transition." In this connection, the initial decade of the 1970s would emphasize the reorientation of national outlooks, the decade of the 1980s would emphasize the growth of certain transnational developments, and the decade of the 1990s would focus upon a new global imperative. The "Prospectus" addresses problems of political consciousness, values changes, and structural modification in world organization during the transition to a world order orientation and relates the successor world order system—the system constituted to give substantial realization to WOMP values—to certain selected patterns of global economics and American foreign policy.

A Study of Future Worlds thus represents a new chapter in the ongoing tradition of federal reformist strategies. While there is still a disturbingly plausible ring to Oswald Spengler's comment that the labors of all "world improvers" are inevitably in vain, *A Study of Future Worlds* goes a long way toward strengthening the institutional case for world order reform. It does this by combining the development of a promising approach to a world order orientation with the elaboration of a specific, carefully articulated global alternative.

INVESTIGATING THE WORLD FEDERALISM IDEA

If the long history of world federal government advocacy is a guide, the world order advantages of global federation are by no means obvious. All of the foregoing recommendations, however carefully conceived, are based upon more or less incompletely examined hypotheses. To remedy this defect, we will now look closely at the internal logic of world federal government.

Reviewing our discussion of notable peace plans, we recognize that despite some significant differences in procedural detail, all of these proposals are based solidly on the following proposition: The effectiveness of power management or war prevention in the world system will be improved to the extent that a decentralized distribution of sovereign authority and force is replaced by a distribution in which these factors are transferred to specially established, centralized institutions.[57]

Several basic analytic models must be constructed in order to examine this hypothesis. Accordingly, these models differ from one another according to the degree of centralization of force and sovereign authority which they imply, and represent what are thought to be successively more effective arrangements for the management of power.

In the following discussion, Model I, balance of power (sovereign authority *and* force decentralized), describes what is believed to be the least effective arrangement for the management of power, while Model III, world federal government (sovereign authority *and* force shared), describes what is believed to be the most effective arrangement. In Model II, collective security, sovereign authority is shared, while force remains decentralized.

Where sovereign authority is decentralized, there exist no specially established central institutions endowed with sovereign authority. Hence, force, or the instruments of international violence, are necessarily (although unevenly) distributed among all of the states. This condition corresponds to the Hobbesian state of nature, the condition that all of the foregoing proposals seek to overcome. Historically, as we have already seen, it has prevailed as the characteristic pattern of modern world politics since the Peace of Westphalia in 1648. Based upon the interplay of sovereign states, this condition of natural liberty manages power according to the operation of a balance mechanism and its associated norms of international law.

The Balance of Power

The balance-of-power world system is, of course, considered to be unsatisfactory. Indeed, it is its intrinsically insecure character that is the very rationale of those arguments that are offered on behalf of world federal government. Joined with the destructiveness of today's strategic weapons technology, the dynamics of this system seem to lead to global catastrophe.

Why is this the case? Consider the following analogy: The condition of states in balance of power world politics is similar to that of a group of herdsmen whose individual members share a common grazing pasture and who feel themselves compelled to increase their respective herds without limit. Even though these herdsmen have determined that the continuing augmentation of their herds constitutes self-interested behavior, the actual effect of such action is an overgrazed commons and financial ruin.

This calamitously erroneous definition of self-interested behavior derives from the uncertainty that each herdsman feels about the probable reciprocity of his fellows. In the absence of assurances that every other herdsman will refrain from increasing the number of animals in his particular herd, each herdsman calculates that he would do best to continue to increase his own herd. The result is already known. In much the same fashion, each state in world politics—however strongly committed it might be to arms control principles and the intentions of international law—inevitably calculates that the costs of its own conformance to these principles and intentions would exceed the benefits because of the uncertainty surrounding the parallel arms-limiting measures by other states.

Tragically, this sort of thinking—the sort that derives from the ironically titled tradition of "realism" in international statecraft—seems only to lead to failure. It spawns a spiraling pattern of hostility and mistrust that progressively forestalls the very objective that it is intended to achieve—the avoidance of war. In a world that is endowed with a veritably limitless capacity to destroy, the consequences of such failure simply cannot be endured.

But what of the overarching "logic" of deterrence? Is there any reason to believe that such deadly logic is incapable of producing global security? To answer this question, we must first consider the meaning of deterrence in world politics.

The Logic of Deterrence

There are two essential modes of producing security in world politics: defense and deterrence. To *defend* itself, a state must be able to prevent an enemy's launched forces and weapons from striking its territory. To *deter*, a state must be able to prevent an enemy, by the threat of an unacceptable response, from making the decision to attack. In the second mode, security is sought by convincing a prospective attacker that the costs of a considered attack will exceed the expected benefits. Mutual deterrence exists between two states when each believes that an attack would bring unacceptable losses to the attacker, no matter which side struck first.

Today, in the nuclear age, defense is no longer a reliable mode of producing security. This is equally true for nuclear and nonnuclear weapon states. There is simply no way in which a determined aggressor's warheads could be kept off an intended victim state's territory once a fair number of them were launched. Offensive weapons technology continues to outdistance attempts at defense.

It follows that the current search for security by states is dependent upon the potential effectiveness of deterrence. In the balance-of-power world, deterrence seeks to produce security by substituting the credible threat of retaliatory destruction for protective defense. It does this by satisfying certain essential expectations of *fear*. Assuming that states (1) always value self-preservation more than any other preference or

96

combination of preferences and (2) always choose rationally between alternative courses of action, it follows that they will always refrain from initiating the use of force against other states that are believed willing and able to deliver an annihilating response.

Two factors communicate such expectations. First, in terms of *ability*, there are two essential components: *payload* and *delivery system*. It must be successfully communicated to the potential attacker that the deterrer's firepower and the means of delivering that firepower are capable of wreaking unacceptable levels of destruction after a first-strike attack. This means that retaliatory forces must appear sufficiently *invulnerable* and sufficiently elusive to *penetrate* the prospective attacker's active and civil defenses. It need *not* be communicated to the potential attacker that such firepower and/or the means of delivery are *superior* to his own. The capacity to deter need not be as great as the capacity to win. In the present nuclear age, an admittedly inferior store of firepower and delivery systems may have considerable deterrence value.

The second factor of communication is *willingness*. How may states convince potential attackers that they possess the resolve to deliver an unacceptably destructive response? The answer to this question lies in the demonstrated strength of the commitment to carry out the threat. States seek to enhance the credibility of their threats by committing themselves to their fulfillment.

These, then, are the basic features of "deadly logic," the system of security through deterrence upon which we depend in a balance-of-power world. It is, however, a system that provides little cause for complaisance. The ingredients of a credible deterrence posture are extraordinarily complex.

The deterrence approach to security management in our decentralized world system is fraught with difficulties that stem from the fact that the logic of deterrence is faulty. In other words, a nuclear weapons capability (defined to include nuclear explosives, associated delivery vehicles, and supporting infrastructure) does not necessarily imply a credible deterrence posture (defined in terms of the perceived ability and resolve to deliver an unacceptably damaging retaliatory blow). In fact, there exists no automatic connection between the two.

In spite of the enormous devastation that nuclear weapons are capable of inflicting, threats of their retaliatory use will not always be believed.

As we now know, the persuasiveness of a retaliatory threat rests not only upon the anticipated level of destruction, but also on the perceived willingness or resolve to carry it out. Such willingness is not always a feature of the nuclear threat.

If prospective aggressor states do not believe that a promised retaliatory strike will actually take place, then they may choose to attack (depending, of course, on the precise value they attach to the expected attack outcome). If their beliefs prove correct, such an attack may still precipitate general hostilities, depending upon the prevailing configuration of international alignments. At the very least, however, a single act of aggression will have taken place.

If a would-be aggressor state does not believe in the promised retaliation, attacks and finds itself incorrect, it will certainly incur high levels of damage and very likely engender systemwide conflict. Whether or not an aggressor is ultimately correct in predicting the likelihood of retaliation, the fact of the matter is that as long as a first strike is actually launched, deterrence has failed. And it has failed even though the victim state was in possession of a nuclear weapons capability.

Another important reason why a nuclear weapons capability need not automatically signal a credible deterrence posture concerns the appearance of *secure* retaliatory forces. A secure retaliatory force is an essential precondition of "assured destruction." It must be judged capable of surviving a first-strike attack by the prospective attacker.

Yet there is no reason to believe that a would-be aggressor will always or even usually make such a judgment. If it does *not* make this judgment, attacks, and is proven correct, a classical case of aggression will have taken place. If the victim state is aligned with certain other states, this aggression may even be unintentionally broadened.

If it does not make this judgment, attacks, and is proven incorrect, it will occasion an unexpected reciprocal strike with destructive by-products that may ultimately prove deleterious for a good part of the world. However accurate the attacker's judgment turns out to be concerning the vulnerability of its victim's retaliatory forces, the resultant decision to attack signifies the failure of deterrence. Once again, deterrence fails even though the attacked state had possessed a nuclear weapons capability.

These comments point to the conclusion that deterrence may fail between rational state actors irrespective of the accuracy of the information processed in their decisional calculi. Still more unsettling, there are additional reasons why the logic of deterrence is incapable of providing for extended global security. The most important of these reasons concerns the assumption of rationality itself. In matters of strategic deterrence, rationality refers to an ordering of preferences believed common to all states wherein self-preservation is consistently valued more highly than any other preference or combination of preferences.

This assumption is unwarranted. On both logical and historical grounds, there is absolutely no reason to base our security hopes on such an idea. A great many national decision makers throughout history have taken steps that were intentionally destructive of their respective sovereignties. There is no reason to believe that this will not happen again.

It is also worth noting that the ability to make rational decisions in world politics is frequently undercut by the consequences of crisis and stress. Even national leaders who deliberately gear their decisions toward the preservation of the state may actually precipitate contrary effects. This might be the result of errors in information or faulty calculations engendered by stress-warping of perception and alertness. In the post-Watergate era in American politics, one can only speculate how closely a president of the United States may have already come to experiencing the level of emotional strain required to upset rational decision making in world politics.

To make matters worse, an increasing number of guerrilla/terrorist actors are beginning to wield significant influence in world affairs. Unlike states, these groups do not always demonstrate a primary concern for self-preservation. Rather, they sometimes reveal a variety of preferences that loom larger than life itself. The recent actions of terrorist organizations in the Middle East corroborate the authenticity of this kind of preference ordering.

As a result, guerrilla/terrorist actors are likely to be substantially less susceptible to threats of retaliatory destruction than state actors. This difference is reinforced by the special geographic difficulties involved in retaliating against terrorists and by the increasing access of these

99

actors to weapons of mass destruction (by bestowal, by self-development, or by hijacking).

A final reason why our deterrence system is apt to fail is *accidental war*. Even where, (a) national decision makers are rational, well-informed, and unwilling to initiate deliberate first-strike attacks, and (b) guerrilla/terrorist behavior parallels that of national actors, nuclear war may still be triggered by mechanical accident or by unauthorized use. The probability of such events actually taking place is increasing along with the steadily growing number of nuclear weapons.

As to the second possibility, one can imagine a variety of entirely plausible scenarios involving mutiny, hijack, or even unauthorized commander-level decisions. For example, notwithstanding the extravagant claims that are usually made for nuclear weapons systems and their guardian personnel, a variety of documented cases exist in which obviously unfit persons have been assigned to the control of strategic weapons. All too often, the greatest danger comes from personnel who demonstrate no evidence of psychiatric disturbance when they are examined.

Perhaps the most terrifying feature of these considerations is that only a *single* instance of unauthorized use is needed to spark systemwide devastation. Our lives now rest precipitously on the assumption that *all* of the individuals involved with nuclear control systems are incapable of recklessness. There are, therefore, certainly enough reasons to strive for a more satisfactory system of world politics than one wherein states continue to coexist in the nuclear variant of a Hobbesian "posture of gladiators."

COLLECTIVE SECURITY AND WORLD GOVERNMENT: THE FEDERAL ALTERNATIVES

Where sovereign authority is shared, the world system is characterized by the presence of a specially established federal center as well as state actors. Here, force may be decentralized or shared. When it is decentralized, all force is distributed among the states alone. Where it is shared, the instruments of violence reside both within the appropriate institutions of the separate federal center and within all of the state actors.

Model II and Model III represent particular versions of global federation, although—strictly speaking—Model II is more of a collective security arrangement. From Dubois, to Kant, to Falk, all of the proposals for world federal government are represented in their basic contours by either of these models. These models are, therefore, indispensable for assessing such proposals.

Model II Global Federation

In Model II global federation, the right to use force is transferred from states to a specially established center of sovereign-authoritative decision making, while the instruments of military force remain decentralized among the states alone. How is power managed in such a system? What manner of limiting interstate violence prevails where states coexist with an authority above them, but where they alone possess the weapons of war? How may the use of force between states be limited where the states no longer are the sole judges of their own conduct, but where force remains exclusively in their own national arsenals? Is there any reason to believe that power would be more effectively managed in such a system than in the existing balance-of-power world?

Through the centuries, the idea of an effective global sovereign unsupported by military force has been widely questioned. The philosopher Hobbes, in Chapter 17 of his *Leviathan,* remarks: "And covenants, without the sword, are but words, and of no strength to secure a man at all." In a similar vein, Freud once commented: "Wars will only be prevented with certainty if mankind unites in setting up a central authority to which the right of giving judgment upon all conflicts of interest shall be handed over. There are clearly two separate requirements involved in this: the creation of a supreme agency and its endowment with the necessary power. One without the other would be useless."

Thus, since the commands of the specially constituted center of sovereign-authoritative decision in Model II global federation would be unsupported by force, there appears no reason to believe that they would be generally heeded because national leaders would always have grave doubts about the reciprocal compliance of other states. Recognizing that such doubts would occasion each state to calculate that the prospective costs of compliance are so great as to outweigh the

101

expected benefits, it seems unlikely that power would be more effectively managed in a Model II global federation than in the present system of decentralized world politics.

This is not to suggest, however, that nothing can be done to make Model II global federation "work." There are certain kinds of changes that might seriously affect the decisional calculi of states, causing them to develop greater confidence in the belief that their own prospective compliance with collective security directives would be generally paralleled. While such changes would certainly be very far-reaching and perhaps even infeasible, they are still worth considering.

Earlier, it was noted that the basis for authority of a "forceless" world federal government might be some *commonly felt need for centralized management*. This "need" must be the compelling element in the relationship between states and the separate center if sovereign-authoritative prerogatives unsupported by force are to be capable of securing compliance. The principal question, then, concerns the "rank" occupied by this need in the states' preference orderings as well as the scope of its claim.

Just how high a position might be assigned to the need for centralized management? And just how commonly felt might this need be? Even a few powerful states that would not concede the importance of centralized management might make its implementation impossible.

Let us first consider the position that states might assign to the need for centralized management of force. If states were to believe that such management was essential to their survival, they might assign this need a very high rank. If the value assigned to self-preservation by states is always higher than that assigned to any other preference or combination of preferences, it would appear that the need for centralized management of force would be allotted the highest possible position. This is true if the preference for self-preservation is tied to the need for centralized management.

To make such an assumption, however, would be foolhardy because it would suppose that states identify their own prospects for survival with the prospects for the creation of a particular organizational scheme of decision making for the world as a whole. While such an identification might appear eminently reasonable in the view of an hypothetical "outside" observer, from the point of view of individual states it is not justified. States do not form their own preferences by first considering the security needs of the entire system. They do not order their preferences in accordance with what they consider these needs to be. The states in Model II global federation would almost certainly prefer to rely on themselves for their security than to rely on the justice and effectiveness of a worldwide system.

States "behave" in this way because each lacks confidence in the others' willingness to work toward realizing a common objective. Moreover, states might fear that even if such willingness were assured, the new arrangement would not be conducted in an acceptable predetermined manner. Thus, even if states did not fear that centralized management would fail because other states would violate the spirit of such an agreement, they still might fear that the resultant distribution of authority would not be equitable and secure. This is because states might fear that without the instruments of violence, the central managers would not be able to assure their safety.

States, then, behave as they do because of the low probability they assign to the securing of security advantages through centralized management of the Model II variety. This probability is so low that the prospect of exclusive security advantage may be preferred even where its perceived value is exceeded by that of security advantages through centralized management. This is true as long as the perceived consequences of security advantages of "private" preference exceed those of security advantages of centralized management.

Where states value an exclusive security-maximizing preference more than they value a centralized management preference, the former prospect is almost certain to be preferred. This is the case as long as the prospect of exclusive security advantage is judged to be at least as likely as the prospect of "public" advantage. Indeed, even where states value the former prospect only as much as the latter, they will always opt for exclusive security advantages where they are judged more likely to be enjoyed.

We see, then, that states do not tie the need for centralized management of force to the preference for self-preservation. Consequently, this need is not assigned the highest possible position in states' preference orderings. The conclusion appears quite clearly: right without force is ineffective in the management of world power. There is no apparent reason to suppose that power would be more effectively managed in a Model II global federation than in a system where both force and right reside solely with the separate states.

Does this mean that spokesmen for Model II global federation have "placed their bets" in error? Not necessarily! Despite the logically consistent character of the above argument, different conclusions could be drawn from different assumptions. We might arrive at a fundamentally different conclusion concerning compliance with centralized management in Model II global federation by substituting a different set of assumptions. For example, the following is a schematic representation of such a set:

- Assumption 1. Each state believes that the cost of compliance for each state must be less than the benefit to it if at least some critical number of states comply with the dictates of centralized management.
- Assumption 2. Each state believes that the cost to a state of complying is greater than the benefit to it of complying if less than some critical number of states comply.
- Assumption 3. Each state believes that each state does better if at least some critical number of states complies than if none comply.
- Assumption 4. Each state believes that each state knows that what it knows about the other states is paralleled by what the other states know about it, and each state believes that each state knows that the other states are rational.

It follows from this set of assumptions that general compliance is the preferred outcome.

Although these assumptions currently require far more of states than we can prudently accept, we must not conclude that they can never be credible. Indeed, students of world order reform must now set out to discover those changes in the character of world politics that might enhance the acceptability of these assumptions. Such changes might include a reduced number of state actors, homogeneity of state governments, "status-quo" rather than "revolutionary-modernizing" states, and a "tight" condition of bipolarity in which the ratio of power between the two blocs is roughly equal. Taken together, these changes might contribute importantly to overcoming the central impediment to

104

the success of collective security: the understanding of states that their own willingness to seek security cooperatively rather than competitively will not be universally (or at least widely enough) imitated.

Model III Global Federation

Model III global federation may improve the prospects for effective power management between states, but this presupposes the fulfillment of a number of antecedent conditions. Where these conditions are not met, Model III may add nothing to the decisional calculi of potentially aggressive states. It follows that in such circumstances, federation would do nothing to ameliorate the hazards of the international state of nature.

What are these conditions? The answer lies in the requirements of successful deterrence, i.e., those factors that affect the credibility of the world federal government's deterrence posture. These factors are defined by would-be "delinquents'" perceptions of the authoritativeness of the world federal government, the amount of force available in its repositories, the nature of those forces, the vulnerability of those forces, and the willingness to use those forces. To the extent that a prospective aggressor would determine that the costs of its planned attack exceed its prospective benefits, world federal government would "work."

However, such an evaluation is hardly apt to be automatic. In fact, it may even be unlikely. The ingredients of a credible deterrence posture are not always easy to satisfy, and world federal government must grapple with the same problems as individual states on this matter. For example, however preponderant its own force reserves, this government might experience difficulty convincing a would-be aggressor that it had both the ability and the resolve to undertake an unacceptably damaging retaliation. For whatever reason, this would signal the failure of deterrence and of the world federal approach to peace and world order reform.

From the standpoint of ability, successful deterrence requires the belief on the part of a prospective aggressor that the world government's capacity to yield unacceptable damage is not vulnerable to preemptive strike or to subsequent attempts at active defense. This means that a would-be offending state must believe that the world government's retaliatory forces have been rendered sufficiently invulnerable to any first-strike attack, and that they are capable of penetrating its own active defenses. A secure retaliatory force is the *sine qua non* of successful deterrence.

The foregoing discussion points to the most unsettling feature of the entire Model III world federal government argument: *its continuing reliance upon the logic of deterrence.* By recommending the creation of a Model III world federal arrangement for managing global power, nothing is done to change the "threat system" dynamics of the prevailing balance of power. True, threats would now be issued "from above" rather than laterally, but this does nothing about eliminating the underlying notion of security through fear. Indeed, the preeminence of this notion is reinforced rather than undercut by Model III world federal government, and the world system would continue its dependence upon the precarious foundations of "deadly logic."

With today's enormously destructive weapons technologies, it is imperative that the above shortcomings of Model III world federal government are widely appreciated. National decision makers must learn to appreciate that the allegedly "realistic" approach to security (an approach that "ties" security to relative power position) is actually unrealistic and that security via deterrence is a contradiction in terms. This is the case whether threats of retaliatory destruction originate "horizontally" from other states (the classical balance of power arrangement) or "vertically" from the specially constituted public authority (Model III-type world federal arrangement).

But what of those conceptions of world federal government that envision disarmed states and a lightly armed world government force? Clark and Sohn call for "universal and complete national disarmament together with the establishment of institutions corresponding in the world field to those which maintain law and order within local communities and nations."[58] And the World Federalists, USA, consistently call for a schedule for universal and complete disarmament rather than for a system whereby order is maintained by the threat of retaliatory destruction "from above."

Even these conceptions, however, are not immune to the foregoing critique of world federal government. How, after all, is such a program for disarmament to be accomplished? Without a prior transfer of strategic and conventional military force to the specially constituted world government center? If so, what reasons exist to believe that individual states will calculate that (1) the benefits of disarmament will exceed the costs if all of the other states are willing to disarm and (2) all of the other states are willing to disarm?

Clearly, unless the specially constituted world government operates on the basis of threat-system dynamics that are supported by the capability to yield "assured destruction," each state contemplating disarmament will entertain grave doubts about the reciprocal behavior of all of the other states. Since the prospect of disarmament can be considered gainful by each state only if it is expected to be generally paralleled, these doubts have fatal implications for the success of disarmament. Without a prior transfer of military force to the world federal government, individual states contemplating disarmament would have every reason to calculate that the prospective costs of compliance with the decision to disarm would outweigh the prospective benefits.

What all of this means is that even those conceptions of world federal government that rest upon designs for disarmament must take earlier criticisms into account because disarmament simply cannot be wished into being. Rather, it must be accomplished incrementally.

The primary stages of disarmament necessarily require conditions whereby the world government center is in a position to effectively influence the decisional calculi of states such that the prospective costs of failing to disarm appear intolerably high. And this necessarily requires a continuation (however temporary) of the long-standing threat system dynamics of deterrence. *A world federal government that fulfills the requirements of a credible deterrence posture in the nuclear age is an essential precursor to a world federal government superintending a disarmed world with light "police-type" forces.* Hence, the weaknesses of the former conception cannot be overlooked by those who favor the latter.

Moreover, from the standpoint of feasibility or attainability, it is exceedingly doubtful that even the "primary" variant of world federal government stands much hope of creation. Recently, this point was accepted by the WFUSA Board of Directors, who declared that world federal government is inconceivable "in the next 200 years." Of course, centralization might be achieved coercively as well as volitionally, and Caesarism as a path to world peace through world government need not be dismissed out of hand. At the same time, it is a path that, as Rousseau recognized long ago, is likely to occasion the very sorts of conflicts and calamities that it is designed to prevent.

WORLD FEDERAL GOVERNMENT: A CONCLUDING APPRAISAL

This chapter has examined world federal government as an institutional strategy of world order reform. How promising does it now appear? What are the prospects for a truly effective world federal government? How might world federal government be adapted to the needs of our own time?

My analysis has included both a comprehensive overview of world federalism proposals and a systematic investigation of the world federalism hypothesis. To accomplish this investigation, several basic models of alternative world systems have been created and inspected. Above all else, we have discovered that there is no necessary connection between the extent to which force and sovereign authority are transferred to systemwide institutions and the effectiveness of global power management. Where a variety of other important conditions are not met, it is unlikely that global federation would provide for significant world order reform.

As determined in the foregoing discussion, these conditions concern matters including perceptions of the value of authoritativeness in securing compliance, the amount of force, the nature of force, the vulnerability of force, and the willingness to use force. In those instances where global federation lacks force, these conditions also concern (1) the extent to which the benefits of compliance are judged to exceed the costs of compliance in circumstances where all or some critical number of states comply, and (2) the extent to which states believe that what they know about other states is paralleled by what the other states know about them. A major shortcoming of proposals for world federal government is that they fail to recognize the enormous changes in effectiveness which accompany even subtle changes in the listed conditions.

What does all of this mean for students of world order reform? Should they regard these findings as cause for dismissal of world federal government as an institutional strategy of world order reform? The answer depends entirely upon the extent to which the conditions necessary for effective global federation are judged capable of fulfillment. Where it is believed that meeting these conditions poses no overwhelming barrier, continued advocacy of world federal arrangements may be warranted. If, however, meeting these conditions is judged unrealistic, world federal government must be viewed with skepticism.

Several options remain open to the latter group. One would involve a shift in orientation. Discouraged with the prospects for reform within the classical framework of assumptions concerning individual and national behavior, the student of world order may focus instead on the creation of alternative frameworks. Rather than seek to understand how specific conditions might be met in a system that assumes fixed forms of behavior, the student might begin to specify and explore alternative forms of behavior. Thereafter, the resultant world systems might be explored in terms of their world order reform potential.

The time is at hand to accept this option. While there is much to be said on behalf of institutional paths to world order reform (they are, to be sure, specific, precise, and relatively unambiguous), students of world order should now turn their attention to *behavioral* paths. These paths of transformation might be examined at the level of individual human beings and at the level of states. Taken together, the institutional and behavioral paths to world order reform can define the modus operandi of a greatly improved strategy for global transformation.

NOTES

1. These cases will be divided into "medieval/classical" and "modern" (twentieth-century) categories.

2. Hannah Arrendt, "What Was Authority," in Carl Friedrich, ed., *Authority* (Cambridge, Mass.: Harvard University Press, 1958), p. 82.

3. Bertrand De Jouvenel, *Sovereignty: An Inquiry Into the Political Good* (Chicago: University of Chicago Press, 1957), p. 33.

4. Emeric Crucé, *The New Cyneas*, translated by Thomas Willing Balch (Philadelphia: Allen, Lane and Scott, 1909), pp. 102, 104.

5. Crucé, *The New Cyneas*, p. 66.

6. James Brown Scott, Introduction to William Ladd, *An Essay on a Congress of Nations for the Adjustment of International Disputes without Resort to Arms* (New York, Oxford University Press, 1916), xiv-xv.

7. Sully, *Grand Design of Henry IV* (London: Grotius Society, 1921), p. 42.

8. See A. Ruth Fry, *John Bellers, 1653-1725: His Writing Reprinted* (London, Cassell, 1935), p. 92.

9. Fry, *John Bellers*, p. 93.

10. Fry, *John Bellers*, pp. 93-94.

11. C.I. Castel de Saint-Pierre, *Abrégé du Project de Paix Perpétuelle*, translated by Hale Beloit, 2d ed. (London: Grotius Society, 1927), p. 27.

12. Saint-Pierre, pp. 28-29.

13. Saint-Pierre, pp. 29.

14. Jean Jacques Rousseau, *A Lasting Peace Through The Federation of Europe*, translated by C.E. Vaughan (London, Constable & Co., 1917), pp. 38-39.

15. Rousseau, *A Lasting Peace*, pp. 59-60.

16. Rousseau, *A Lasting Peace*, p. 112.

17. Jean Jacques Rousseau, *The Social Contract*, translated by Charles Frankel (New York, Hafner, 1947), p. 24.

18. Jeremy Bentham, *Plan for an Universal and Perpetual Peace* (London: Grotius Society, 1927), p. 11.

19. Bentham, *Plan for an Universal and Perpetual Peace*, p. 26.

20. Bentham, *Plan for an Universal and Perpetual Peace*, p. 27.

21. Bentham, *Plan for an Universal and Perpetual Peace*, p. 30.

22. Bentham, *Plan for an Universal and Perpetual Peace*, p. 31.

23. See Benjamin Franklin Trueblood, *The Federation of the World* (New York: Hougton Mifflin, 1899); Raymond L. Bridgman, *World Organization* (Boston, Ginn & Co., 1905); and John A. Hobson, *Towards International Government* (New York: Macmillan, 1915).

24. See H.G. Wells, *The Outline of History*, vol. II (New York: Macmillan, 1920), p. 580.

25. See H.G. Wells, *The Common Sense of World Peace* (London, L. & V. Woolf, 1929), p. 18.

26. See Clarence K. Streit, *For Union Now* (Washington: Harper & Bros., 1939).

27. See Philip Curtis Nash, *An Adventure in World Order* (Boston: Beacon, 1944), p. 14.

28. See W.B. Curry, *The Case for a Federal Union* (Harmondsworth, England: Penguin, 1939).

29. See address delivered at the banquet given by the International Club in honor of the European Committee of the Carnegie Endowment for International Peace, Geneva, Switzerland, June 14, 1937. Reprinted in Nicholas Murray Butler, *The Family of Nations: Its Needs and Its Problems* (New York: C. Scribner's, 1939), p. 362.

30. See *A Memorandum With Regard to a New Effort to Organize Peace and Containing a Proposal for a "Federation of Free Peoples" in the Form of a Draft of a Constitution for the Proposed Federation* (New York, December, 1939).

31. C.E.M. Joad, in Preface to Duncan and Elizabeth Wilson, *Federation and World Order* (London, T.Nelson & Sons, 1939), xiii.

32. See William C. Brewer, *Permanent Peace* (Philadelphia, Dorrance & Co., 1940).

33. See David H. Munroe, *Hang Together: The Union Now Primer* (New York: Union Press, 1940).

34. See Oscar Newfang, *World Government* (New York: Barnes & Noble, 1942).

35. In empirical terms, one cannot help but wonder why it is so widely believed that government ensures order in domestic society. Anthropologists have been telling us for some time that several of the most secure, best-ordered domestic societies are anarchic, while some of the most disordered ones have long-since abandoned self-help conceptions of security for the specially constituted central agencies of government. This point is argued strongly by the movie, *Death Wish*, a film that has as its theme an urgent plea for increasing *decentralization* of power and authority in American cities as the only way to battle crime. If, at the municipal level, the failure of government is attributable to deep cleavages and distinctions in the social fabric, can we not assume that the problem would only be *magnified* at the global level? After all, the world system is *the* heterogeneous social system, the fractionated, discordant social system *par excellence.*

36. See P.E. Corbett, *Post War Worlds* (New York: Farrar & Rinehart, 1942).

37. Corbett, *Post War Worlds,* p. 187.

38. Corbett, *Post War Worlds,* p. 189.

39. See Ely Culbertson, *Summary of the World Federation Plan: An Outline of a Practical and Detailed Plan for World Settlement* (Garden City: Garden City Publishing Co., 1943).

40. See Emery Reves, *Anatomy of Peace,* reprinted in David Brook, ed., *Search for Peace* (New York: Dodd, Mead, 1970), p. 364.

41. From an interview on June 23, 1946; cited in Linus Pauling, *No More War* (New York: Dodd, Mead, 1958), p. 213.

42. See Cord Meyer, Jr., *Peace or Anarchy* (Boston: Little, Brown, 1947); and *Beliefs, Purposes, and Aims* (New York, 1948).

43. See Robert Maynard Hutchins, "The Constitutional Foundations for World Order," in *Foundations for World Order* (Denver, 1949), p. 100.

44. Hutchins, "Consitutional Foundations for World Order," p. 105.

45. See Clarence Streit, *Union Now: A Proposal for an Atlantic Federal Union of the Free* (New York: Harper & Bros., 1949).

46. See Owen J. Roberts, John F. Schmidt, and Clarence Streit, *The New Federalist* (New York: Harper, 1950). The authors characterized themselves as Publius II.

47. It is worth noting that in *Federalist* no. 6, Alexander Hamilton addresses the problem of international hostility directly, focusing on the "dismembered" and "alienated" character of states as the prima facie cause of war between them.

48. See Grenville Clark, *A Plan for Peace* (New York: Harper, 1950).

49. See Grenville Clark and Louis Sohn, *World Peace Through World Law* (Cambridge: Harvard University Press, 1966).

50. Linus Pauling, *No More War*, p. 149.

51. Bertrand Russell, *Has Man a Future?* (Baltimore: Penguin, 1961), p. 71.

52. Grenville Clark and Louis Sohn, *World Peace Through World Law*. The year 1966 is also the publication year of David Mitrany's *A Working Peace System* (Chicago: Quadrangle, 1966), which challenges the reasonableness of the "constitutional" approach to peace. Instead, Mitrany offers a "functional" approach, i.e., one that seeks true international community and security via nonpolitical sorts of association and cooperation. Authority is linked to a specific activity rather than to a definite territory.

53. Betty Reardon and Saul H. Mendlovitz, "World Law and Models of World Order," in Charles R. Beitz and Theodore Herman, eds., *Peace and War* (San Francisco: W.H. Freeman, 1973), p. 159.

54. Reardon and Mendlovitz, p. 160. The identification of the world law model with world federal government reflects a narrow definition of international law, i.e., a definition that ties international law to the presence of government.

55. See Richard A. Falk, *A Study of Future Worlds* (New York: The Free Press, 1975).

56. Falk, *A Study of Future Worlds*, p. 11.

57. The effectiveness of an arrangement for managing power is evaluated in terms of the likelihood of interactor violence. By world system I mean the most comprehensive system whose component parts are human aggregates. By sovereign authority I mean the ultimate right to make decisions and enforce obedience in the world system. By force I mean the weapons of war—guns, battleships, missiles, etc.

58. See Charles R. Beitz and Theodore Herman, eds., *Peace and War, op. cit.*, p. 163.

CHAPTER 3

World Order Reform Through Behavioral Change
TRANSFORMING PEOPLE

Scholars historically have responded to the continuing crises of global society with *institutional* proposals for world order reform. Even today, with few exceptions, students of world affairs seek solutions to pressing problems in new norms and procedures for global regulation. This chapter and the next rest on the understanding that a new orientation is needed, one that would not replace institutional strategies of world order reform, but augment them. This orientation, which I will call "behavioral," shifts attention from the longstanding emphasis on the invention and implementation of institutions to the very nature of human beings and the characteristic inclinations of states. This shift will lead to new and promising strategies for improved global relations.

THE POLITICAL PERSPECTIVE

In the study of political matters, great weight in the explanation of major international problems has always been assigned to humankind's basic imperfections and intrinsic unworthiness. Writing nearly four hundred years before the birth of Christ, Thucydides, the great historian of the Peloponnesian War, offers the following explanation of the conflict's convulsive effects on the Hellenic world:

. . . with the ordinary conventions of civilized life thrown into confusion, human nature, always ready to offend even where laws exist, showed itself proudly in its true colors, as something incapable of controlling passion, insubordinate to the idea of justice, the enemy to anything superior to itself; for, if it had not been for the pernicious power of envy, men would not have so exalted vengeance above innocence and profit above justice.[1]

Plato's theory, offered in the fourth century B.C., seeks to explain politics as an unstable realm of sense and matter, an arena formed and sustained by half-truths and distorted perceptions. In contrast to the stable realm of immaterial Forms, from which all genuine knowledge must be derived, the political realm is dominated by the uncertainties of the sensible world. At the basis of this political theory is a physical-mental analogy that establishes a correlation between the head, the heart, and the abdomen, and the virtues of intelligence, courage, and moderation.[2]

For Plato, the central problem of the political realm lies in the failure to join political authority with philosophy. In what is perhaps the best-known passage in the *Republic*, Plato contends that human improvement is contingent upon philosophers acquiring political authority or upon kings becoming true philosophers. In a truly ideal state, the philosopher-king—nurtured and sustained by an educational system that recognizes virtue as knowledge—would embody the rule of pure reason.

In early Christendom, Saint Augustine offered a system of thought that identifies the locus of global problems in the human potentiality for evil. Combining the philosophy of Neoplatonism with a view of the universe as a struggle between good and evil, Augustine attributed the tribulations of humanity to the taint of original sin. This view, transformed into a secular political philosophy, is now reflected by all exponents of the school of *realism* or *realpolitik*.

It should not be surprising, therefore, that St. Augustine—who is largely responsible for the idea of a *respublica Christiana* or Christian Commonwealth discussed earlier in this book—should have had such a cynical view of the state or polity. Writing at the beginning of the fifth century A.D., he sets out, in the *City of God,* to describe human history as a contest of two societies, the intrinsically debased City of Man and the eternally peaceful City of God. In this contest, the state, the product of

114

humankind's most base tendencies, is devoid of justice and destructive of salvation. A mirror image of human wickedness, the state is little more than a "large gang of robbers." Indeed, in an oft-quoted passage, St. Augustine recalls the answer offered by a pirate captured by Alexander the Great, who asked him what right he had to infest the seas: "The same right that you have to infest the world. But because I do it in a small boat I am called a robber, while because you do it with a large fleet you are called an emperor."

The sixteenth-century Florentine philosopher, Niccolo Machiavelli, joined Aristotle's foundations for the scientific study of politics with the assumptions of *realpolitik* to reach certain conclusions about the behavioral bases of politics. One of his most important conclusions underscores the dilemma of practicing goodness in an essentially evil world: "A man who wishes to make a profession of goodness in everything must necessarily come to grief among so many who are not good."[3] Recognizing this tragic state of affairs, Machiavelli proceeds to advance the arguments for expediency that have become synonymous with his name.

With the placing of the idea of force at the center of his political theory, the author of the *Prince* and the *Discourses on the First Ten Books of Titus Livius* stands in sharp contrast to the Platonic and early Christian concepts of the "good." Rejecting both Plato's argument that there is a knowable objective "good" that leads to virtue and St. Augustine's otherworldly idea of absolute goodness, Machiavelli constructs his political theory from the assumption that "all men are potential criminals, and always ready to realize their evil intentions whenever they are free to do so." Small wonder, then, that in his instructions to the statesman on how to rule in a world dominated by force, he advises "to learn how not to be good."

The seventeenth-century materialist and social philosopher, Thomas Hobbes, elaborated a complex system of thought in which man was reduced to a state of nature and then reconstructed. Seeking a science of human nature that would have the rigor of physics, Hobbes looked to introspection as the source of genuine understanding: "Whosoever looketh into himself and considereth what he doth when he does think, opine, reason, hope, fear, etc., and upon what grounds; he shall thereby read and know, what are the thoughts and passions of all other men, upon the like occasions."[4] The results of such an analysis of one's own thought processes led Hobbes to his celebrated theory of the social contract: the natural egoism of man produces a "war of all against all" in the absence of civil government and must be tempered by absolute monarchy. Moreover, the condition of nature, which is also called a condition of war marked by "continual fear, and danger of violent death," has been the characteristic condition of world politics:

> But though there had never been any time, wherein particular men were in a condition of war one against another; yet in all times, kings, and persons of sovereign-authority, because of their independency, are in continual jealousies, and in the state and posture of gladiators; having their weapons pointing, and their eyes fixed on one another; that is, their forts, garrisons, and guns upon the frontiers of their kingdoms; and continual spies upon their neighbors; which is a posture of war.[5]

WAR AND HUMAN BEHAVIOR

War, above all other world order concerns, has been identified prominently with behavioral origins. In addition to those thinkers already mentioned, the human roots of war are examined in the works of Erasmus, Confucius, Isaiah, Epictetus, Jesus, Tertullian, St. Francis, Aristophanes, and Tolstoy among almost countless others. Today legions of behavioral scientists continue the quest, spurred on by the idea expressed in the Preambleto the UNESCO charter: ". . . Since wars begin in the minds of men, it is in the minds of men that the defences of peace must be constructed."

But what sort of defenses must they be? Is war an ineradicable aspect of humankind's biological endowment, an affliction of the germ plasm to be endured with resignation? Is it aggression, rather than war, that man carries from birth to death, and which may or may not produce organized intergroup conflict? Or is even personal aggression a product of humankind's twisted and stressful cultural environment rather than of its instinctual, animal heritage?

History, as we all know, is the record of a continuous bath of blood. From the ancient recitals of Homer's *Iliad* to the more carefully documented cruelties of modern times, the story of humankind relates an orgy of power and plunder, of jingoism and imperialism, of killing and enslavement. Must this story continue without interruption until the species itself has become extinct, or can it be stopped in time? And if it can be stopped, must the stopping mechanism including transforming people?

To answer these questions, let us consider some of the better-known commentaries on the question of war and human behavior.

Writing in 1929, George Malcolm Stratton offers the following observation:

> Those who declare that war comes from human nature and that human nature does not change, have weighty evidence in their favor. Wars have occurred since the remotest time of history and were doubtless waged long before history began. Fighting less organized than war reaches still farther back . . . . into the animal world.[6]

Almost a generation later, Sir Arthur Keith reaffirmed Stratton's view that humanity seems pugnacious in its very nerve and muscle, that "fierce war must be attributed to an inborn fierce nature which has developed in tribes long subjected to the rigors of competitive evolution."[7]

A contemporary proponent of this view is Robert Ardrey, who is particularly concerned with man's instincts, specifically with the instinctual force exerted on human life by territory. Ardrey concludes that "a common cause for war lies in the aggressor's ignorance of the enormous animal energies which his intrusion will release in a seemingly weak territorial defender."[8]

Commenting on this view in his own discussion of native aggressiveness as a cause of war, social psychologist Otto Klineberg says the following:

> A variant of the view that human aggressiveness causes wars is represented by the theory that in animals as well as in humans, a fundamental impulse is to maintain "territoriality." Ardrey (1961) argues that fights arise when one's territory is attacked or threatened, and that throughout the animal kingdom this is what causes individual and group conflict, and many ways of resolving it, and the exclusive emphasis on one motive and one outcome hardly carries conviction.[9]

In another context he states:

> . . . aggressiveness, whether or not it has an innate basis, may be modified by the culture in many ways. It may be stimulated in one society

and relatively lacking in another. It may arise as the result of any one of a number of different causes. It may express itself in violent physical combat or in a socially regulated contest in which no one is harmed. There is no justification, therefore, for the attempt to explain any specific type of aggressive behavior on the ground that it has a biological basis. To the question as to whether war is inevitable because of the existence of such an aggressive instinct, the ethnologist and the social-psychologist have reason to give a categorical negative. War is an institution, and must be explained in relation to the whole structure in which it occurs.[10]

According to Klineberg, the capacity for aggressive behavior may be a necessary antecedent to war, but it certainly is not the sole effective cause. There is nothing in human nature that makes war inevitable; thus, "personal aggressiveness . . . is definitely not an adequate explanation of war."[11]

This view is seconded by Clyde Kluckhohn:

Nothing can be further from the truth than the shibboleth that "human nature is unalterable" if by human nature is meant the specific form and content of personality. Any theory of personality which rests upon such a basis is necessarily weak, for personality is preeminently a social product and human society is ever on the march.[12]

Perhaps the most prominent modern student of human aggression and war is the Nobel laureate ethologist, Konrad Lorenz.[13] Recognizing that aggression between individuals cannot automatically explain aggression between states, Lorenz argues that the aggressive "instinct" finds an important outlet in war. However, aggression need not cause war if it can be redirected. In this conclusion, which favors the cathartic discharge of aggression through sublimation, Lorenz is reminiscent of Freud, who argues that "complete suppression of man's aggressive tendencies is not in issue; what we may try is to divert it into a channel other than that of warfare."[14]

While differing with Freud and Lorenz on the issue of a general aggressive drive, Edward O. Wilson, who describes aggression as an "ill-defined array of different responses with separate controls in the nervous system," shares the belief that human aggression is innate. According to Wilson, whose extension of population biology and evolutionary theory to social organization has produced the philosophy of sociobiology:

118

Are human beings innately aggressive? This is a favorite question of college seminars and cocktail party conversations, and one that raises emotion in political ideologues of all stripes. The answer to it is yes. Throughout history, warfare, representing only the most organized technique of aggression, has been endemic to every form of society, from hunter-gatherer bands to industrial states.[15]

But how are we to deal with human aggression? Today's "answers," none of which seems particularly practical or, for the matter, particularly desirable, range from psychosurgical intervention to a Skinnerian "technology of behavior." One polar extreme suggests visions of an "ablatarchy" and an end to war by the electric excision of aggression-regions of the brain.[16] The other suggests arranged environments to produce sought-after patterns of behavior through selected reinforcement.[17]

Under certain natural conditions, aggression helps any particular animal species to survive. For our own species, however, aggression has become maladaptive. Rather than serve our survival goals, it now threatens to destroy them through the use of highly destructive weapons technologies. This is the case because our collective development of such technologies has now outstripped our behavioral mechanisms of inhibition and containment.

For students of world order reform, this suggests a need for diverting human aggression toward more productive pursuits. Earlier in this century, William James recognized this need and suggested a rechanneling of warlike virtues in peaceful directions. It is likely, however, that something more is needed, some strategy of behavioral transformation that seeks not only less socially destructive outlets for aggression but also the development and improvement of certain human institutions. Such a strategy could prove to be a most promising fusion of two previously distinct paths to a more harmonious world order.

THE PROBLEM OF NUCLEAR WAR

The human roots of war have sometimes been explained in terms of the psychoanalytic mechanism known as *denial*, whereby a dangerous situation is dismissed as nonexistent. Nowhere is this maladaptive response more striking than in the current worldwide unconcern for

119

nuclear war. Unless the human population comes to understand the full implications of the nuclear war threat, denial may ultimately prove to be the single most important cause of world order collapse. Unless we begin to experience some widespread shocks of recognition about our current nuclear collision course, there is little hope that humankind can escape its last paroxysm.

Spasmodic instances of awareness are not enough. If we are to prevent nuclear catastrophe in world politics, we must begin immediately to hone our anticipatory imagination of a shattered planet. The wreckage of moral, spiritual, and physical being that would descend in the wake of nuclear war must be made more visible if it is to be avoided.

The ground is slowly dissolving under our feet, but we are either unaware of the situation or pretend not to notice. Our pretences that irretrievable nuclear disaster cannot happen represent a fatal flight from reality. Our only hope for survival lies in facing the awesome possibilities squarely and in transforming our primal terrors into constructive strategies of prevention.

Humankind's tendency to flee from a seemingly intolerable reality is communicated brilliantly in Doris Lessing's novel, *The Memoirs of a Survivor*. Amidst a dark vision of the not-so-distant future, when humanity gropes for security in a rapidly disintegrating world, the narrator captures our species' peculiar penchant for collective denial.

> For instance, on the newscasts and in the papers they would pursue for days the story of a single kidnapped child, taken from its pram perhaps by some poor unhappy woman. The police would be combing the suburbs and the countryside in hundreds, looking for the child, and for the woman, to punish her. But the next news flash would be about the mass deaths of hundreds, thousands, or even millions of people. We still believed, wanted to believe, that the first—the concern about the single child, the need to punish the individual criminal, even if it took days and weeks and hundreds of our hard-worked police force to do it—was what really represented us; the second, about the catastrophe, was, as such items of news had always been for people not actually in the threatened area, an unfortunate and minor—or at least not crucial—accident, which interrupted the even flow, the development, of civilization.

There are fissures in the columns of false hopes that sustain our global civilization. These fissures must be enlarged and the entire edifice of empty expectations destroyed if a more enduring structure of world order is to be erected. Humankind must learn to spark and nurture deep intimations of a post-holocaust future as an essential first step toward averting such a future. To accomplish this, we must look unflinchingly at the full, unvarnished consequences of nuclear war.

Sapere aude! Dare to know! This motto for the Enlightenment suggested by the philosopher Kant acquires a special meaning in the late twentieth-century study of nuclear war. Just as denial of the fear of death by individual human beings can occasion activities that impair the forces of self-preservation, so can states impair their prospects for survival by insulating themselves from reasonable fears of collective disintegration. While it is true that the fear of death must be tempered in both individual and national drives lest it create paralysis, to deny the effect of such fear altogether is to make the threat of extinction *more imminent.*

The prospect of nuclear war is also tied very closely to the *rationality* of national leaders. Although the assumption of rationality lies at the very heart of the "logic" of nuclear deterrence, it is altogether likely that *irrationality* and nuclear weapons capability will sometime overlap. When this happens, the relationship between human nature and world order will become explosively apparent.

We live in a world in which the security of more than four billion people rests on the continuing rationality of only a handful of national leaders. This handful is bound to multiply several fold before the year 2000. While we must now contend with the possibility of no more than a half dozen potentially irrational nuclear leaders, tomorrow we may have to contend with at least fifty. The odds are not very encouraging. As the distinguished psychiatrist Jerome Frank has pointed out, "At least seventy-five chiefs of state in the last four centuries led their countries while suffering from severe mental disturbances."[18] Are we really entitled to assume that such leadership can never take place in a nuclear weapons country? The present system of nuclear deterrence *is* explicitly based upon precisely this assumption. If it is unreasonable, then we are rapidly approaching the end of the "fuse."

And unreasonable it appears to be. An irrational order to use nuclear weapons can stem from a variety of personal ills. It need not necessarily derive from the "usual" characteristics of mental illness or madness.

For example, what Dr. Frank has described as the "creeping

incapacity under the pressure of age" can have the same effect as flagrant mental illness. According to Frank:

> The characteristic manifestations of hardening of the arteries of the brain are general loss of energy and adaptive capacity, impairment of ability to concentrate, lapses of memory . . . . periods of confusion, emotional liability, and irritability. A leader with such disabilities is poorly equipped to meet the demands of modern leadership, especially when he is apt to be faced with prolonged crises in which decisions must be made under emotional stress and without sufficient sleep.[19]

The peculiar *stress* of national leadership, especially in such dangerous times, may have a very important effect upon the probability of irrational decisions. In this connection, Dr. Frank points out an interesting, but terrifying fact: Because of the great strides that are being made by modern medicine, we are entering into an epoch wherein all human organs *except the brain* can be repaired or replaced altogether. The predicted result of this uneven progress is "an increasing proportion of national leaders with vigorous bodies and potentially failing minds."[20]

But the problem predates this new epoch. Even the American experience reveals a number of presidents who were expected to discharge their responsibilities while suffering from various kinds of incapacities. Woodrow Wilson suffered a severe stroke during his incumbency. Franklin Roosevelt, during his fourth term, was obviously a very weak man suffering from advanced hardening of the arteries of the brain. And Eisenhower had both a heart attack and a stroke. According to Dr. Frank, Roosevelt was "a dying man at Yalta, unable to brief himself adequately for the conference . . .," while Eisenhower, after his slight stroke in 1957, described his own mental state as follows:

> . . . a confusion of mind. I just couldn't pick up a pen. I messed some papers off the desk. I went down to pick them up. I didn't know where to put them.[21]

These are sobering revelations for students of world order reform, not so much for what they suggest about what might have happened at the time as for what they suggest about the future—a future of many national leaders with a nuclear weapons capability who might exercise that capability out of madness, stress, or other form of body impairment. To take this sort of future seriously, we needn't confine our attention to such distant examples as Caligula, Nero, or Mad Ludwig of Bavaria. Nor do we have to point to the much more recent historical example of Hitler, which indicates that madness and consummate political skill are easily joined. Although no American president seems to have displayed the obviously delusional traits of James Forrestal, the first American Secretary of Defense, who feared that the sockets of beach umbrellas recorded everything he was saying and who finally jumped out of a window, the examples of Wilson, Roosevelt, and Eisenhower frankly point to disturbing possibilities of irrationality. The fact that these possibilities stemmed neither from malevolence nor madness does little to temper the understanding that such incapacities can take their victims down very dangerous paths.

Finally, the prospect of nuclear war is tied very closely to the *language* human beings have adopted for strategic studies. Such euphemisms as "limited nuclear war," "collateral damage," "countervalue" and "counterforce" strategies, and "enhanced radiation warfare"[22] are insidious to the cause of peace because they tend to make the currency of nuclear warfighting valid coin. Just as the barbarisms of the Nazis were made possible through such linguistic disguises as "final solution," "resettlement," "special treatment," and "selections," so do the euphemisms of the nuclear age make nuclear war more likely. To counter the current euphemisms that may etherize an unwitting humanity into accepting nuclear war, humankind must come to understand how much it is already lost in its own gibberish. In doing this, the species may eradicate still one more behavioral obstacle to survival and world order reform.

WAR AND DISORDER

Other approaches to the human roots of war have focused on the concepts of frustration, insecurity, and anxiety.[23] *Frustration* has become especially well-known for its part in what is known as "frustration-aggression theory."[24] Proponents of this theory argue that "frustrations in early childhood create adults who, often unconsciously, want war; consequently, the best way to prevent war is to reduce such early frustrations, and thereby remove the need to find an 'enemy' upon whom to exercise one's latent hostility."[25]

Not unlike such theories are those which make use of *insecurity* as an explanatory concept. Says Harold Lasswell:

Wars and revolutions are avenues of discharge for collective insecurities and stand in competition with every alternative means of dissipating mass tension. The reduction of violence in world politics means strengthening the competitive power of activities whose human costs are less . . . . The politics of prevention calls for a continuing audit of the world level of insecurity. The political psychiatrist, assuming the desirability of enabling human activities to evolve at a minimum of human cost, approaches the problem of war and revolution as one detail of the whole task of mastering the sources and mitigating the consequences of human insecurity in our unstable world.[26]

And according to Clyde Kluckhohn:

When the *security* of individuals or the cohesion of a group is threatened, scapegoats are almost always sought and found. They may be either other individuals within the group or they may be an outside group. The first phenomenon may be observed alike in the chicken yard and in any human society. The second phenomenon seems to be the principal psychological basis for modern wars. This question of "what to do about hate satisfaction" faces every social order.[27]

Frustration, however, has been the focus of attention not only for those concerned with the problem of war, but also for those interested in the study of disorder and mass social movements.[28] One such example is Eric Hoffer, whose basic hypothesis is that the frustrated predominate among the early adherents of all mass movements and that they usually join of their own accord. According to Hoffer:

1. Frustration, of itself, without any proselytizing prompting from the outside, can generate most of the peculiar characteristics of the true believer.
2. An effective technique of conversion consists basically in the inculcation and fixation of proclivities and responses indigenous to the frustrated mind.[29]

According to Zevedei Barbu, frustration and insecurity together help to explain the social, political, and spiritual movement of Nazism:

It answered a state of frustration and insecurity widespread in all strata of the population during this period. It would also be right to infer from this that the cadres, and particularly the leadership of the party, were made up of individuals and groups who suffered more than others from frustration and insecurity.[30]

One of the most distinguished political scientiests to focus upon the explanatory concept of *anxiety* has been Franz Neumann. According to Neumann, the conspiracy theory of history is closely related to "caesaristic identification and false concreteness."[31] First, one must make distinctions. There are nonaffective identifications, i.e., those in which coercion or common material interests play an essential role and which involve a minimal libidinal tie, if any, and affective, i.e., libido-charged, identifications. Of the latter, two additional subtypes may be identified:

> One may call them cooperative and caesaristic. It is conceivable . . . that many equals identify themselves cooperatively with one another in such a manner that their egos are merged in the collective ego. But this cooperative form is rare . . . . The decisive affective identification is that of masses with leaders. It is—as I have said—the most regressive form, for it is built upon a nearly total ego-shrinkage. It is the form which is of decisive significance for us. We call it caesaristic identification.[32]

Neumann argues that wherever caesaristic, affective leader identification occurs in politics, both masses and leaders share a conspiratorial theory of history. Thus, "that the distress which has befallen the masses has been brought about exclusively by a conspiracy of certain persons or groups against the people. With this view of history, true anxiety, which had been produced by war, want, hunger, anarchy, is to be transformed into neurotic anxiety, and is to be overcome by means of identification with the leader demagogue through total ego-renunciation, to the advantage of the leader and his clique, whose true interests do not necessarily have to correspond to those of the masses."[33]

In his own discussion of conspiratorial theories of history, historian Richard Hofstadter has evaluated the "style" of American politics as "paranoid." Hofstadter resorts to psychological description "simply because no other word adequately evokes the qualities of heated exaggeration, suspiciousness, and conspiratorial fantasy that I have in mind."[34] The basic elements of this paranoid style, according to Hofstadter, are:

. . . vast and sinister conspiracy, a gigantic and yet subtle machinery of influence set in motion to undermine and destroy a way of life . . . . The distinguishing thing about the paranoid style is not that its exponents see conspiracies or plots here and there in history, but that they regard a "vast" or "gigantic" conspiracy as *the motive force* in historical events.[35]

Just as Hofstadter described "paranoid style," Erich Fromm, commenting on political and social problems—categorized all political thinking into two classes: sane and pathological. In his discussion of sane versus pathological thinking in politics, Fromm begins with a description of one of the more extreme forms of pathological thinking—"paranoid thinking." Hofstadter's reference to "conspiracy as the motive force" closely resembles Fromm's reference to the confusion over the difference between what is possible and what is probable:

It is easy for people to recognize paranoid thinking in the individual case of a paranoid psychotic. But to recognize paranoid thinking when it is shared by millions of other people and approved by the authorities who lead them, is more difficult. A case in point is the conventional thinking about Russia. Most Americans today think about Russia in a paranoid fashion, namely, they ask what is *possible* rather than what is *probable* . . . . If we only think of *possibilities*, then indeed, there is no chance for realistic and sensible political action. Sane thinking means not only to think of possibilities, which are in fact always relatively easy to recognize, but to think also of probabilities.[36]

Fromm similarly regards "fanatical" political thinking as a pathological thought process, different from conventional pathology only in that political thoughts are shared by a group rather than one or two individuals. "The fanatic," says Fromm,

. . can be described as a highly narcissistic person who is disengaged from the world outside. He does not really feel anything since authentic feeling is always the result of the interrelation between oneself *and* the world. The fanatic's pathology is similar to that of a depressed person who suffers not from sadness (which would be a relief) but from the incapacity to feel anything. The fanatic is different from the depressed person (and in some ways similar to the maniac) inasmuch as he has found a way out of acute depression. He has built for himself an idol, an absolute, to which he surrenders completely but of which he also makes himself a part.[37]

STATUS AND WORLD ORDER

Just as frustration, insecurity, and anxiety have been particularly common focal points of international political analysis, so has an explanatory emphasis on "deference" become widespread. In fact, the opinion that one cannot explain political behavior except by reference to status has been offered by Davies and others who speak of both "the unequal distribution of deference" and "status politics." According to Davies, "It may have been usually true that, as Madison and Marx have said, inequality of property is the most enduring cause of political conflict. But it may be better to broaden the concept to status and say that differences in status, when these become rigid and socially enforced, have been and remain an enduring source of conflict." Further, continues Davies,

> From time to time noneconomic issues emerge which can quite overwhelm the importance of economic issues. People neither live nor vote by bread alone . . . . The difficulty is that politics is fraught with explosive force when people rise above the subsistence level, want more goods and more liberty, and fear they may lose either or both. And people now are in that frame of mind all over the world, . . . A trying time for the psyches of men.[38]

The notion that "status politics" grows in importance when phenomena of interest politics and ideological politics decrease in importance has been expressed by sociologists and historians as well as by political scientists. In the opinion of Daniel Bell:

> The politics of conflict in any country inevitably has some emotional dimension, but in the United States, lacking a historically defined doctrinal basis—as against the ideological divisions of Europe—it takes on, when economic-interest group issues are lacking, a psychological or status dimension.[39]

A frequent manifestation of status politics is a particular group or class that is threatened by loss of status while failing to understand the reasons for this threat. According to Franz Neumann, this situation can best be understood in terms of anxiety: "The intensification of anxiety into persecutory anxiety is successful when a group (class, religion, race) is threatened by loss of status, without understanding the process which leads to its degradation."[40]

To Erich Fromm, status politics is best understood not in terms of anxiety, but in terms of fear of "change." Says Fromm, "Man, in each society, seems to absolutize the way of life and the way of thought produced by his culture and to be willing to die rather than to change, since change, to him, is equated with death. Thus, the history of man is a graveyard of great cultures that came to catastrophic ends because of their incapacity for planned, rational, voluntary reaction to challenge."[41]

POLITICAL MAN

Students of politics have also begun to consider the human roots of our world order crisis by studying the problem of why people enter politics in the first place and why, once they have entered politics, they direct their energies in the particular way that they do. According to Robert E. Lane, man seeks political involvement as a means of relieving "intrapsychic tensions,"[42] while Robert Dahl suggests that an individual is unlikely to get involved in politics "if he places a low valuation on the rewards to be gained from political involvement relative to the rewards expected from other kinds of activity."[43] This statement is based, says Professor Dahl,

> . . . on the fact that man is not by instinct a reasonable, reasoning, civic-minded being. Many of his most imperious desires and the source of many of his most powerful gratifications can be traced to ancient and persistent biological and psychological drives, needs, and wants . . . . To avoid pain, discomfort, and hunger; to satisfy drives for sexual gratification, love, security and respect—these needs are insistent and primordial. The means of satisfying them quickly and concretely lie outside political life.[44]

Beginning with a lengthy scrutiny of the histories of specific individuals, and relying upon the procedures and findings of psychopathology, Harold Lasswell has attempted to generate hypotheses specifying links between the development of human personality (especially the direction and strength of "unconscious" factors in this development) and the nature of political participation.[45] Making use of a "Lasswellian" type of analysis, Gabriel Almond attempted to generate some hypotheses about reasons for joining the Communist Party by interviewing a group of American psychoanalysts who had Communists as patients and subsequently examining thirty-five clinical case histories of Communists.[46]

Power and Personality

Students of the power phenomenon, the central concept of international relations studies, also have found psychological categories of explanation useful. According to Bertrand Russell, the impulse to power is distinctive to man in that, unlike an animal, his drives cannot be fully satisfied. Man is insatiable. While animal activity, with few exceptions, is inspired by primary needs such as survival and reproduction, human activity is not. Man seeks something beyond the abatement of primary needs. He seeks power, but as such desires are infinite, repose may be found only "in the infinitude of God."[47]

Regarding the power impulse in some form or other as an integral libidinal component, certain elements of Russell's scheme are roughly analagous to the Freudian model. Both Freud and Russell affirm the inherent difficulty of reconciling man's drives to his universe. Yet Russell identifies the dilemma with infinitude (human drives and impulses to power are simply too numerous ever to be fully realized), while Freud locates the impediment in the conflict between individual claims and societal restrictions. The decisive step of civilization is, in fact, the substitution of community power for individual power.[48]

While Russell cannot conceive of satisfying the human impulse to power, Freud allows for the amelioration of suffering by recognizing the employment of libidinal displacements. Here, the impulse to power is displaced on to socially acceptable activities, representing a way out of the "dilemma."[49] Cravings for power are socially proscribed when openly proclaimed.[50] Hence, there is a displacement of these drives that is legitimized in the name of plausible symbols. The individual does not act openly with the intention of securing gestures of deference for his ego. Rather, he implies that he strives for the "glory of God, the sanctity of the Home, the independence of the Nation, the emancipation of the Class."[51] Private motives are displaced on to public objects and the displacement is rationalized in terms of public advantage.[52]

The so-called "liberal" attitude, nurtured in the climate of the Thomistic notion that power is not unnatural, represents a culmination of the view that power is a "natural" phenomenon.[53] However, its recognition is coupled with distrust. Power must be rendered both predictable and accountable. Metaphorically, fences must be erected around power centers and the sources of such traditional historical restraints as the state and church. The central question to be asked concerns the relation of power to responsibility. Currently, the pluralist society is seen by many as the modern analog of the classic liberal society.

One of the first to recognize the vital interaction between personality and power was Charles Merriam:

> . . . many of the secrets of political power may be found in the penetralia of the human personality, which we are just beginning to explore, and from which we may hope to return with far deeper insight into the riddles of human behavior. Psychology, psychiatry, psychoanalysis—will unlock the door to many chambers of life hitherto barred to the observer and give us a new basis for the understanding and interpretations of human activity in the political and social realm.[54]

According to Harold Lasswell, there exists a particular "political personality type."[55] This type is characterized by the accentuation of power in relation to other values, and an intense and ungratified craving for deference. Such cravings, having either been frustrated or overindulged within the primary sphere, are displaced upon public objects and rationalized in terms of public advantage. As Merriam has pointed out:

> It may also prove true that the profession of general interest and responsibility is merely a verbalism to cover selfish exploitation. In any case, deference to the "common interest" is a tribute to the basis of authority .. . . The tyrant will not admit that he is a tyrant . . . for he is always the vicar or someone or something, God or the Nation, or the Class or the Mass or the customs of his Folk.[56]

The power seeker thus pursues power as a means of compensation against deprivation. Politics is a substitutive reaction and power is expected to overcome low estimates of the self. In short, power is resorted to when it (as a representative value) is expected to contribute to overcoming low valuations of the self more than would the acquisition of any alternative value.[57]

130

In their seminal work on "political culture" and "political socialization," Gabriel Almond, James Coleman, and Sidney Verba have made considerable progress in exploring and explaining the behavioral bases of world order problems. The notion of "political culture," which makes use of concepts involving learning, is employed in only one of its many meanings as follows: "that of *psychological orientation toward social objects*. When we speak of the political culture of a society, we refer to the political system as internalized in the cognitions, feelings, and evaluations of its population."[58]

The field of public opinion research also has made considerable use of psychological categories, especially with regard to attitude and intelligence tests and measurements as well as with substantive concepts and propositions. Bernard Berelson has been particularly concerned with the relationships between democratic theory and public opinion research. More specifically, he has been concerned with particular requirements in democratic theory that refer to those characteristics demanded of the electorate as it initially comes to make a political decision, i.e., preconditions for electoral decisions. One of these preconditions—a suitable personality structure—is an area that is particularly amenable to psychological investigation. Says Berelson: "The influence of character on political democracy has been perceived in general terms by a number of theorists, and some psychologists and sociologists have begun to work on this topic."[59]

The Problem of Terrorism

Nowhere is the study of political character more central to world order reform than in the problem of terrorism. The individuals who comprise today's terrorist groups are spurred on by a great variety of motives. Some are moved by a genuine desire to remedy the terrible inequalities of an unjust social-political order. Others, in the fashion of bandits, are moved by the selfish search for material gain. Still others base their motive, consciously or unconsciously, on the need to escape from one form or another of private anguish. In this last category, we discover the "incapacity for authentic relatedness" described by Erich Fromm and the rage that is brought on by repeated doses of misfortune.

Occasionally, some combination of traits foments a genuinely psychopathic breed of terrorist, one who says, with Jerry Rubin, "When

131

in doubt, burn," or one who feels, with Kozo Okamoto, the surviving terrorist of the Lydda Airport massacre, "a strange ecstasy" in meting out death to innocents. In certain cases, such terrorists bear a bizarre resemblance to today's punk rockers, whose dominant rationale is to move, to shock, to goad, to outrage, to reveal potency without any real underlying ideology. For punk rockers, the essential tools of the trade are guitar, bass, and drums amplified to a neurologically destructive volume. For psychopathic terrorists, the essential implements are the instruments of violence, readied for indiscriminate slaughter. It would surely be a fatal mistake to conclude that such terrorists are incapable of wreaking profound unhappiness because of their condition. As Freud points out:

> Fools, visionaries, sufferers from delusions, neurotics, and lunatics have played great roles at all times in the history of mankind, and not merely when the accident of birth had bequeathed them sovereignty. Usually, they have wreaked havoc . . . .

Exhibiting an orientation to violence that has been shaped largely by the preachings of Bakunin, Fanon, and Sorel, many of today's terrorist groups have abandoned the idea of distinguishing between combatants and noncombatants in the selection of victims. Rather, these groups are engaged in total war against various countries, religions, and ethnic groups, and their choice of targets is typically unaffected by considerations of age, sex, or innocence. As a result of this calculus, terrorist activities have involved the killing and maiming of many people who have no particular part in the problem the terrorists seek to resolve.

In short, the imperative to create "boundaries" in the application of violence is ignored by many modern terrorist groups. This orientation stems in part from the romanticization of brutality that is a dominant motif of terrorist thinking. Even where it is doubtful that arbitrary violence will be productive of their desired goals, terrorists are sometimes moved by Bakunin's statement, "The passion for destruction is a constructive passion," and by the equally cathartic remark of Franz Fanon:

> Violence is a purifying force. It frees the native from his inferiority

132

REFORM: TRANSFORMING PEOPLE

complex and from despair and inaction. It makes him fearless and restores his self-respect.[60]

Such romanticizing breeds a cold-blooded view of the role of force. The ultimate expression of this view is a blind and nihilistic devotion to the "creativity" of violence. In its extreme form, this devotion reveals still another basis of the no-holds-barred orientation to violence that is characteristic of so much modern terrorism—the presence of psychopaths and sociopaths who enjoy carnage for its own sake. Here, the complete inversion of Judeo-Christian principles flows not from any devotion to the "creativity" of violence, but from purely psychotic motive. Where such motive is present among terrorists who are suicidal schizophrenics, the problems of effective counterterrorist action are greatly exacerbated. This is the case because such terrorists—whose incentive it is to use violence nihilistically rather than politically—are apt to regard the threat of death as a stimulus rather than as a deterrent.

A principal basis of the no-holds-barred orientation to violence that is present in modern terrorism lies in the position, articulated by many terrorist groups, that the overwhelming righteousness of their objectives justifies any means whatsoever; i.e., "The ends justify the means." As long as terrorist groups assume such a stance on violent excesses, they are susceptible to what political theorist Hannah Arendt has called the "banality of evil": individuals are capable of engaging in evil without experiencing it as evil.

In certain instances, this logic has led terrorists to displace responsibility for their own violent acts upon their victims. The statement by the leader of the Black September band concerning responsibility for the helicopter deaths in Munich is an example: "No Israelis would have been killed if the Germans had not trapped the operation. No one at all would have been killed if the Israelis had released their prisoners." Here, terrorist reasoning disclaims responsibility because the victim countries—West Germany and Israel—did not agree to blackmail. Such patterns of thinking, of course, contribute greatly to the logic of excessive violence of many terrorist groups.

To curb terrorist excesses before they consume even more lives, an effective behavioral strategy of counterterrorism must be formulated. Such a strategy must be based upon the understanding that there is no such thing as "the terrorist mind." Rather, there are a great many terrorist

133

minds, an unbelievably variegated potpourri of ideas and ideologies embraced by a tangled skein of participants and personalities. What must be established, therefore, is a limited and manageable number of basic strategies formed according to the principal types of terrorist group behavior. By adopting this means of "blueprinting" effective counterterrorist action, policy makers can be presented with a decision-making program in which strategies are differentiated according to the particular category of risk involved.

This is not to suggest that each terrorist group is comprised of individuals who exhibit the same pattern of behavior. Rather, each terrorist group is made up, in varying degrees, of persons with a wide variety of motives. Since, from the point of view of creating the necessary behavioral strategy, each terrorist group must be categorized according to a particular type of risk calculation, the "trick" is to identify and evaluate the leadership strata of each terrorist group in order to determine the predominant ordering of preferences. In so organizing their counterterrorist activity, governments can begin to develop a rationally conceived "behavioral technology" that distinguishes contingencies of reinforcement according to the particular type of terrorists involved. To deal effectively with the problem of terrorism, it is essential to correlate deterrent and remedial measures with the character and *modus operandi* of the particular terrorist group(s) in question.

For students of world order reform, however, it must also be kept in mind that terrorism is not inherently evil and that—in fact—it sometimes issues from very just causes. Indeed, where it is understood as resistance to despotism, terrorism has been defended in the Bible and in the writings of ancient and medieval texts. The right to rid society of tyrants is countenanced in Aristotle's *Politics,* Plutarch's *Lives,* and Cicero's *De Officiis.* According to Cicero:

> There can be no such thing as fellowship with tyrants, nothing but bitter feud is possible: and it is not repugnant to nature to despoil, if you can, those whom it is a virtue to kill; nay, this pestilent and godless brood should be utterly banished from human society. For, as we amputate a limb in which the blood and the vital spirit have ceased to circulate, because it injures the rest of the body, so monsters, who, under human guise, conceal the cruelty and ferocity of a wild beast, should be severed from the common body of humanity.[61]

134

As was noted earlier in this book, the legitimacy of certain forms of insurgency is also codified in modern international law. Both the 1973 General Assembly "Report of the Ad Hoc Committee on International Terrorism" and the General Assembly's 1974 Definition of Aggression protect the "inalienable right" to self-determination and independence of all peoples and the right of these peoples to struggle toward those ends. This "inalienable right" stems from a prevailing international consensus that recognizes basic human rights and obligations owed by all governments to their peoples and is reinforced by the Universal Declaration of Human Rights, the International Covenant on Civil and Political Rights, the International Covenant on Economic, Social and Cultural Rights, and by other international and regional human rights agreements. It follows that any concern for world order reform through behavioral change must include the elimination of repressive regimes as well as the balanced management of insurgent terror.

THE PHILOSOPHIC PERSPECTIVE

In the philosophy of human affairs, greater importance has usually been cast on the side of humankind's base and unruly character than upon its virtues. The kind of sentiment expressed by Moliere's *The Misanthrope*, which parallels the sentiments of *realpolitik* cited earlier, is typical of this view:

> All are corrupt; there's nothing to be seen
> In court or town but aggravates my spleen.
> I fall into deep gloom and melancholy
> When I survey the scene of human folly,
> Finding on every hand base flattery,
> Injustice, fraud, self-interest, treachery . . .
> Ah, it's too much; mankind has grown so base,
> I mean to break with the whole human race.

Students of world order reform must now begin to consider modifying the characteristic ways in which human beings structure their interactions with each other. Such an orientation would signal a new regard for some essential bases of global improvement.

The principal theme of this orientation must be maximal individual development balanced by the demands of interpersonal harmony. While a continuing antagonism seems to exist between the search for

135

personal progress and the requirements of social accord, it needn't be an irremediable sort of antagonism. We might explore the desirability and the feasibility of certain compromise "trade offs" between these competing claims and begin to set forth the basic behavioral underpinnings of a new world order.

The ancient philosopher Heraclitus tells us that opposition is the surest path to concert and that from things that differ and compete comes the most beautiful and complete harmony. The unceasing tension between individual and social fulfillment provides an exciting area of exploration for those students who are committed to heightening the chances for survival on this endangered planet. Humankind must perpetually cultivate its sense of boundless aspiration and energy, but how can this be accomplished in the absence of unrestrained egoism? Human beings must strive to become something unique and incomparable, but how can they accomplish this without producing antisocial effects?

To answer this question, the student of the "human transformation" route to world order reform must examine the means by which private wishes, once encouraged, can be tempered by public claims. He or she must seek to understand ways in which the character of these claims can be transformed from a relationship of competition to one of partnership. With such an understanding he or she may extend himself/herself beyond prevailing conceptions of a preferred world into a new vision of creative planetary improvement.

We know that it is not our fate to understand the universe. But we also know that it is not entirely unreasonable to try and cope with the "human condition." The shortcomings of our species are imprinted indelibly upon the works of our greatest thinkers. From Dante's *Divine Comedy* we have a remarkably comprehensive ordering of vices and virtues. From Swift's firm grip on the human creature in *Gulliver's Travels* we capture the essence of the odious Yahoos. And from Voltaire's *Candide* we discover an astounding truth: that of all the fantastic and horrible episodes in this tale—of the continuing rapine, shipwreck, and slaughter—only the brief interlude in the harmonious society of Eldorado is fictitious. The venal behavior and constant brutalization that transpire in "the best of all possible worlds" are historically accurate and painfully real. Only a land of congenial social interaction is fable.

What greater satisfaction can there be than to begin to unravel the

136

human roots of such accounts? What more productive approach to world order reform can the "behaviorally" oriented student claim for his/her efforts? This student can be aware that the essence of worthy planetary life lies promisingly at its human beginnings. To grope constantly for this essence is one notable manner in which a new world order may be fashioned and sustained. A good place to begin our search for a behavioral "way" is with a look at the Faust legend. The adjective *Faustian* signifies a continuing and restless striving for fulfillment, a search for the fullest and most profound appreciation of human existence. But it also signifies a willingness to pursue this search at all costs.

Humanity's search for individual development may run counter to its idea of community well-being. This dilemma, of course, revolves about the centuries-old conflict between the benefits of unfettered personal growth and the demands of interpersonal harmony. Too often, as Freud and others have pointed out, an irremediable antagonism is created between the search for unbridled personal progress and the wish for congenial modes of social interaction. Recognizing this, we must learn to accept certain restrictions on this progress as a world order objective. We must learn to accept a certain measure of incompatibility between such personal development and social harmony. This points to the acceptance of certain compromise "trade offs" between competing values and signifies an unwillingness to define improved world orders without regard for interdependence.

The world order student, therefore, must learn to steer a steady course between the sheer rock of Scylla and the whirlpool of Charybdis, between the fully egoistic pole of human development and the extreme condition of social accord at any price. Humanity must perpetually cultivate a sense of boundless aspiration and energy, but it must avoid unrestrained egotism. Goethe intended such egotism as Faust's undoing, and there is lasting wisdom in his meaning for students of world order: Individual striving must be tempered by an ongoing concern for its cumulative effects. Where these effects are markedly antisocial, striving has exceeded its proper bounds and become counterproductive to an improved global community.

How, then, can humankind achieve true fulfillment without abiding the presence of excessive self-centeredness? How must humanity strive?

Surely there is enormous pretense in venturing an answer, as Faust himself understood:

> I don't imagine I know anything worth while;
> I don't suppose I can teach anything
> To improve or convert the race of man.

But there is also enormous promise wrapped up in the effort. And there is no lack of places at which to begin. If the hour has not yet come to prove in people a genuinely heightened stature, we may at least explore what is needed to hasten its coming.

A suitable starting point is Goethe's dictum that a perfect creation must transcend itself and go on to become something very special. Applied to our species, this means an advance in the evolution of human consciousness toward a condition whereby each person achieves his/her highest being, not only in his/her individual life, but also in his/her collective life. It is this growth of consciousness that defines the behavioral key to an improved system of world order.

The beginning of an improved system of world order will come when growing numbers of people learn to develop their minds to the point where extant powers and capacities are pushed farther and farther back to new and more distant human boundaries. We must learn to understand that there exist much higher reaches of the mind than we are currently prepared to appreciate, and that these reaches must be continually sought and carefully cultivated. Only then will an appropriate transformation of self be possible.

This brings us back to an essential concern for the whole. To fulfill a preferred vision of human transformation, the progressive development of individual potentials must be carried out without losing sight of its cumulative effects. This we must always bear in mind. With the Roman emperor Marcus Aurelius, we must never cease asking the basic questions of *Meditations:*

> what is the nature of the whole, and what is my nature, and how is this related to that, and what kind of part is it of what kind of whole.

When we continue to ask these questions, we lessen the likelihood of personal growth becoming contrary to interpersonal harmony, of world

138

order reform developing in a fashion that is contrary to what people often recognize as "good."

Although this suggests that movement toward goodness in world order reform necessarily parallels movement toward a holistic awareness of the world, the core of a *good* world order inheres originally in each individual person. Here, however, we must resist the tendency to compartmentalize good and evil. We must remain aware of the interweaving strands of base character and lofty vision. We must recognize the *duality* of man's righteousness and wretchedness, the *coexistence* of good and evil in every person.

Looking back to what has just been considered, we see that world order improvement must proceed along "behavioral" lines and that individual human transformation must take account of the demands of social harmony. Paradoxically, a better system of world order must rest upon both personal development and on the willing renunciation of certain features of such development. To assist in binding this "partnership," humankind must renew its awareness of "oneness" or "connectedness." Each person's future is tied intimately to the whole. All people are linked to their fellows and to the larger universe of which they are a part. There are no unrelated beings.

The tradition of human unity and cosmopolis has a long and persuasive history. We have already noted that the great Roman stoic, Marcus Aurelius, understood the universe as one living being with one substance and all people as actors within a web of single texture. And we have already seen that by the Middle Ages, the idea of universality had fused with the idea of a *respublica Christiana,* a Christian Commonwealth, and Thomas, John of Salisbury, and Dante were contemplating Europe as a unified Christian community. This whole universe was tidy and orderly. At its center lay the earth, at once both a mere part of creation and a single, unified whole unto itself. Such a conception of human oneness ultimately set the stage for the cosmopolitanism of the Enlightenment.

Recently, the writings of Pierre Teilhard de Chardin appear in this tradition. As he states in his major work, *The Phenomenon of Man,* "Each element of the cosmos is positively woven from all the others. . . ." There is no way in which the network of cosmic matter can be sliced up into distinct, isolable units. Only one way of considering the universe is really possible, that is, "to take it as a whole, in one piece."

From the overarching singularity of their kind, men and women may learn that positive transformation requires an "opening out" to something beyond oneself. This singularity does not oppose the enriching function of differentiation, but it does point to an ordering of objectives in which confluence and convergence are uppermost. Whether or not we can actually conceive of a moment in which all peoples will consolidate and complete one another by cultural cross-fertilization, humankind's task must center about cohesion. Its future requires the understanding that any cause is subordinate to the aim of coming together.

With respect to the potential evolutionary future and prospects of the human race, we are born into a world of inconscience. But we are capable of an upward development of consciousness and an ascent into reaches wherein personal growth is easily harmonized with the good of the whole. To unloose this capability we must appreciate that a oneness lies hidden beneath the diversities of a seemingly fractionated world. People are cemented to each other not by haphazard aggregation, but by the certainty of their basic likeness and by their increasing interdependence.

We must aim at the realization of the unique and fulfilled Self in harmony with all others; an integral vision sparked by an impulse of human singularity. With the manifestation of the One in the Many, each individual may begin to pursue a progressive development of consciousness to ever-higher levels of mind without disregard for its cumulative effects. The world order consequences of this synthetic principle may embrace the beginnings of a new humanity.

NOTES

1. Thucydides, *The Peloponnesian War*, translated by Rex Warner (Baltimore: Penguin Books, 1954), p. 211.
2. Charles Merriam, "The Significance of Psychology for the Study of Politics," *The American Political Science Review*, XVIII, no. 3 (August 1924): 470.
3. See *The Prince*, Chapter XV.
4. See Introduction to *Leviathan*.
5. See *Leviathan*, Chapter XIII.
6. George Malcolm Stratton, *Social Psychology of International Conduct*

(New York, 1929), p. 245. "The fallacy of this purely personal explanation," says Gordon W. Allport, "lies in the fact that, however pugnacious or frustrated an individual may be, he lacks the capacity to make organized warfare. He is capable of temper tantrums, chronic nagging, biting sarcasm and personal cruelty; but he alone cannot invade an alien land or drop bombs upon a distant enemy to give vent to his own emotions. Furthermore, whereas national aggressiveness is total—all citizens being involved in offensive and defensive efforts—relatively few citizens feel personally hostile toward the enemy. Studies of soldiers in combat show that hate and aggression are less commonly felt than fear, homesickness, and boredom. Few citizens in an aggressive nation actually *feel* aggressive. Thus their warlike activity cannot be due solely to their personal motivations." [*Personality and Social Encounter* (Boston, Beacon Press, 1960), p. 328].

7. Sir Arthur Keith, *Evolution and Ethics* (New York, G.P. Putnam's, 1946). Citation is from Elton Atwater, Kent Forster, and Jan S. Prybla, *World Tensions: Conflict and Accommodation* (New York, Appleton, Century, Crofts, 1967), p. 94.

8. From the Introduction to Robert Ardrey, *The Territorial Imperative* (New York, Atheneum, 1966).

9. Otto Klineberg, *The Human Dimension in International Relations* (New York, Holt, Rinehart, & Winston, 1964), p. 16.

10. Otto Klineberg, *Social Psychology* (New York, Holt, 1954), p. 96.

11. Klineberg, *The Human Dimension in International Relations*, p. 15.

12. Clyde Kluckhohn, *Mirror For Man* (New York: Whittlesey House, 1944), p. 194.

13. See Konrad Lorenz, *On Aggression* (New York: Bantam Books, 1966).

14. Sigmund Freud's letter to Albert Einstein, Vienna, September 1932, reprinted in Leon Branson and George W. Goethals, eds., *War: Studies From Psychology, Sociology, Anthropology* (New York: Basic Books, 1968), p. 77

15. Edward O. Wilson, *On Human Nature* (Cambridge, Mass.: Harvard University Press, 1978), p. 99.

16. Ralph Pettman, *Human Behavior and World Politics* (New York: St. Martin's Press, 1975), p. 168.

17. B.F. Skinner, *Beyond Freedom and Dignity* (New York: Bantam Books, 1971).

18. Jerome D. Frank, *Sanity and Survival: Psychological Aspects of War and Peace* (New York: Random House, 1967), p. 59.

19. Frank, *Sanity and Survival*, p. 61.

20. Frank, *Sanity and Survival*, p. 62.

21. Frank, *Sanity and Survival*, pp. 60-61.

22. "Limited nuclear war" refers to a measured and strictly controlled strategic exchange confined to military and industrial targets. The consequences of such a war, if it were a real possibility, could involve tens of millions of fatalities.

"Collateral damage" refers to the damage done to human and nonhuman resources as a consequence of strategic strikes directed at enemy forces or military facilities. This damage could involve tens of millions of fatalities.

"Countervalue strategies" refers to targeting of an opponent's cities and/or industries, in other words, the targeting of millions of innocent civilians.

"Counterforce strategies" refers to targeting of an adversary's strategic military facilities. Such strategies are dangerous not only because of the "collateral damage" that they might produce, but also because they heighten the likelihood of first-strike attacks.

"Enhanced radiation warfare" refers to the use of thermonuclear weapons (commonly called the neutron bomb) that kill primarily through the distribution of radioactive neutrons while leaving buildings and other structures intact.

23. According to James C. Davies *(Human Nature in Politics,* New York: Wiley, 1963), all three of these categories—frustration, insecurity, and anxiety—may be subsumed under the heading of "tension." Says Davies, "As I will use the term, tension, it includes insecurity, anxiety, and frustration, but it includes both the disagreeable and the agreeable sensations of wanting. I use the term to describe a general, somewhat diffuse, mental state that is not identical with the need or needs that produced it" (p. 64).

24. See especially Pryns Hopkins, *The Psychology of Social Movements* (London, G. Allen & Unwin, 1938); Durbin and Bowlby, *Personal Aggressiveness and War* (London, Kegan Paul, 1939); and Alix Strachey, *The Unconscious Motives of War* (New York: International Universities Press, 1956).

25. Klineberg, *The Human Dimension,* p. 14.

26. Harold Lasswell, *World Politics and Personal Insecurity* (New York, McGraw, Hill, 1935), pp. 19-20.

27. Kluckhohn, *Mirror for Man,* p. 120.

28. Major works in this area include Hadley Cantril, *The Politics of Despair* (New York: Basic Books, 1958); *The Psychology of Social Movements* (New York, Wiley, 1941); *Tensions that Cause War* (Urbana: University of Illinois Press, 1950). Interesting also is the work by Gustav LeBon, *The Crowd* (New York, Viking, 1960); and the work of Hans Toch, *The Social Psychology of Social Movements* (Indianapolis, Bobbs-Merrill, 1965). Toch, a student of Cantril's, tends to corroborate Hoffer's notion that the core of every social movement is made up of zealots and fanatics who are, in fact, unconcerned with the movement's particular ideology.

29. From the Preface of Eric Hoffer, *The True Believer* (New York, Harper, 1951).

30. Zevedei Barbu, "The Uniqueness of the German Psyche, 1918-1933" in J. L. Snell, ed., *The Nazi Revolution* (Boston, D.C.Heath, 1959), p. 87.

31. Neumann, "Anxiety and Politics," in *The Democratic and the Authoritarian State* (London, Free Press, 1957), p. 279.

32. Neumann, "Anxiety and Politics," p. 278.

33. Neumann, "Anxiety and Politics," pp. 279-280.

34. Hofstadter, *The Paranoid Style in American Politics* (New York, Knopf, 1965), p. 3.

35. Hofstadter, *The Paranoid Style in American Politics*, pp. 29-30.

36. Fromm, *May Man Prevail?* (New York, Anchor Books, 1961), pp. 20-21.

37. Fromm, *May Man Prevail?* pp. 24-25.

38. Davies, *Human Nature in Politics*, p. 273.

39. Daniel Bell, in *The Radical Right* (New York, 1964), p. 41.

40. Neumann, "Anxiety and Politics," p. 293.

41. Fromm, *May Man Prevail?*, p. 5.

42. Robert E. Lane, *Political Life* (Glencoe: Free Press, 1959), p. 102.

43. Robert Dahl, *Modern Political Analysis* (Englewood Cliffs, N.J.: Prentice Hall, 1964), pp. 60-61.

44. Dahl, *Modern Political Analysis*.

45. See especially Harold D. Lasswell, *Psychopathology and Politics* (Chicago, University of Chicago Press, 1930).

46. See Gabriel A. Almond, *The Appeals of Communism* (Princeton, Princeton University Press, 1954).

47. Bertrand Russell, *Power: A New Social Analysis* (New York, W.W. Norton, 1938), p. 11.

48. Sigmund Freud, *Civilization and Its Discontents* (New York, W.W. Norton, 1961), p. 42.

49. Freud, *Civilization and Its Discontents*, p. 26.

50. This point is noted by Harold Lasswell, *Politics: Who Gets What, When, How*, (N.Y., McGraw-Hill, 1936); and Charles Merriam, *Political Power* (New York: McGraw Hill, 1934).

51. Lasswell, *Politics: Who Gets What, When, How*, p. 22.

52. Lasswell, *Politics*, p. 133.

53. Neumann, "Anxiety and Politics," p. 6.

54. Charles Merriam, *A Study of Power* (Glencoe, The Free Press, 1950), p. 6.

55. Much of Lasswell's work on the personalities of major political figures resembles the published "psychological study" of Woodrow Wilson by Sigmund Freud and W.C. Bullitt: "Born of unique collaboration," say the publishers, "this biography is a profound study of Woodrow Wilson's life and career based uncompromisingly upon Sigmund Freud's insights as the founder of psychoanalysis and upon the records of first-hand witnesses, including Mr. Bullitt himself. The authors reveal with devastating clarity how deeply disturbed a man Wilson was and how his inner conflicts altered the lives of all of us." (From the cover of *Thomas Woodrow Wilson*, Cambridge, Houghton, Mifflin Co., 1967).

56. Merriam, *A Study of Power*, p. 19.

57. Lasswell, *Power and Personality* (New York, W.W. Norton, 1948), p. 40.

58. See G.A. Almond and S. Verba, *The Civil Culture* (Boston, Little, Brown, 1963), p. 13. See also G.A. Almond and J.S. Coleman, *The Politics of the Developing Areas* (Princeton, Princeton University Press, 1960), for a discussion of "political socialization"; G.A. Almond, *The American People and Foreign*

Policy (New York, Harcourt, Brace, 1950); and Gabriel A. Almond, "Comparative Political Systems," *The Journal of Politics,* 18 (1956): 391-409.

59. Bernard Berelson, *Democratic Theory and Public Opinion in Political Behavior: A Reader in Theory and Research,* edited by Heinz Eulau, Samuel J. Eldersveld, & Morris Janowitz (Glencoe, Illinois, The Free Press, 1956), p. 108.

60. Constance Farrington, trans., *The Wretched of the Earth* (New York: Grove Press, 1963), p. 73.

61. Walter Laqueuv, *The Terrorism Reader: A Historical Anthology From Aristotle to the IRA and the PLO* (New York: New American Library, 1978), p. 16.

CHAPTER 4

World Order Reform Through Behavioral Change
TRANSFORMING STATES

States continue to be the basic units within which human beings structure their global interactions. States also continue to "behave" in a manner that can only be described as "egoistic." As is the case with individuals, such egoism is a primary barrier to world order reform. It follows that students of global affairs who seek to improve the quality of international political life must now begin to explore ways of changing the characteristically competitive nature of states.

The underlying problem is simple to understand. In a world system that lacks government, each state feels bound to increase its relative power position. In a world of "all against all" and "everyone for himself," each state feels obligated to pursue its goals on an intensely competitive basis even if the course of such competition should involve a high risk of worldwide impoverishment, disillusionment or even disintegration.

Ironically, such thinking and behavior by states continues to be called "realism." An international relations legacy from the time of Thucydides, the principles of *realpolitik* generate a spiraling pattern of fear and mistrust that progressively inhibit opportunities for general cooperation, freeze developing hostilities into fixed and intractable

145

camps, and ultimately explode into war. All in all, history has shown very clearly that "realism" is a predictable formula for global catastrophe. In view of the enormous powers of destruction now available to states, we can no longer tolerate the *realpolitiker's* model of international statecraft.

In order to avert the dangers inherent in this model, steps must be taken to transform states. This transformation must put an end to the characteristically self-centered course of national policy by involving world leaders in a redefinition of national interest. To apply the vision of Pierre Teilhard de Chardin, no state can prosper and grow except with and by all the others with itself.

In general terms, this redefinition rests on an awareness of the *systemic* underpinnings of each state's interests. Realizing that national survival requires a renunciation of the principles of "everyone for himself," national decision makers must create a system whereby their own particular judgments of self-interest are tied to their judgments of what is best for all states. In such a system, these decision makers would recognize that what is best for the entire system is necessarily best for their own sovereignties. There can be no policy of national gain that is at cross-purposes with the spirit of worldwide well-being.

By defining national interests in terms of strategies that secure and sustain the entire system, world leaders can begin the crucial process of supplanting competitive self-seeking with cooperative self-seeking. By building upon the understanding that it is in the best interests of individual states to develop policies from a systemic vantage point, national decision makers can take a decisive step in the direction of world order reform, not by abandoning their self-interested pattern of action, but by rerouting this pattern to a global orientation.

But what exactly does all of this really mean? Exactly what is involved in this recommended redefinition of national interest? In the most general sense, the answer lies in a self-conscious attempt to create an alternative configuration of world politics with which every nation feels able to identify the support of its own major preferences. Since there is bound to be a multiplicity of competing values involved, such a configuration must necessarily fall short of any one nation's optimal design; yet it still must be acceptable to all of them. This implies an expansive exploration of alternative patterns in an effort to settle upon

146

an appropriate "mix." *The new world order must be based upon a broad variety of compromises between state actors.*

To begin its design, scholars must set forth a series of basic dimensions in terms of which more secure world forms can be described. At a minimum, these dimensions should correspond to (1) the kinds of *nonstate actors* in world politics; (2) the *structure* of world politics (i.e., the prevailing pattern of global power; and (3) the weapons technology *context* of world politics. By characterizing world order models along these three dimensions, the infrastructure of another sort of behaviorally transformed world might be "blueprinted." Such a system would represent the outcome of large-scale trade offs between competing national preferences and would permit the development of reoriented national decision making.

What this means, of course, is that institutional transformation must necessarily precede this particular kind of behavioral transformation. Until a new configuration is brought about with which every state can identify the preservation and advancement of its own major preferences, no one can reasonably expect states to redefine their judgments of self-interest along systemic lines. It follows that this transformation of the characteristic behavior of state actors is not a distinct alternative to institutional change, but rather "one step further along" a continuous path to world order reform.[1] And since institutional transformation might itself depend upon prior successes in transforming people, the transformation of states may also require individual human kinds of changes. Where this is the case, the alteration of national behavior represents a convergence of seemingly discrete strategies of planetary renewal. It reflects the culminating effect of transformations at both higher levels of organization and lower levels of comprehensiveness.

DESIGN DIMENSIONS

Nonstate Actors

The principal nonstate actors in world politics are the *United Nations,* an interstate organization whose world order role has already been

147

discussed; *regional organizations; guerrilla/terrorist organizations;* and the *multinational coporations* (MNCs).

The United Nations. The United Nations represents humankind's most ambitious experiment in international organization and world order. During the critical decade of the 1980s, states will have to decide whether to maximize their goals cooperatively through a progressive surrender of sovereign authority to the United Nations or competitively through traditional strategies of confrontation and conflict. To a significant extent, the prospects for transforming states from a *realpolitik* to a world order point of view will depend upon the degree of support for U.N. activities concerning peacekeeping, human rights, education, economic development, health care, and ecological stability.

More than any other actor in world politics, the United Nations offers states the opportunity to transform in the interests of world order improvement. Faced with what certain prominent scholars at The Trilateral Commission have called "the steady expansion and tightening of the web of inter-dependence," states must learn to manage this "web" as an essential precondition to long-term survival.[2] To accomplish this objective, states must give the imperatives of cooperative interaction precedence over the persistent claims of national autonomy, domestic politics, and the deep-seated antagonisms of East-West and North-South relations.[3]

Understood within the framework of the United Nations, this means that states must begin a steady retreat from the prerogatives of "statist" world politics. Although it would be unfair to describe the United Nations as merely an "instrument" of states, the world organization is still effectively denied an independent capacity for authoritative decision making. This capacity remains in the hands of national actors.

How can this condition be changed? How can the processes of authoritative decision making be transferred from states to the United Nations organization? The answers range from what is generally called "piecemeal functionalism"[4] to drastic system transformation creating collective security or world government.

In the case of "piecemeal functionalism," cooperation on specific issue areas (e.g., international monetary arrangements, environmental pollution, peaceful use of nuclear energy) is expected to "spill over" into cooperation on matters of far-reaching political concern. The ultimate

148

objective of functionalist strategies is the *evolutionary* transfer of sovereignty through incremental patterns of cooperation between states on all matters that concern their common well-being. In the case of collective security or world government advocacy, the United Nations would be transformed into a truly authoritative source of decision making by the volitional and constitutional surrender of sovereignty by individual states. Such a transfer would not take place gradually, but through a single series of concerted legal and political measures.

The advantages of a functionalist strategy of world order, which seeks increasing global centralization gradually or by "installments," are highlighted by the manageability of issues. Since the issues are relatively concrete and well-defined, bypassing the more controversial matters of "high politics" and national security, states may organize their cooperative activities around the specific requirements of technical interaction, trade liberalization, and international monetary arrangements. Although such cooperation between states is simpler on essentially nonpolitical issues, e.g., the Universal Postal Union and the World Health Organization, it is still feasible for such functionally specific economic institutions as the International Monetary Fund (IMF) and the General Agreement on Tariffs and Trade (GATT).[5]

According to the authors of a report of the Trilateral Integrators Task Force to The Trilateral Commission:

> Where cooperation on a functional issue offers all participating countries potential specific gains, these gains are most likely to be achieved by focusing on the issue in question rather than combining it with negotiations cutting across many areas. By narrowing the negotiation, it can be kept concrete and deal with specific arrangements and procedures. In such cases, specialists (who are more likely to dominate more limited discussions) may be better able to reach agreement than political generalists for whom issues are more likely to become symbolic of victory or defeat for particular national or regional political viewpoints. Specialization creates common bodies of knowledge and intellectual frameworks among experts from many nations. Coalitions of specialists can be built across national boundaries in specific functional areas, blunting the nationalism that might otherwise hinder international agreement. These factors do not mean that the issues may not be "political" or involve political choices. Indeed, the choice of specialist negotiations is itself a political decision. It is a matter of how political leadership is exercised.[6]

Of course, functionalist theory is not without its problems. For one, it is by no means clear that a hard-and-fast distinction can be drawn between political and nonpolitical areas of involvement. For another, the prospects for cooperative "spill over" from economic and social matters to political ones are hardly assured. Nevertheless, a functional approach to world order reform is effectively built into the structure of the United Nations, especially the specialized agencies of the Economic and Social Council and the many nongovernmental organizations that work with these agencies. Among the most important of the spcialized agencies are the International Labor Organization (ILO); the Food and Agriculture Organization (FAO); the United Nations Educational, Scientific and Cultural Organization (UNESCO); the World Health Organization (WHO); the International Monetary Fund (IMF); and the Universal Postal Union (UPU).

Drastic system transformation leading to collective security or world federal government has been the second path to centralization of global authority processes. Among the many advocates of such transformation, the most prominent and comprehensive has been the thoroughgoing revision of the United Nations Charter by Grenville Clark and Louis B. Sohn, *World Peace Through World Law*.[7] The authors, legal scholars, set forth an article by article revision that is designed to replace the current anarchy of world politics with the law of a "world authority." According to Clark and Sohn, such law "would be uniformly applicable to all nations and all individuals in the world and would definitely forbid violence or the threat of it as a means for dealing with any international dispute. This world law must also be law in the sense of law which is capable of enforcement, as distinguished from a mere set of exhortations or injunctions which it is desirable to observe but for the enforcement of which there is no effective machinery."[8]

Clark and Sohn's underlying principles are the following: an enforceable law of war prevention resting upon general and complete disarmament; clearly stated rules against violence, courts to interpret these rules, and police to enforce them; constitutional and statutory prohibitions against the use of force by any nation except for self-defense; creation of the world peace organization through ratification of the constitutional document by a preponderant majority of all the nations and peoples of the world; and applicability of the revised

150

Charter to all states in the system, irrespective of membership in the revised United Nations system.

With respect to the existing organs and agencies of the United Nations, *World Peace Through World Law* seeks, generally, to preserve and to strengthen them. The centrality of the General Assembly, which has been established through behavioral expansion of Charter mandate, would be codified. Thus, the General Assembly would have the final responsibility for the maintenance of peace, a responsibility supported by a new system of representation and voting and through a new power to legislate. While the voting procedure in the existing General Assembly is one vote per member, *World Peace Through World Law* calls for a system of "weighted voting." This system is based on relative populations but is qualified by the provision that no state, however large, shall have more than thirty representatives and that even the smallest state shall have one representative.

The Security Council, which under the present Charter has primary responsibility within the United Nations for the "maintenance of international peace and security," would be abolished. In its place, Clark and Sohn offer a veto-less Executive Council (in the Security Council, any one of the five states entitled to "permanent" membership has a veto power in all nonprocedural matters), chosen by and responsible to the General Assembly. To be comprised of seventeen representatives, two more than in the present Security Council, the Executive Council would make special provision for representation of the largest states and would function as the "executive arm" of the strengthened United Nations. According to Clark and Sohn, it would hold much the same relation to the General Assembly as that of the British Cabinet to the House of Commons. Subject to its responsibility to the General Assembly, "the new Council would have broad powers to supervise and direct the disarmament process and other aspects of the whole system for the maintenance of peace provided for in the revised Charter."[9]

The Economic and Social Council and the Trusteeship Council would be continued by Clark and Sohn, but with major changes regarding their composition, function, and financial support. The Economic and Social Council (ECOSOC) would continue in its mission to promote human welfare throughout the system of states, carrying out studies and preparing reports on international economic, social, cultural, educational, health, and human rights concerns. The Trusteeship Council would maintain its role to provide supervision of those non-self-governing territories that are designated as trust territories. However, by 1981, if the independence of the Trust Territory of the Pacific Islands is granted as planned, the Trusteeship Council will have no further business and will therefore cease to function.

As to the International Court of Justice, Clark and Sohn envision a vastly enlarged arena of jurisdiction and degree of authority. Unlike the present International Court of Justice, which often lacks the compulsory jurisdiction to hear cases between states, the revised "judicial and conciliation system" would compel states to submit cases for hearing and decision. *World Peace Through World Law* proposes to empower the General Assembly to *direct* the submission of international disputes that are susceptible to legal settlement to the International Court of Justice whenever the General Assembly finds that such disputes are apt to endanger world peace. In case of such submission, the International Court of Justice would have obligatory jurisdiction to decide the case, even if one of the parties should refuse to appear before the Court.

Drastic system transformation leading to collective security or world federal government has also been recommended by a number of policy-oriented interest groups. In this connection, the Policy Statement of the World Federalists, USA, is instructive and warrants close comparison with the more scholarly program of Clark and Sohn:[10]

WORLD FEDERALISTS, USA
POLICY STATEMENT

WHAT WE SEEK

We are people and we live on the planet Earth.
We live here with billions of other people.
Our problems, dangers, hopes, and destinies are one with all of theirs.
Planet earth is the only possible home for any of us—or for our children and our children's children.
Yet this home is becoming increasingly crowded.
The waters of the earth are threatened by pollution. Its atmosphere is threatened with destruction. Its resources are being exhausted with wasteful usage. The quality of human life deteriorates even as its quantity multiplies. And the obsolete war system, arch-enemy of man, threatens the extinction of our human race.

We believe this need not be our destiny.

Against its possibility we raise our united voice in righteous anger, in dedicated determination, in desperate hope.

And we shall be heard.

We believe these lethal dangers to ourselves and our Earth home require an agency of all people on the planet.

We believe the times demand—as no earlier times have done—a worldwide governmental institution with power to stop the pollution of the air and waters of the Earth, to conserve its exhaustible resources, to promote social and economic justice, to abolish the war system, to enforce disarmament simultaneously upon all nations, and to establish peace with justice under law, without which we can no longer live.

We believe that such an institution must be federalist in nature. Our forefathers established the United States Constitution on this principle.

We believe that the United Nations, imperfect as it is, can become the framework on which such a structure of peace under law can be established.

Today the right of people to decide their own destiny is denied. The right of nations to be sovereign within their own borders is also denied. And the thing that denies, indeed destroys, these rights is the false claim of nations to a license to make war at will. As long as that license is allowed to exist, no nation can be free. Nations tax their people to the breaking point, not to do what they should and would like to do, but solely and obediently to outmatch other nations in the creation of even more frightful weapons for destruction of the human race.

We believe that the measures we propose can stop such madness.

We believe the right of domestic sovereignty can be restored to the people of the Earth and to their nations.

And we propose to see it done.

For we believe in the inalienable right of all people of Planet Earth to life, liberty, and the pursuit of happiness.

WE FURTHER BELIEVE

Peace is more than the absence of war. It is more than disarmament. Peace is a world system of law and justice—a world community wherein every nation *must* respect the rights of all other nations. Each nation could thus develop its own culture, institutions, and ways of living and working free of danger of outside attack.

Peace requires a structured world society in which resources are freed to clean its environment, and end hunger, and malnutrition wherever they exist, provide education for all people everywhere, and establish justice in the affairs of man. Such a peace is the one hope for man.

The existing war system—and the international anarchy in which that

153

system breeds—is strangling that hope. It must be destroyed. As the stockpiles of bombs, missiles and chemical agents of universal death grow greater, so does the utter insecurity of the people of the world, including especially the very ones which possess the stockpile. Never can these weapons be used unless the user is ready to commit national suicide.

We believe that war system can be replaced by peace system; that the present rule of violence can be replaced by a rule of law.

HENCE WE DECLARE THAT

The policy and purpose of World Federalists, USA is the establishment of an enforceable law of peace with justice in the world. It is a policy and purpose for all mankind.

Our path to the goal is the creation of a world federal government, either established through a transformation of the United Nations, a world constitutional convention, or other legal means. But we believe the most direct path lies in strengthening the United Nations.

The United Nations should be given adequate power to make, interpret and enforce world law with justice. This requires a comprehensive revision of the UN Charter.

The United Nations must be strengthened to a point where it can, on its own authority, make, interpret and enforce a world law of peace and justice.

To do this we must:

1. Grant the United Nations effective power to make laws which prohibit any nation from using force or threats of force in international disputes, and which also prohibit the manufacture, possession, or use of armaments beyond those small arms required for internal policing. These laws must be binding on individuals as well as on nations. At the same time, a scheduling for universal and complete disarmament must be adopted.
2. Provide for universal membership without right of secession.
3. Give the world organization the means to raise living standards through economic and technical aid, more equitable trade terms, monetary reform, and such other measures as may be necessary to increase production, purchasing power, and markets for goods and services.
4. Grant the United Nations power to govern the seabed, the high seas, and outer space, as well as other carefully defined international jurisdictions.
5. Grant the United Nations authority to control those aspects of the environment which cannot or will not be adequately regulated by private or national action.
6. Grant the United Nations authority to raise adequate and dependable revenue, including a carefully defined and limited taxing power.

7. Establish a system for enforcing world law with justice through inspectors, civilian policy, courts, and an adequate armed peace force under civilian control.
8. Establish a responsible civilian executive branch of the UN.
9. Provide a voting system on legislative matters more just and realistic than the present one-nation-one-vote formula in the General Assembly, and encourage direct popular election of United Nations representatives.
10. Confer on an expanded United Nations judiciary the final authority to interpret the Charter and world laws, including existing international law; to settle disputes between nations and to try all individuals accused of violating world laws.
11. Provide a Bill of Rights protecting individuals against arbitrary or unjust action by the United Nations, and prohibiting United Nations interference with civil rights or liberties guaranteed to citizens by their own nation or state institutions.
12. Reserve to individuals, nations and their people all powers not expressly delegated to the United Nations, thus guaranteeing each nation freedom to manage its domestic affairs and to choose its own political, economic, and social institutions.

Not all plans for drastic system transformation leading to collective security or world federal government, however, are cast in terms of reforming the United Nations. Even Clark and Sohn recognize that the decision to revise the United Nations Charter or to create a whole new world organization is a question not of principle, but of policy:

It must be recognized that if the creation of adequate world institutions for the prevention of war is to be achieved through the medium of the United Nations, numerous amendments of the Charter will be required which would together amount to a fundamental change in the structure and powers of the United Nations. And if it should develop that for technical or psychological reasons it would be more difficult to accomplish these amendments than to create a wholly new world organization to take over the peace-maintenance functions of the United Nations, we wish to make it clear that we would not object to that alternative method. In other words, a thorough revision of the Charter is merely, as we see it, the most reasonable means to the end in view and not an end in itself.[11]

One prominent example of drastic system transformation advocacy that by-passes the existing United Nations is the World Constitution and Parliament Association's "Universal Call for Ratification of The Constitution For The Federation Of Earth."[12] With members in fifty countries, the World Constitution and Parliament Association seeks the establishment of a democratic federal world government founded upon a constitution that defines the powers, structure, and composition of the new organization as well as the procedure by which it would be brought into being. At a World Constituent Assembly meeting in June 1977 at Innsbruck, Austria, participants from many countries debated and adopted the draft of *A Constitution For The Federation of Earth*. Supporters of the Constitution have submitted the document for worldwide ratification by the "nations and peoples of Earth." The procedure for ratification is defined in the Constitution itself. Preliminary ratification is requested by the national legislatures or by the national governments of each country, and final ratification is requested by the people of each country through popular referendums. Figure 4-1 presents an overview of world government under the proposed Constitution. (See page 157.)

Whatever the proposed path to centralization of global authority processes, be it piecemeal functionalism, revision of the U.N. Charter, or calls for a wholly new world organization, the end product represents some form of collective security or world federal government arrangement. And as has already been shown in Chapter 2, the alleged world order advantages of such an arrangement are by no means obvious. Indeed, unless a number of important conditions are met, a transfer of sovereignty from states to supranational institutions may be no better than the prevailing balance of power.

What are these conditions? Overall, they involve the supranational authority's ability to appear both willing and able to influence the decisional calculi of states such that the prospective cost of non-compliance with its rulings always exceeds the benefits of non-compliance. This ability concerns the so-called "tragedy of the commons," which is defined here as the problem of decision making that arises when states calculate that a particular course of action is to be preferred only where it is expected to be generally imitated.[13] From the standpoint of collective security or world government, the tragedy of the commons refers to the difficulty of securing general compliance with the commands of a supranational authority as long as each state is uncertain about the reciprocal behavior of other states. Unless each state believes that its own willingness to comply is generally paralleled, it is

Figure 4-1.
Diagram of World Government under the Constitution for the Federation of Earth

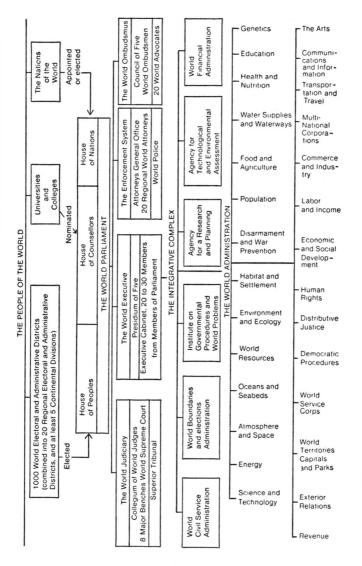

SOURCE: World Constitution and Parliament Association.

apt to calculate that the benefits of compliance are exceeded by its costs.

In collective security arrangements for supranational authority, sovereignty is transferred to a specially constituted central institution while military force remains exclusively in the hands of individual states. It is an arrangement, as we know, whereby sovereignty is unsupported by force. Upon inspection, it becomes apparent that the absence of centralized military force in the collective security arrangement will raise grave doubts in each state about the reciprocal compliance of every other state.

This does not mean, however, that collective security can never succeed as a basis of a supranational authority. A variety of changes might seriously affect the decisional calculi of states, causing them to develop far greater confidence in the belief that their own compliance with supranational directives would be generally paralleled. These changes include a diminished number of states, a far-reaching consensus among states about the goals, norms, and procedures of international statecraft, and a "tight" bipolar structure of world politics.

This last change is important because the preeminence of two major states would have the effect of reducing the number of individual national decisions needed to achieve widespread compliance with supranational authority. The more limited the freedom of action of individual states, the greater the likelihood that major powers can ensure broad compliance. Of course, the preeminence of two major states can contribute to undercutting the tragedy of the commons only if both favor the success of collective security and are willing to act accordingly.

Taken together, these changes could contribute importantly to overcoming the central impediment to collective security success. In so doing, they could make it reasonable for nations to seriously consider the collective security model. Nonetheless, these changes are not of the sort that can be brought about by design. Rather, they represent conditions that could develop "on their own" and that could therefore make collective security more plausible.

In world federal government arrangements for supranational authority, both sovereignty and military force are transferred from states to a specially constituted central institution. Unlike the collective security arrangement, therefore, sovereign directives emanating from the central authority would be supported by force. It follows that world federal government would be apt to provide a better chance for overcoming the tragedy of the commons. Because there would be central force to enforce compliance, each state would probably be less uncertain about the reciprocal compliance of other states.

Yet, as was already shown in Chapter 2, the existence of its own military forces would not necessarily be enough to ensure widespread compliance with world federal government. No less than individual states in a balance of power arrangement, the federal supranational authority would need to satisfy the requirements of a credible deterrence posture. That is, the world federal government would have to convince potential delinquent states that it has the ability and the resolve to punish noncompliance severely.

Since these requirements would be difficult to satisfy, scholars exploring the "national transformation" prospects for world order reform along the lines of the world federalism model must be cautious in their assessments. At the same time, they must not be unduly pessimistic. As in the case of collective security, there are conditions that can contribute to the success of world federal arrangements for supranational authority. These conditions are highlighted by a widespread awareness of the dangers of noncompliance and by widespread perceptions of the supranational authority's deterrent effectiveness. Such perceptions, in turn, would depend upon the way in which individual states judge the supranational authority's own image of its proper purpose, the way in which these states judge the nature and measure of force involved in threats of punishment, and the way in which these states assess the disutility which the supranational authority attaches to whatever destruction it might suffer as a consequence of carrying out a threat.

Regional Organizations

World order reform via the transformation of state "behavior" must also take into account the form and function of regional organizations. Like the United Nations, such organizations can contribute to the replacement of balance-of-power world politics by a new world politics of globalism and community. They can do this by contributing to the management of interdependence between states.

The precise world order role of a regional organization, however, depends on its particular purpose. Since the end of World War II, there has been rapid growth in all categories of regional organizations. While there have been many schemes for classifying such organizations, the most useful has been offered by A. LeRoy Bennett, whose fourfold scheme includes (1) multipurpose organizations, (2) alliance systems, (3) functional organizations, and (4) United Nations regional commissions.[14]

Multipurpose Organizations. In promoting the transformation of national behavior and world order reform, the multipurpose regional organizations have certain special advantages, including the size and scope of their functions, the size of their memberships, and the formal institutionalization of their structures. For example, the Organization of American States (OAS), with twenty-four members, operates through a number of units that parallel the organs of the United Nations: a General Assembly, a Permanent Council with security functions, an Inter-American Economic and Social Council, and an Inter-American Council for Education, Science and Culture. Moreover, an Inter-American Juridical Committee serves to promote the progressive development and codification of international law, making it a hemispheric counterpart of the United Nations' International Law Commission.

Similarly, the Organization of African Unity (OAU), with forty-seven members, functions through an Assembly of Heads of State and Government, a Council of Ministers, a permanent General Secretariat, five functional specialized commissions, and a Commission of Mediation, Conciliation, and Arbitration. And the League of Arab States (Arab League), with twenty member states, operates through a Council, a Political Committee, a Joint Defense Council, a Permanent Military Committee, and an Economic Council.

Nevertheless, the world order potential of such multipurpose regional organizations is far from being realized. In fact, because of their particularistic and segmented vision of objectives, these organizations have often proved to be more of an impediment to world order reform than a useful catalyst. The problem has been aggravated by the primary commitment of these organizations to the sovereignty-centered system of international relations.

Another problem has been the tendency of such organizations to promote regional solidarity at the expense of universal cohesion.

Although the U.N. Charter expressly permits regional arrangements that are consistent with the purposes and principles of the United Nations, the operation of regional organizations has sometimes undermined the world organization. In the future, regionalism and universalism will have to become mutually supporting if either strategy is to contribute to world order reform.

How can the cleavage between universalism and regionalism be resolved harmoniously? The answer lies in a more complete understanding of the fact that both orientations to formalized international relations stem from a primary commitment to the international law of cooperation. Unlike the international law of coexistence, which aims at reinforcement of long-standing principles of sovereignty, jurisdiction, and immunities, the international law of cooperation aims at all elements of *human welfare*. Although it is still at an embryonic stage, the international law of cooperation provides the "cement" between universal and regional organizations. Taken seriously, it can contribute importantly to the understanding that regionalism serves world order reform only when its activities serve the interests of the world system as a whole.[15]

To date, there have already been promising examples of movement toward such an understanding. The OAS played a major role in resolving several inter-American disputes, e.g., Costa Rica and Nicaragua (1948-49, 1955-56, 1959); Honduras and Nicaragua (1957); Venezuela and the Dominican Republic (1960-61); and the so-called soccer war between El Salvador and Honduras in 1969-70.[16] Similarly, the OAU worked closely with the United Nations on the Rhodesia issue (now Zimbabwe) and on establishing mutual cooperation to facilitate economic and social development in Africa.[17]

Alliance Systems. While several of the multipurpose organizations have alliance or collective defense functions, another type of regional organization draws its central purpose from these functions. Nurtured and sustained by the Cold War, these alliance systems, especially the North Atlantic Treaty Organization (NATO) and the Warsaw Pact (WP) reflect the most long-standing means of producing security in decentralized world politics. Unlike existing collective security arrangements, which rest upon a presumption of impartiality until a wrongdoer has been identified, alliances are characterized by the advance identification of friend and foe.

161

It follows from the different purposes of collective security and collective defense that the two forms of collaboration may compete. Although it may first appear that collective security and collective defense typically supplement each other, harmony between the two types of arrangements may be ended whenever a situation of contradictory commitments develops. In such an event, the reliability of one arrangement may be decisively undermined by the other.

For example, a state may be faced with a choice in which satisfying the requirements of a U.N. or multipurpose regional organization arrangement means defaulting on an alliance agreement or vice-versa. Whatever the choice made, one or more states in the system may suffer because of the dual presence of arrangements for collective security and collective defense. As Arnold Wolfers, the distinguished international relations scholar, has suggested, the cases in which the two forms of collaboration are complementary and helpful to each other "are largely a matter of happy coincidence."[18]

Although defenders of military security alliances are quick to point out that such arrangements are compatible with the U.N. Charter, especially the Article 51 provision that refers to the "inherent right of individual or collective self-defense," there is little doubt that collective defense arrangements undermine the impartiality of collective security. Alliances do not create hostile divisions between states, but they do reinforce and institutionalize such divisions. As a result, the "objective" functioning of the United Nations and of certain multipurpose regional organizations is effectively compromised.

How can this situation be remedied? Surely, the answer does *not* lie in getting rid of alliance systems. The use of such systems to produce security has been of enormous popularity throughout history. States that are themselves uncertain of their security status have always looked to stronger states for support.

The commitment to collective defense has been affirmed repeatedly in theory as well as in practice. Indeed, it has even been suggested that membership in an alliance is *always* essential to the maintenance of a credible deterrence posture; that no single state, however powerful, can always persuade other states that it possesses the capacity to prevent aggression. According to Lord Bolingbroke, for example, who had been intimately involved in the delicate negotiations leading to the Peace of Utrecht early in the eighteenth century, "occasional union, by alliances with other states . . . is so necessary to all the nations on the continent, that even the most powerful cannot subsist without it. . . ."[19]

Somewhat less convinced than Bolingbroke that membership in an alliance is *always* necessary for national security, Emmerich de Vattel, the eighteenth-century Swiss legal scholar, was still convinced of the importance of alliances to the *lesser* powers. In this respect, his position more closely resembles that of the British statesman, Robert Walpole, who referred to alliances as a means by which "the weak are defended against the strong."[20] Thus, we have Vattel's statement: ". . . force of arms is not the only expedient by which we may guard against a formidable power. There are other means, of a gentler nature, and which are at all times lawful. The most effectual is a confederacy of the less powerful sovereigns, who, by this coalition of strength, become able to hold the balance against that potentate whose power exictes their alarms. Let them be firm and faithful in their alliance; and their union will prove the safety of each."[21]

But states have not always been "firm and faithful" in their alliances, and the history of international relations theorizing is replete with skepticism concerning the reliability of alliances. Not surprisingly, the origin of such skepticism lies in the demonstrated unreliability of states to comply with alliance obligations that are judged contrary to their own self-interest. One of the earliest doubters of alliance reliability was Sir Thomas More, author of *Utopia*:

> Treaties, which all other nations so often conclude among themselves, break, and renew, they (the Utopians) never make with any nation. "What is the use of a treaty," they ask, "as though nature of herself did not sufficiently bind one man to another? If a person does not regard nature, do you suppose he will care anything about words?" They are led to this opinion chiefly because in those parts of the world treaties and alliances between kings are not observed with much good faith.[22]

Sir Francis Bacon, the great thinker of the seventeenth century, shared More's assessment of alliances. No matter how solemn the oaths which confirm treaties of alliance, contended Bacon, such treaties cannot be counted upon "as they seem used rather for decorum, reputation, and ceremony, than for fidelity, security, and effectuating."[23] Similarly, Edmund Burke, the eighteenth-century conservative philosopher, argued that in the interaction between states, "We are apt to rely too much on the instrumental part. We lay too much weight upon the formality of treaties and compacts."[24]

Thomas Paine, too, commented upon the flagrant disregard among states for treaties of alliance:

> Perhaps there is not a greater instance of the folly of calculating upon events than are to be found in the treaties of alliance. As soon as they have answered the immediate purpose of either of the parties they are but little regarded. Pretences afterwards are never wanting to explain them away, nor reasons to render them abortive. And if half the money which nations lavish on speculative alliances were reserved for their own immediate purpose, whenever the occasion shall arrive, it would be more productively and advantageously employed.[25]

And let us consider the opinion of Alexander Hamilton:

> There is nothing absurd or impracticable in the idea of a league or alliance between independent nations . . . . With a view to establishing the equilibrium of power and the peace of that part of the world, all the resources of negotiations were exhausted, and triple and quadruple alliances were formed; but they were scarcely formed before they were broken, giving an instructive but afflicting lesson to mankind, how little dependence is to be placed on treaties which have no other sanction than the obligations of good faith, and which oppose general considerations of peace and justice to the impulse of any immediate interest or passion.[26]

The key to understanding why alliances are unreliable can be found in the close of Hamilton's argument. Since it is axiomatic that rational states will always act in a self-interested manner, it follows that a state will fail to fulfill its obligations when they are deemed to be more costly than gainful. This kind of calculation becomes more probable in the nuclear age, where honoring alliance guarantees of nuclear retaliation may invite overwhelmingly destructive nuclear counter-retaliation.

In the final analysis, the very nature of nuclear weapons makes the threat of nuclear retaliation by a state's allies difficult to believe. Such weapons are not simply more modern versions of conventional weaponry. Unlike conventional weapons, the use of nuclear weapons is an all-or-none proposition; they cannot be used effectively in a graduated way.

From the standpoint of reliability, however, existing collective

164

security arrangements suffer from the same deficiencies as alliance systems. While such arrangements substitute the principle of "all for all" for the notion of "some for some," the obligations incurred still depend on each state's consent. And consent is based upon perceived judgments of self-interest.

Understood in terms of the world order reform potential of alliance systems, these points suggest a need for the continuing harmonization of collective defense objectives of alliance systems with the aims of the U.N. Charter and the multipurpose regional organizations. While both the North Atlantic Treaty (1949) and the Warsaw Pact (1955) pledge compliance with the U.N. Charter, both also affirm the right of collective self-defense recognized by Article 51. In the nuclear age, the promise that measures involving the use of armed force will be reported to the Security Council in accordance with Article 51 is hardly reassuring. Instead, both major systems of collective defense must begin to take steps that would ultimately replace the prerogatives of Article 51 with the provisions for collective security uses of armed force already offered in Chapter VII of the Charter. Such steps would not amount to a dismantling of the alliance systems generally, since both systems would continue consultation, cooperation, and discussion on economic, political, scientific, and cultural affairs.

Functional Organizations. As was already shown in the discussion of the United Nations in this chapter, a functionalist strategy of world order reform can contribute to the transformation of national behavior through "piecemeal" increases in global centralization. Such transformation, however, need not only be undertaken within the specialized agencies of the world organization, nor does it need to focus exclusively on alterations of the United Nations. Rather, a number of functional regional organizations can contribute directly to systemic redefinitions of national interest.

A review of the functional regional organizations listed in Table 4-1 indicates that, for most of them, their primary purpose is the achievement of mutual economic advantages. Unlike the United Nations, multipurpose regional organizations, or alliance systems, the functional organizations do not seek to promote security advantages for their own sake. However, these organizations do foster the "habits of cooperation" that might ultimately "spill over" from one sphere to another.

Table 4-1

MAJOR INTERGOVERNMENTAL REGIONAL ORGANIZATIONS

I. Multipurpose Organizations

Title	Acronym	Established	Membership (1976)
Organization of American States (originally, International Union of American Republics)	OAS	1948 (1890)	24
League of Arab States (Arab League)		1945	20
Organization of African Unity	OAU	1963	47
Commonwealth (formerly, British Commonwealth of Nations)		1926	36
French Community		1958	19
Council of Europe		1949	18
Organization of Central American States	ODECA, or OCAS	1952	5
Common Afro-Mauritian Organization	OCAM	1966	10

II. Alliance Systems

Title	Acronym	Established	Membership (1976)
North Atlantic Treaty Organization	NATO	1949	15
Warsaw Treaty Organization	WTO	1955	7
Australia, New Zealand, United States Security Treaty Organization	ANZUS	1952	3
Western European Union	WEU	1954	7
Central Treaty Organization (formerly, Baghdad Pact)	CENTO	1959 (1955)	4

III. Functional Organizations

Title	Acronym	Established	Membership (1976)
Benelux Economic Union	BENELUX	1948	3
European Coal and Steel Community	ECSC	1952	9
European Economic Community	EEC	1958	9 + 6 assoc.
European Free Trade Association	EFTA	1960	6 + 1 assoc.
European Atomic Energy Community	EURATOM	1958	9

166

Table 4-1 (Continued)

III. Functional Organizations (Continued)

Title	Acronym	Established	Membership (1976)
Organization for Economic Co-operation and Development	OECD	1961	24
Latin American Free Trade Association	LAFTA	1961	11
Association of Southeast Asian Nations	ASEAN	1967	5
Central American Common Market	CACM	1961	5
Council for Technical Cooperation in South and Southeast Asia (Colombo Plan)		1950	27
Council for Mutual Economic Assistance	COMECON, or CMEA	1949	9
Inter-American Development Bank	IDB	1959	24
African Development Bank	AFDB	1964	41
Asian Development Bank	ASDB	1966	41
Central American Bank of Economic Integration	CABEI	1961	5
European Investment Bank	EIB	1958	9
Nordic Council	NC	1952	5
Conseil de l'Entente	CE	1959	5
Organization of Petroleum Exporting Countries	OPEC	1960	13

IV. United Nations Regional Commissions

Title	Acronym	Established	Membership (1976)
Economic Commission for Europe	ECE	1947	34
Economic and Social Commission for Asia and the Pacific	ESCAP	1947	32 + 4 assoc.
Economic Commission for Latin America	ECLA	1948	32 + 2 assoc.
Economic Commission for Africa	ECA	1958	47 + 4 assoc.
Economic Commission for Western Asia	ECWA	1974	12

SOURCE: Bennett, *International Organizations*, pp. 375-76.

The three European communities—the European Economic Community (EEC or Common Market); the European Coal and Steel Community (ECSC); and the European Atomic Energy Community (EURATOM)—represent the most far-reaching experiments in regional advances toward supranationalism. The European Free Trade Association (EFTA) was an outgrowth of the inability of certain members of the Organization for European Economic Cooperation (established in 1948 to implement the European recovery program) to agree with the six members of the EEC on plans for broad economic recovery. The Council for Mutual Economic Aid (COMECON), which is the Soviet bloc counterpart of the economic organizations of the Six and Seven of Western Europe, has not achieved equivalent supranational character.[27]

Despite certain changes in membership within the EEC and EFTA (on January 1, 1973, Denmark and the United Kingdom withdrew from the EFTA and joined the EEC, Ireland joined the EEC in 1973, and Greece became the tenth member in 1981), both organizations seek a sustained expansion of economic activity, increased productivity and employment, an expansion of free trade, and broadly improved living conditions. But while broad decision-making authority within the economic sphere has been surrendered to collective agencies within the EEC, the organs of the EFTA lack extensive supranational powers. Similarly, COMECON, whose purpose is to coordinate the development efforts of its members, increase productivity, and assist in the establishment of improved economic relations, is unable to issue regulations that are directly binding on national agencies in its member states.

The European Coal and Steel Community, proposed by Robert Schuman, then French foreign minister, on May 9, 1950, was established by a treaty signed in Paris on April 18, 1951. In order to assure adequate supplies of coal and steel, the expansion and production of international trade, and the broad improvement of living conditions, the treaty established specialized institutions designed to abolish import and export duties with in the Community, prohibit discriminatory practices and state subsidies, and eliminate other restrictive practices. The executive organ of the ECSC, the Commission, has been merged with the counterpart institutions of the European Economic Community and the European Atomic Energy Community, and is comprised of persons whose instructions come only from the Community, not from the constituent governments. The Council of Ministers, the Assembly, and the Court of Justice are all shared with the other European Communities.

The European Atomic Energy Community (EURATOM) was established by a treaty signed in Rome on March 25, 1957. Sharing its institutions with the two other European Communities, EURATOM is designed to develop research, disseminate information, enforce uniform safety standards, facilitate investment, ensure regular and equitable distribution of supplies of nuclear material, guarantee that nuclear materials are not improperly diverted, and generally promote the peaceful uses of atomic energy.[28] In these functions, EURATOM overlaps to a significant extent with the International Atomic Energy Agency (IAEA), an autonomous international organization within the family of the specialized agencies that have ties to the United Nations. Established on July 29, 1957, the IAEA has as its stated objective to:

> . . . accelerate and enlarge the contribution of atomic energy to peace, health and prosperity throughout the world. It shall ensure, so far as it is able, that assistance provided by it or at its request or under its supervision or control is not used in such a way as to further any military purposes.[29]

Not under U.N. direction or control, the IAEA reports annually to the General Assembly and, in some cases, to the Security Council and to the Economic and Social Council. IAEA membership is open to any state, whether or not it is a member of the United Nations, and any IAEA member can withdraw at any time by written notice.

Regrettably, EURATOM's encouraging moves toward European unity, augmented by IAEA safeguards and procedures, have been steadily eroded by independent national moves toward a nuclear energy capability. Since 1961, a marked trend toward nuclear nationalism among its member nations has left EURATOM with greatly reduced funding and without a meaningful function in the application of nuclear power technology in Europe.[30] This suggests problems not only in terms of the Community's world order reform potential, but also in terms of controlling the spread of nuclear weapons.

How can functional organizations like the three European Communities, the European Free Trade Association, and COMECON, contribute to the transformation of national behavior along world order lines? The answer lies in a steady and progressive harmonization of their aims and procedures with those of the United Nations and the other regional organizations. Of course, this is more easily said than done, and students of world order reform will have to look very closely at ways in which the forces of integration can prevail over the forces of disintegration, at ways in which the enhancement of national interests can be served by cooperative involvement within the functional organizations.

In this connection, special attention needs to be directed to the slowing down of the national development of nuclear power in certain countries and to a reproduction—in other spheres of international relations—of the jurisdiction of the European Court of Justice. (Unlike the International Court of Justice, this Court always has compulsory jurisdiction.) Attention also needs to be directed towards the resolution of intra-organizational political warfare. Within the Common Market, for example, relations have been strained by disagreements over Britain's share of the organization's running costs (Britain pays the largest net share while it has a lower standard of living than West Germany, France, the Netherlands, Belgium, Luxembourg, and Denmark); the protectionist farm policy (which accounts for 70 percent of Common Market spending); and plans for missile modernization in Western Europe. Unless such strains are relieved, the Western European drive for unity could be permanently thwarted.

Moreover, there is special need for cooperation between the European organizations and COMECON. As a specific instance of the more general problem of constructive collaboration with Communist countries, such cooperation could follow naturally from the greatly increased volume of East-West economic transactions during the 1970s. While such cooperation is apt to elicit cries of protest from those who would regard it as unreasonable support of Soviet power and influence, the net benefits in terms of effectively managed interdependence would almost certainly outweigh the costs.

In a report to the Trilateral Commission on "Collaboration with Communist Countries in Managing Global Problems: An Examination of the Options," Chihiro Hosoya, Henry Owen, and Andrew Shonfield, three distinguished international relations scholars, offer the following summary judgment: "Constructive cooperation with Communist countries in a number of areas of global concern could make a significant contribution to solutions of the substantive problems involved without causing undue risks or intrusion in the internal affairs of participating countries."[31] To advance such cooperation, the report recommends encouraging bilateral commercial agreements with members of COMECON, but notes that such agreements must be subjected to minimum ground rules, i.e., an internationally-negotiated set of trade rules or at least an internationally-negotiated set of procedures for arbitrating trade disputes. We should not, therefore, seek East-West economic collaboration at the expense of European Community common external commercial policy or if it promotes the power of a centralized organization in COMECON over the trade of individual Eastern European countries.[32]

Other functional organizations that can contribute to a more cooperative system of international relations are the Organization for Economic Cooperation and Development (OECD) and the regional development banks. The OECD was established in 1961 as the successor to the Organization for European Economic Cooperation (OEEC), and aims at an improved world economic order via the promotion of financial stability, economic development, and nondiscriminatory expansion of trade. The regional development banks, which were established primarily to expand financing opportunities for development purposes, include the Inter-American Development Bank (IDB), the African Development Bank (AFDB), and the Asian Development Bank (ASDB). Subregional development banks include the European Investment Bank (EIB), the International Bank for Economic Cooperation (IBEC), the International Investment Bank (IIB), the Central American Bank for Economic Integration (CABEI), and the East African Development Bank.[33]

The World Bank, known formally as the International Bank for Reconstruction and Development (IBRD) is a specialized agency of the United Nations. Founded in 1946 as one of the pillars of the Bretton Woods postwar economic structure, it now lends about $8 billion a year. By 1979 it had received capital subscriptions from 135 countries and made loans to 99 of the poorest of these countries to finance such projects as dams and roads. In recent years it has channeled increasing

171

amounts of money into programs that expand food and water supplies, improve educational systems, and support other basic needs.[34]

Yet, the World Bank, together with the other Bretton Woods institutions—the International Monetary Fund (IMF) and the General Agreement on Tariffs and Trade (GATT)—is in need of reform. The World Bank, in order to continue to exercise a vital leadership position in providing assistance to developing countries, must direct more of its lending to "middle-range" countries with growing capital needs while revising its voting system to permit greater participation by developing countries.[35] The IMF, in cooperation with the World Bank, must continue to adjust to sharp rises in world oil prices with adaptations that keep the monetary system orderly. In this connection, the recommendation of the Trilateral Task Force on International Institutions is instructive: "The International Monetary Fund (IMF) needs new arrangements to effect multilateral surveillance over the system of flexible exchange ranges and control over the growth of international liquidity."[96] And new arrangements are needed in GATT to govern export controls.

There are, however, certain functional organizations with seemingly limited world order potential. Indeed, one such organization seems more likely to impede the progressive transformation of national behavior along world order lines than to encourage such transformation. This organization is the Organization of Petroleum Exporting Countries (OPEC). In its critical role as a world energy supplier, OPEC has rendered a vast number of states vulnerable to its economic and political interests. As a cartel that controls 85 percent of the oil moving in international commerce, OPEC's strength in the energy field has already outdistanced OECD and the European Common Market. If it is to be successfully integrated into the "new international economic order," OPEC will need to become increasingly sensitive to the expanding linkages of inter-dependence, joining in collective leadership of common problems with the United States, Japan, and the European communities. In this connection, special attention must be given to cooperation between OPEC and the International Energy Agency, a group of 20 leading oil-buying states that developed out of a U.S. response to the 1974 Arab oil embargo and that serves as an institutional mechanism for long-term energy cooperation.

Before such cooperation can begin, however, the members of the IEA must demonstrate to OPEC nations their willingness to provide a collective counterweight to the petroleum exporters. They can do this by setting individual ceilings on their oil imports and by strengthening conservation efforts. These steps must be led by the United States, which can no longer afford to consume twice as much oil per capita as its European allies.

United Nations Regional Commissions. A final category of regional organization that must be examined for its world order reform potential concerns the regional commissions of the United Nations. These commissions are the Economic Commission for Europe (ECE), the Economic and Social Commission for Asia and the Pacific (ESCAP), the Economic Commission for Latin America (ECLA), the Economic Commission for Africa (ECA), and the Economic Commission for Western Asia (ECWA). Each of the regional commissions functions as a subsidiary of the Economic and Social Council and works closely with the Department of Economic and Social Affairs of the U.N. Secretariat, the U.N. Development Program, the U.N. Conference on Trade and Development (UNCTAD), the U.N. specialized agencies, and other regional organizations. And as is the case with other regional organizations discussed in this chapter, the central objective of the U.N. regional commissions is to promote intraregional economic well-being and strengthened economic ties with other states and regions.[37]

Ideally, the world order reform potential of the United Nations regional commissions would lie in their capacity to reinforce the objectives and operations of other regional organizations. Unfortunately, this potential is undercut, in fact, by ordinary rivalries of international statecraft, both with other organizations and with individual states themselves. To improve this condition, the authority processes of the regional commissions will have to be clarified vis-à-vis the other regional organizations and the entire network of cross-cutting regional authority structures will have to be rendered more coherent.

Guerrilla/Terrorist Organizations

It is now widely understood that guerrilla/terrorist actors exert a major destabilizing influence on world order. Unlike the other categories of nonstate actors discussed thus far, therefore, guerrilla/terrorist actors can serve the objective of world order reform not through an expansion of their activities, but through a moderation of their claims and tactics. This is not to suggest that such actors never have a just cause for their activities (the principle of "just cause" is even recognized by existing international law); however, irrespective of the reasonableness of their claims, the resort to indiscriminate, excessive violence cannot be tolerated.

Who, exactly, are today's guerrilla/terrorist groups? While there are extraordinary differences in power, purpose, and popular support for different groups, they include such far-flung organizations as Japan's Red Army (Sekigun), which has mounted operations in Malaysia, Lebanon, Israel, Mexico, Cuba, West Germany, and Libya; West Germany's Baader-Meinhof Group, sometimes known as the Red Army Faction; Northern Ireland's Provisional Irish Republican Army; Italy's Red Brigades; and the various organizations that coexist uneasily under the loose umbrella of the Palestine Liberation Organization—Al Fatah, the Popular Front for the Liberation of Palestine (PFLP), the Popular Front for the Liberation of Palestine-General Command (PFLP-GC), and the Popular Democratic Front for the Liberation of Palestine (PDFLP).

Ideologically, these groups are a tangled mixture of purpose and composition. Their intellectual and spiritual mentors include Bakunin, Marx, Lenin, Sorel, Marighella, Mao, Giap, Fanon, Marcuse, Guevara, Debray, Trotsky, and Guillen. And their motives range from genuine and deeply rooted political convictions to nihilistic/psychopathic feelings.

The destabilizing influence of guerrilla/terrorist actors is aggravated by a new phenomenon in world politics—systematic cooperation and collaboration between these groups. Terrorists have always formed associations with sympathetic states, but now they are also beginning to cement patterns of alliance with each other. In recent years, they have launched a significant number of joint operations. Most of these cooperative cadres of multinational operational teams have involved the Popular Front for the Liberation of Palestine (PFLP). The following events are some examples:

- May 1972—JRA/PFLP/German collaboration in attacking Lod Airport, Israel.

- July 1973—PFLP/JRA/Latin American cooperation in hijacking a Japan Air Lines 747 in Europe.
- January 1974—PFLP/JRA operation against Shell oil facilities in Singapore.
- September 1974—JRA/PFLP/Baader-Meinhof collaboration in assault on the French Embassy, The Hague.
- January 1975—PFLP/German cooperation in attempted attack against El Al aircraft, Orly Airport, Paris.
- December 1975—German/Palestinian collaboration in the Vienna assault on the ministerial conference of the Organization of Petroleum Exporting Countries (OPEC).
- June 1976—PFLP/Latin American/German effort culminating at Entebbe.

Ironically, while terrorists are engaged in "total war" with much of humanity, the prevailing attitude in many countries is one of tolerance or open support. The following are just two prominent examples: (1) In the wake of the July 4, 1976, Israeli commando raid at Entebbe, which freed 105 hostages taken by pro-Palestinian skyjackers, African members of the Security Council proposed a resolution to condemn the raid as a "flagrant violation" of Uganda's sovereignty. In view of long-standing international law, such a proposal was unjustified since all states have a responsibility to protect nationals of other countries and a corresponding obligation to protect their own nationals *in extremis* abroad. (2) In the aftermath of Munich, a number of Arab governments heaped lavish praise upon Black September for its attack on the Israeli athletes in the Olympic Village.

In international relations, the tolerance and support of terrorism by certain states stems from the belief that terrorist groups often work in their own national interest. Issues of morality are overshadowed by the presumption that terrorists, however inadvertently, are useful surrogates in the ongoing struggle for international power and influence. The predictable end of such narrow-minded notions of this struggle has been presaged by earlier periods of human history in which global society has lost its center of values.

At the moment, a number of countries—e.g., Libya, Saudi Arabia, Somalia, Kuwait, Iraq, Syria, South Yemen, Algeria, Vietnam, and the Soviet bloc—are sponsors of terrorist groups. Recently, these countries were joined by Iran, which, under the Islamic government of the

175

Ayatollah Khomeini, has pledged its support to the Palestinian insurgency against Israel and turned over the Israeli embassy to Yasser Arafat's PLO. As long as this situation prevails, many terrorist groups will continue to interpret aid from sponsor states as an incentive to violence.

The idea of terrorism as surrogate political warfare is hardly a recent development. Even before the 1960s, when state-supported terrorism became commonplace in the Middle East and North Africa, Italian fascists supported the Croatian *Ustasha* in the assassination of King Alexander in 1934. Today, the surrogate phenomenon has been widely termed "a new type of war" and has received considerable attention in the scholarly literature.

In a Rand Corporation paper published in June 1974, Brian Jenkins points out that "Although the actual amount of violence caused by international terrorism is small compared with war, it has had a destabilizing effect on international order and could become a surrogate for conventional warfare against a nation."[38] According to Jenkins:

> Terrorists, whatever their origin or cause, have demonstrated the possibilities of . . . "surrogate warfare." Terrorism, though now rejected as a legitimate mode of warfare by most conventional military establishments, could become an accepted form of warfare in the future. Terrorists could be employed to provoke international incidents, create alarm in an adversary's country, compel it to divert valuable resources to protect itself, destroy its morale, and carry out specific acts of sabotage. Governments could employ existing terrorist groups to attack their opponents, or they could create their own terrorists. Terrorism requires only a small investment, certainly far less than what it costs to wage conventional war. It can be debilitating to the enemy.[39]

A recent CIA study, however, takes exception to the idea that surrogate warfare will become increasingly likely. According to the study, ". . . barring total collapse of world order and consequent international anarchy (something that no state actor has reason to promote), international terrorism is highly unlikely to gain acceptance as an admissible form of behavior in the foreseeable future. All told, in fact, it seems likely that the employment of terrorist groups in a surrogate warfare role will continue to be more the exception than the rule for some time to come."[40] This conclusion is regrettably unconvincing, however, since it flows from the erroneous premises that: (1) states identify their own interests with the continued operation of the international legal order, and (2) states identify their support of terrorism with the total collapse of that order.

A more compelling argument is offered by Russell E. Bigney in "Exploration of the Nature of Future Warfare":

> The costs and destructiveness of modern warfare, including insurgent wars, are becoming prohibitive and may exceed net gains. As a result, many nations are looking for alternative means to achieve political and economic dominance over adversary nations. The relative low cost of sponsored terrorism and the disproportionate influence that a small well-trained terrorist group can exert becomes an attractive alternative to war.[41]

Support of international terrorism is also increased to the extent that terrorists influence the foreign policies of "host" states. For example, the host states, sometimes in combination with allied countries, may act as advocates of the terrorist groups before the "tribunal" of the state system itself. Such advocacy further legitimizes terrorists as actors in world politics, extending their arena of acceptance and influence.

In 1974, the Palestine Liberation Organization was internationally recognized as the sole legitimate representative of the Palestinian people. The PLO has also been admitted into the U.N.'s Economic Commission of Western Asia (ECWA) and has been granted observer status with such other U.N.-affiliated agencies as WHO, ILO, UPU, ITU, and UNESCO. Moreover, it has been able to open offices in over fifty nations. Such action, like the Khomeini transfer of Israel's embassy to the PLO, has the effect of making a terrorist organization a "juristic person" and may heighten terrorist incentives to violence.

Proposals to sever the bonds between states and terrorist groups are often based on the idea that all states have a common interest in combating terrorism. These proposals rest on the mistaken idea that all states value the secure operation of the international diplomatic system more than any objective that might be obtained via terrorist surrogates. This idea has its roots in a basic principle of international law: that is, the legal systems embodied in the constitutions of particular states are part of the international legal order, and are therefore an interest which all states must defend against attack.

What can be done to limit the influence and moderate the claims of guerrilla/terrorist actors in world politics? Of course, there are special difficulties. These difficulties center on the fact that certain states sponsor and host terrorist groups and that such states extend the privileges of sovereignty to insurgents on their land. While it is true that international law forbids a state to allow its territory to be used as a base for aggressive operations against another state with which it is not at war, a state that seeks to deal with terrorists hosted in another state is still in a very difficult position.

To cope with these difficulties, like-minded governments must create special patterns of international cooperation. These patterns must be based upon the idea that even sovereignty must yield to gross inversions of the norms expressed in the United Nations Charter; the Universal Declaration of Human Rights; the International Covenant on Economic, Social and Cultural Rights; the International Covenant on Civil and Political Rights; the Convention on the Prevention and Punishment of the Crime of Genocide; the European Convention for the Protection of Human Rights and Fundamental Freedoms; the American Convention on Human Rights; the Nuremberg Principles; and the 1949 Geneva Conventions. They must, therefore, take the form of specialized collective defense arrangements between particular states which promise protection and support for responsible acts of counter-terrorism.

Such arrangements must entail plans for cooperative intelligence gathering on the subject of terrorism and for exchange of the information produced; an expanded and refined tapestry of agreements on extradition of terrorists; multilateral forces to infiltrate terrorist organizations and, if necessary, to take action against them; concerted use of the media to publicize terrorist activities and intentions; and counterterrorism emergency medical networks. Such arrangements might also entail limited and particular acts directed toward effective counterterrorism. Examples of such acts include the willingness of Kenya to allow Israeli planes refueling privileges during the Entebbe mission and the assistance of three ambassadors from Moslem states during the Hanafi Muslim siege of Washington, D.C., in March 1977.

Other arrangements might center on encouraging dissension among the various terrorist groups. Such arrangements would seem to be especially promising if applied to the various factions of the Palestinian movement. Internecine struggles within this movement have been obvious since the mid-1970s, when Arafat's PLO faction of Fatah, Al Saiqa, and PDFLP drew opposition from PFLP, ALF and PFLP-GC "rejectionists."

Above all else, however, international arrangements for counterterrorist cooperation must include sanctions for states that sponsor or support terrorist groups and activities. As in the case of sanctions applied to terrorists, such sanctions may include "carrots" as well as "sticks." Until every state in the world system calculates that support of counterterrorist measures is in its own interest, individual terrorist groups will have reason and opportunity to escalate their violent excursions.

The international legal order has tried to cope with transnational terrorism since 1937, when the League of Nations produced two conventions to deal with the problem. These conventions proscribed acts of terror-violence against public officials, criminalized the impairment of property and the infliction of general injuries by citizens of one state against those of another, and sought to create an International Criminal Court with jurisdiction over terrorist crimes. The advent of World War II, however, prevented the ratification of either document.

An International Criminal Court is unlikely to come into being, but there are other measures under international law that could and should be used in the arsenal of international counter-terrorism measures.

First, the principle of *aut dedere aut punire* (extradite or prosecute) needs to be applied to terrorists. And the customary excepting of political offenses as reason for extradition must be abolished for most acts of terrorism. In this connection, the Canadian standard for political crimes, set down by the Canadian Federal Court of Appeal in 1972, would be a suitable model. By this standard, the elements of a political act are so narrowly defined that virtually all acts of terrorism are patently criminal.

Although such a standard would appear to impair the prospects of even those legitimate rights to self-determination and human rights, actors proclaiming such rights cannot be exempted from the prevailing norms of humanitarian law. At the moment, the ideological motives of

179

the accused are given far too much weight by states acting upon extradition requests. While ideological motive should be considered as a mitigating factor in the imposition of punishment, it must not be regarded as the basis for automatic immunity.

Second, states must creatively interpret the Definition of Aggression approved by the General Assembly in 1974. This definition condemns the use of "armed bands, groups, irregulars or mercenaries, which carry out acts of armed force against another State" but supports wars of national liberation against "colonial and racist regimes or other forms of alien domination." Where it is interpreted too broadly, such a distinction leaves international law with too little leverage in counterterrorist strategies. But where it is interpreted too narrowly, it places international law in the position of defending the status quo at all costs.

The problem is allowing international law to serve the interests of world order without impairing the legitimate objectives of international justice. It is an age-old problem not adequately answered by identifying the institutional responsibility of the Security Council. The deliberate vagueness of the language of the Definition of Aggression is less of an obstacle than an opportunity if states can see their way clear to sensible ad hoc judgments.

But how can they make such judgments? What criteria can be applied to distinguish between legitimate claims for human rights and illegitimate acts of terror? Given the context of a decentralized system of international law, individual states must bear the ultimate responsibility for distinguishing between terrorists and "freedom fighters." At the moment, the only hope for appropriate criteria seems to lie in a deep and abiding concern for *discrimination* and *proportionality* in the use of force.

Multinational Corporations

Of all the nonstate actors in world politics, none is more controversial as an instrument of world order reform than the multinational corporation. The entrepreneurial networks that control activities and assets in more than one country have been described as both an essential agent of and a principal impediment to global improvement. Whatever one's position on the desirability of multinational corporations, however, one thing is clear: This form of economic and political relationship is having an

180

impact that is worldwide and profound. Dedicated to centralized planning on a global scale, the multinational corporations have been experiencing a rate of growth that almost makes them serious contenders for the title, "the new sovereigns."[42]

In this connection, it is sobering to point out that the annual sales of many large corporations exceed the gross national products of many countries and that the growth rates of the most successful global corporations are several times greater than that of most advanced industrial countries.[43] With the resultant power that derives from control of the means of creating wealth on a worldwide basis, the multinational corporations are now able to transform the world political economy and the effective role of the state. According to Richard J. Barnet and Ronald E. Muller:

> In the process of developing a new world, the managers of firms like GM, IBM, Pepsico, GE, Pfizer, Shell, Volkswagen, Exxon, and a few hundred others are making daily business decisions which have more impact than those of most sovereign governments on where people live; what work, if any, they will do; what they will eat, drink, and wear; what sorts of knowledge schools and universities will encourage; and what kind of society their children will inherit.[44]

But what, exactly, will be the nature of this impact? How will these decisions alter the state system that has organized international life since the seventeenth century? What do the prevailing patterns of investment and activity of the multinational corporations suggest about the prospects for peace, social justice, and world economic development?

The answers to such questions are many and varied. They depend upon a number of factors. For example, they depend upon whether the multinational corporations assessed are "ethnocentric" (home-country oriented), "polycentric" (host-country oriented) or "geocentric" (world oriented). Furthermore, a multinational enterprise that takes internationalism to the outermost limit may be considered "anational" and described as "denationalized," "supranational," or "cosmocorp."[45]

An assessment of the world order reform impact of multinational corporations will also be influenced by the particular vantage point of the observer, i.e., home country or host country. From the home country point of view, multinationals foster worldwide welfare by encouraging global specialization and optimal global economic efficiency.

Moreover, by creating transnational economic interdependence, multinationals promote a more stable global society. At the same time, however, multinationals may contribute to a destabilizing global concentration of economic and political power and to a proliferation of unethical business practices.

From the host country point of view, multinationals provide a "package" of capital, technology, and managerial "know-how"; supply needed opportunities for employment; encourage investments that lead to increased levels of GNP; and optimize global economic efficiency. At the same time, however, multinationals are often presumed to exploit the resources of the host country (especially if it is a less-developed country, an LDC); to absorb scarce local capital; to place investment decisions in the hands of foreign managers; to repatriate profits to the home country; to foster corrupt business practices; and to interfere in the internal politics of the host country.[46]

If the world order reform potential of the multinational corporation is to be realized, this nonstate actor must begin to assume a form with which state actors can identify the support of their own major goals. At present, the global corporation continues to erode the state-centered image of world politics, but it has yet to replace it with an alternative image of systemwide and pluralistic cooperation. To prevent the replacement of one conflictual dynamic with another, the progressive demise of the state-centered view of world affairs must be accompanied by a *planetary* perspective on transnational economic relations.

Such a perspective is already evident in the many existing international instruments that involve dealings with transnational enterprises and their activities.[47] These instruments include *nongovernmental efforts* (sponsored by such organizations as UNCTAD, the Pugwash Conferences on Science and World Affairs, the International Chamber of Commerce, the Japan Federation of Economic Organizations, and individual enterprises such as Turner and Newall, Caterpillar Tractor Co., Union Carbide, Motorola, and Ciba Geigy); *bilateral governmental efforts* (implemented by bilateral treaties); *multilateral governmental efforts* (sponsored by such organizations as the Non-Aligned Movement, OAS, the European Community, and OECD); *United Nations efforts* (sponsored by UNCTAD, ILO, and IBRD); and *labor union efforts* (sponsored by such organizations as the

International Confederation of Free Trade Unions, the World Federation of Trade Unions, and the Council of Nordic Trade Unions).

Perhaps the most significant attempts at regulating and refashioning the activities of transnational enterprises have taken place under the aegis of the United Nations. Stemming from its overarching commitment to a New International Economic Order (NIEO), the world organization in May 1974 laid the groundwork for dealing with multinationals with the following proposals:

All efforts should be made to formulate, adopt, and implement an international code of conduct for transnational corporations:
(a) To prevent interference in the internal affairs of the countries where they operate and their collaboration with racist regimes and colonial administrations;
(b) To regulate their activities in host countries to eliminate restrictive business practices and to conform to the national development plan and objectives of developing countries, and in this context facilitate, as necessary, the review and revision of previously concluded arrangements;
(c) To bring about assistance, transfer of technology, and management skills to developing countries on equitable and favourable terms;
(d) To regulate the repatriation of the profits accruing from their operations, taking into account the legitimate interests of all parties concerned;
(e) To promote reinvestment of their profits in developing countries.[48]

In September 1975, the resolution of the Seventh Special Session on the New International Economic Order elaborated on the goal of limiting restrictive business practices:

Restrictive business practices adversely affecting international trade, particularly that of developing countries, should be eliminated and efforts should be made at the national and international levels with the objective of negotiating a set of equitable principles and rules.[49]

Recognizing the national imperative to support developing international guidelines or principles of behavior for multinational corporations, the United States has affirmed its respect for an open international economic system. Favoring a liberal and stable investment climate that facilitates international flows of capital and technology, it supports codes relating to multinational corporations that are voluntary;

183

do not discriminate against multinationals, as compared to purely national enterprises; are balanced to include references to the responsibilities of governments as well as of multinationals; and apply to all enterprises regardless of whether their ownership is private, government, or mixed.[50]

U.S. policy on this issue reflects OECD guidelines for multinational corporations, whose several interrelated elements are contained in the June 21, 1976, OECD Ministers' Declaration on International Investment and Multinational Enterprises:

> —a reaffirmation by OECD members that a liberal international investment climate is in the common interest of the industrial countries;
> —an agreement that they should give equal treatment to foreign-controlled and national enterprises;
> —a decision to cooperate to avoid "beggar-thy-neighbor" actions pulling or pushing particular investments in or out of their jurisdictions;
> —a set of voluntary guidelines, defining standards for good business conduct which the Ministers collectively recommended to MNCs operating in their territories;
> —a consultative process under each of the above elements of the investment agreement.[51]

Growth and profitability continue to be the primary objective of the multinational corporation. From the point of view of world order reform, the task ahead is not to alter these objectives, but to harmonize them with the requirements for transformed national behavior. To existing claimants on the functioning of multinational corporations must be added the overriding interest of the world system as a whole. In this connection, there must be a continuous search for the coincidence of planetary, national, and corporate interests that can encourage far-reaching patterns of global cooperation. In the words of the authors of a recent report to the Club of Rome, there is evidence that such a search is already well underway, that multinational corporations "show flexibility and adaptability in strategies when faced with changing conditions, and these qualities could be harnessed to create more long-term benefits for the international community."[52]

STRUCTURE

The second basic dimension in terms of which more secure world forms can be described is *structure*—the prevailing pattern of global power. By describing world order models along this dimension, as well as in terms of *nonstate actors* and *weapons technology context,* students of international relations can contribute to the eventual transformation of national behavior and to world order reform. In the attempt to create alternative systems of world politics with which states can identify their major values and goals, a full understanding of structure must precede the disappearance of *realpolitik.*

The beginnings of such an understanding can be discovered in much of the existing literature of international relations theory, which contains many arguments favoring one or another form of global structure. The best known arguments, and the best place to begin this discussion, center on the relative merits of bipolar and multipolar configurations.[53]

Bipolarity

States might favor a "duopolistic" arrangement of global power for a variety of reasons. Perhaps the best known reason concerns the four factors offered by Kenneth Waltz: the absence of peripheries, the particular range and intensity of competition, the persistence of pressure and crisis, and the preeminent power position of two major actors. Professor Waltz suggests that these four characteristics of bipolarity combine to create a uniquely stable condition in world politics. Indeed, the bipolar balance is allegedly more stable than the multipolar one irrespective of weapons technology context.

Multipolarity

Alternatively, states might favor an "oligopolistic" arrangement of global power. In this case, they would side with the "classical" position in international relations theory, which suggests that a multipolar system is more stable than a bipolar one unless the system is characterized by a proliferating nuclear weapons technology. This is the position of such well-known theorists as Hans Morgenthau and Morton Kaplan.[54]

The crux of the classical argument suggests that the shift from bipolarity to multipolarity in the absence of nuclear proliferation is accompanied by a diminished likelihood of war. This is generally attributed to the greater flexibility of alignment identified with

185

multipolar systems. In their widely read piece on the matter, Karl Deutsch and J. David Singer present a formal argument supportive of multipolar security. Nevertheless, they are acutely sensitive to problems of nuclear arms competition and long-run instability in multipolar systems that world leaders involved with planetary design would have to consider.

Bipolarity, Multipolarity, and the Reliability of Alliances

As has already been shown, the use of alliances represents a long-standing means of protection in world politics. At the same time, the history of international political theorizing is replete with skepticism concerning the deterrent capacity of alliances. Most often, the crux of such skepticism lies in what is believed to be the demonstrated unreliability of states to faithfully honor their alliance commitments once the inducement of expected benefits has been replaced by the expectation of injury or loss. The following will determine the extent to which alliance reliability varies in accordance with the structure of world politics.

There are several reasons why it would appear that alliance reliability is greater in the bipolar system than in the multipolar one. One of these reasons centers on the difference in the shifting of alignments. As the benefits of common purpose are more equitably distributed in a lasting or fixed coalition than in a transient one,[55] states are more apt to identify their own particular interests with the more permanent coalitions of the bipolar configuration.[56] It follows from what is known of the self-interested manner of national decision making that so far as structure is concerned, states in a bipolar system are more likely to honor their alliance commitments than are states in a multipolar system.

Why are alignments considered more susceptible to shift and more impermanent in the multipolar setting? So long as the definition of bipolarity isn't tied to the number of independent actors,[57] there appears to be no logical reason why the number of interaction opportunities should be greater in a multipolar setting than in a bipolar one. The number of states able to enter into alliance agreements seems to be just as large in the latter setting.

In the bipolar system, however, alignments are fixed around two points with little or no movement of states from one point to another.

This is because moving between poles in the bipolar system for purposes of fixing alignments is restricted by the peculiarly intense and fundamentally antagonistic nature of interbloc rivalry. Such movement is inhibited even further where this basic polar antagonism is reinforced by hostile ideologies.

If it is assumed, then, that the shifting of alignments in the bipolar setting takes place around two fixed points with little or no movement of states from one point to another, the structure of bipolarity *does* tend to limit the number of alignments. A bipolar configuration effectively reduces the number of states with which any particular state may align itself. Applying the standard formula for possible pairs, $N(N-1)/2$, and assuming no movement of states between poles, it can easily be seen that in a bipolar system consisting of the same number of states as a multipolar system, there are fewer possible alignments. Thus, the multipolar system is characterized by a greater number and diversity of interaction opportunities than the bipolar one.[58] Consequently, states will be more likely to become subject to a greater variety of cross-loyalties in the multipolar configuration; these loyalties will tend to weaken the reliability of any one particular alliance commitment.

Depending upon one's particular ordering of the conditions believed to minimize the likelihood of interstate conflict, an increased variety of cross-loyalties may be regarded as either desirable or undesirable in the world system. From the standpoint of classical international relations theory (e.g., Hans Morgenthau and Morton Kaplan), the greater variety of cross-loyalties that characterizes the multipolar configuration represents a *conflict-mitigating* factor. No primary link is assumed between the effectiveness of conflict mitigation and alliance reliability—quite the contrary. At the same time, the greater variety of cross-loyalties that characterizes the multipolar configuration may be deemed *conflict aggravating*. This is the case where analysis emphasizes a primary connection between (1) the effectiveness of conflict mitigation and the credibility of particular deterrence postures and (2) the credibility of particular deterrence postures and the reliability of alliances.[59]

It may also be that the greater diversity of interest which characterizes the multipolar system vis-à-vis the bipolar one makes for greater reliability of alliances in the latter for a reason other than the pressure of cross-loyalties. Whether such diversity of interest is considered the result of the greater number and diversity of interaction opportunities *or* as the outcome of a situation in which there is a larger number of significant states, its inhibiting effect on alliance reliability may also be in evidence where no contradictory alliance commitments exist. That is, it may be due solely to the increased difficulty for states to identify their own judgments of self-interest with the interests of their alliance partners. (The wider the range of particular interests, the harder it is for any one state to reconcile them with its own.) Thus, alliance reliability in the multipolar setting vis-à-vis bipolarity suffers from the increased extent of particularity in the world system.

Yet another reason why it might be argued that alliance reliability is greater in the bipolar system than it is in the multipolar one centers on the differences in alliance structure. The shift from multipolarity to bipolarity involves the shift of the "hard shell" from the individual member state to the entire rim of the region circumscribed by the alliance. According to John Herz:

> The chief characteristics of the bipolar system lie in its trend toward an extension of the hard shell, the protective wall which used to surround single territorial units, so as to include (in tendency, if not in actuality) approximately one half of the world in the case of each of the two blocs. In this way, the unit of defense and protection is being shifted from the nation to the bloc.[60]

Together with this extension of the "hard shell," bipolar bloc alliances involve structural changes that go significantly beyond those that characterize multipolar alliances.[61] As the latter type of alliance typically provides only declarations of mutual commitment to assist one another under specified circumstances by the member parties, individual states remain separate units of power. Implementation of an integrated military establishment is not undertaken. In a bipolar situation, on the other hand, alliance agreements function under significantly different sutructural premises. What really matters is not the alliance agreements as such, but rather the implementation of the particular system that they foster. This system is founded upon arrangements for integrated defense, bases, stationing of troops, and related matters undertaken by superpower and particular "rim" countries. According to Herz:

> . . . in place of some scattered outposts, bases, and other garrisoned

188

places, all of which were parts of individual defense systems of various powers and which had their guns turned against each other, under bipolarity they are rearranged into one comprehensive hard-shell system opposing the only other one extant. The guns within each system are now lined up parallel to each other. . . .[62]

A final reason for arguing that alliance reliability is greater in the bipolar than in the multipolar system centers on the increased extent of alliance penetration of intrastate processes of decision making. Once again, while there is no logical reason why such penetration might not also characterize multipolar alliance arrangements, the uniquely powerful position of the leading states in a bipolar system coupled with their particularly expansive range of concern suggests that such penetration is *more likely* within the bipolar configuration. Moreover, active intervention in the realm of intrastate affairs by alliance leaders will be all the more likely to the extent that (1) states represent not only repositories of power to members of the other bloc, but also a particular economic, social, and political system of beliefs and (2) the superpower at the head of each bloc is interested in preserving and advancing the basic features of this system. To a greater extent than in multipolar systems, then, alliance leaders in a bipolar configuration tamper with decision-making processes *within* states. Consequently, individual members are more "amenable" to honoring their obligations to the alliance than would ordinarily be the case.

Thus far, in focusing upon the implications of structure for alliance reliability the importance of the number of axes of conflict has been stressed. Structure, then, has been conceptualized quite narrowly in terms of bipolar and multipolar world systems. Now alliance reliability in terms of more complex conceptualizations of the world system in terms of structure must be determined.

Four Variations of Bipolarity. One particularly interesting set of conceptions of bipolarity is provided by Wolfram Hanrieder.[63] In effect, Hanrieder creates his four alternative models by introducing two additional explanatory variables: (1) the ratio of power between the two poles and (2) the extent to which secondary states share in power. Each of the resultant models will be considered in terms of alliance reliability.

Hanrieder's first configuration is referred to as a *symmetrical* system. This is a pronounced or "tight" bipolar system, with no states in the system existing apart from the two blocs and with a situation of

189

approximate equilibrium existing between the two poles. Moreover, the two poles occupy a position of joint preponderance within the system. As this pattern represents conceptions of bipolarity discussed in the preceding pages, the second proposed configuration will be considered immediately.

The second model is referred to as an *asymmetrical system*. In this system the two poles still predominate at the expense of the secondary states, but one pole occupies a position of predominance over the other. What does this suggest for alliance reliability? Is there any reason to believe that the introduction of an inequality of power factor will alter an evaluation of bipolar alliance reliability?

Insofar as none of the features of a bipolar configuration cited as factors making for greater alliance reliability is changed with the introduction of the inequality of power factor, there is no reason to suppose that such introduction will affect an evaluation of bipolar alliance reliability vis-à-vis multipolar alliance reliability. For example, the fixing of alignments still takes place around two fixed points, and the rate of alignment shifts is thereby still slowed down. The uniquely powerful position of the leading state in each bloc vis-à-vis the secondary states is still preserved. This, too, results in the limiting of alignment shifts. The greater extent of functional integration of facilities, which is associated with bipolar alignments and which inhibits the shifting of alignments (as well as having a more *direct* effect on the credibility of particular deterrence postures), is unaffected as well by imbalance between poles. And the extent of penetration into intrastate decision processes is also unaffected by such imbalance.

But even if the introduction of power ratio between blocs as an "intervening variable" has no bearing on one's conclusions about bipolar alliances as opposed to multipolar ones, it does make possible an effective difference in alliance reliability between blocs within the same bipolar system. In the first place, if the acknowledged inequality is due to fewer members, states in the bloc with the fewer number of states have fewer possible interaction opportunities. For reasons discussed earlier, this will tend to make for more permanent or lasting alignments and, consequently, for greater reliability. Fewer interaction opportunities also mean fewer cross-loyalties, which tend to weaken the reliability of any one particular alliance commitment. Moreover, even where the pressures of cross-loyalties are absent, an increase in the

190

number of states within a given bloc may inhibit alliance reliability because the resultant growth of particular interests makes it increasingly difficult for states to identify their own interests with those of their partners. Finally, it ought also to be pointed out that while decreasing the number of states decreases the number of interaction opportunities, it also increases the ratio of the number of alliances to which any given state may belong to the total number of possible alliances. In this sense, a decrease in the number of states may be judged to increase the ability of alliances to assist states in projecting the image of a credible deterrence posture.

What might be said about differences in alliance reliability between the two blocs that are unequal in terms of weapons systems and military hardware? What effect, if any, can be associated with predominance in force level, skill, and systems of delivery? And will the answer to this question depend on the particular manner in which these factors are distributed within each bloc?

If, for example, the state of inequality is due to a more or less significant disparity between the leading states with no real difference between the secondary states of the two blocs, would not the state contemplating alignments around the less powerful pole be inclined to be less than enthusiastic about the prospects of collective action? So long as it is assumed that the purpose of alignment is tied to the prospects for *deterrence* and not for victory and so long as alignment around the inferior pole is judged capable of producing the image of sufficient means for delivering an unacceptably destructive or annihilating response, the answer to this question is certainly no. There is, then, no reason to suppose that alliance agreements based upon alignment with the inferior leading state in an asymmetrical bipolar system are less reliable than agreements based upon alignment with the superior state in this system. Similarly, where the situation of inequality between poles is due to a disparity between the secondary states with no real disparity between the leading states or where it is due to a disparity between both the leading states *and* the secondary states, there is still no reason to suppose a consequent difference in alliance reliability between the two blocs.

Hanrieder's third and fourth models represent two variants of a bipolar configuration in which a more or less sizable number of states exist apart from the membership of the two blocs. Each variant of this configuration resembles the most rudimentary formulation of what Morton Kaplan has termed the "loose" bipolar system. The difference between these variants is the ratio of power between the two blocs (equal in the hetero-symmetrical system and unequal in the hetero-asymmetrical system). What follows, then, is a look at two forms of "loose" bipolarity in terms of alliance reliability.

In the "loose" bipolar configuration several changes in the features of bipolarity increase greater alliance reliability. In the first place, the fixing of alignments is no longer restricted to taking place around two fixed points in the system. Alignments may shift around points located apart from the system's two poles, and states may move from one pole to another in the shifting of alignments. It follows that there exists a greater number of interaction opportunities here than in the "tight" bipolar world and a greater likelihood of shifts in alignments. This increased likelihood is further reinforced by the diminished power position of the leading states that accompanies the transition from "tight" to "loose" bipolarity. And in the light of the connection between "permanence" and reliability, which was discussed previously, it appears that states in a "tight" bipolar system are more likely to honor their alliance commitments than are the states in a "loose" bipolar system.

Moreover, the increased number of interaction opportunities will also tend to weaken the reliability of individual commitments insofar as it produces a greater variety of cross-loyalties in the system. And even in the absence of contradictory alliance commitments that might be engendered by an increase in cross-loyalties, the increased diversity of interest associated with the shift from "tight" to "loose" bipolarity may itself make alliance commitments in the latter system less reliable. This is because even where the increased diversity of interest does not produce a conflict of commitments, such an increase still makes it more difficult for states to equate their interests with those of their partners. Finally, the increased number of alignments may affect the protective character of alliances in ways other than those that are stated in terms of honoring obligations. That is to say, alliances may be less helpful in the "loose" bipolar system than in the "tight" bipolar system not only because commitments tend to be more reliable in the latter type of configuration, but also because the increased number of possible alignments in the "loose" bipolar system tends to decrease the ratio of the number of

192

alliances to which any given state may belong to the total number of possible alliances.

What is the effective difference of alliance reliability *within* the "loose" bipolar system? First, as the definition of "loose" bipolarity excludes the situation where nonmember actors constitute a separate bloc (this situation would represent a fundamental transformation of the underlying bipolar structure of the system), the problem becomes one of determining the differences in reliability prevailing between bloc alliances, nonbloc alliances, and alliances between member states and nonmember states.

Determining these differences requires an assessment of the power position of the leading state of a nonbloc alliance. Despite the fact that the transition from "tight" to "loose" bipolarity diminishes the power position of the leading states in each bloc, such states may still be in a more powerful position vis-à-vis their partners than are the leading states of nonbloc alliances. Where this is the case, despite the fact that in the "loose" bipolar system member states may move from one pole to another and from one pole to a nonmember state in fixing alignments as readily as nonmember states may move between other nonmember states, it is likely that alignment shifts of the last category would still be the most common. It appears, then, that *within* the "loose" bipolar system described above, bloc alliances may be characterized by greater reliability than (1) nonbloc alliances and (2) alliances between member states and nonmember states.

A Variation of Multipolarity. One interesting variation of the *multipolar* model is the multibloc configuration proposed by Roger Masters.[64] According to Masters, this model is best described as Kaplan's "balance-of-power" model with five or more regional blocs as actors. So long as regional bloc actors are tied definitionally to larger units of territory than state actors, the effective result is a smaller number of larger actors.

What does this mean in terms of alliance reliability? Since the multibloc system would have fewer actors than the balance-of-power one, alliances would be apt to be considerably more reliable because fewer actors means fewer interaction opportunities and consequently greater value attached to any one particular alignment. Fewer interaction opportunities also means fewer cross-loyalties, which tend to weaken the reliability of any one particular alliance commitment. Moreover, insofar as there is less particularity, fewer actors makes it more likely for any given actor to equate its own interests with those of its partners. And fewer actors also means an increased ratio of the number of alliances to which any given actor may belong to the total number of possible alliances.

This discussion has been concerned with the effects of structure on alliance reliability. Needless to say, there are many other conceptualizations of the world system that might be examined for their alliance reliability features. Aside from the vast number of *possible* models that have never even been developed in the body of professional literature, one might consider the vertically layered system of Richard Rosecrance (which has both a bipolar and multipolar realm) and the discontinuities model of Oran Young.[65] Whatever set of conceptions is ultimately selected for examination, the analyst will be focusing upon a particularly crucial relationship concerning national transformation and world order reform.

Bipolarity, Multipolarity, and Collective Security

Earlier in this chapter the difficulties surrounding collective security from the standpoint of the "tragedy of the commons"—the problem of securing general compliance with the commands of a supranational authority as long as each state is uncertain about the reciprocal compliance of other states—was explored. As will now be shown, the extent to which this problem can be overcome—and, therefore, the extent to which collective security can succeed—will depend largely on the structure of world politics. In this case, understanding the effects of structure on the tragedy of the commons is essential to world order reform of the United Nations.

In examining the relationship between structure and the tragedy of the commons, one may encounter convincing reasons for favoring *either one* of the two principal configurations. Depending upon the character of the investigator's assumptions, one might reasonably conclude that bipolarity *or* multipolarity constitutes the most favorable arrangement for overcoming the tragedy. Given the assumptions that direct this particular analysis, however, the following argument will favor the *former* type of structure. The full contours of this argument for bipolar world systems will now be elaborated.

The bipolar world system, of course, represents a "duopolistic" arrangement of global power. Virtually all international processes in this configuration are undercut by a single, systemwide axis of conflict. As a result, the diminished number of "peripheries" is accompanied by a decline in uncertainty. Such a decline is necessary to overcoming the tragedy of the commons. From what is already known about this tragedy, it is clear that for each state to believe that its own compliance with agencies of collective security will be generally paralleled, its understanding of other states' behavior must be maximized. And the decline in peripheral alignments and interactions that accompanies the shift from multipolarity to bipolarity suggests that this is more easily accomplished in bipolar world systems than in multipolar ones.

Together with the decline in peripheries, there is another feature of bipolar systems that may be decidedly favorable to collective security. This feature is the *preeminent power position* of the two major states, which has the effect of limiting the number of individual decisions needed to achieve general compliance with collective security dictates. The "harder" the dualism of power, the more limited the freedom of action left available to individual states. Hence, as the bipolarization of power becomes complete, the ability of the major states to assure broad compliance with collective security directives is heightened.

The relationship between a dualism of power and the evaporation of allies' freedom of action can be illustrated by the development of Spartan and Athenian alliance systems during the era of Thucydides. As the hegemonial powers came closer and closer to final confrontation, they both exercised increasing amounts of control over their alliance partners. Toward the end, the lines between empire and alliance blurred almost indistinguishably, and allies were reduced to virtual satellites.

But why is it necessary to argue that the range and intensity of competition between blocs in bipolar systems will *always* have the effect of augmenting the power positions of the two leading states? Even where interbloc rivalry is extremely intense, might not individual states be freer to exercise autonomous judgments than is ordinarily believed? Indeed, might not this greater freedom occasionally be a *consequence* of *heightened* rivalry?

These questions derive from the assumption that heightened interbloc rivalry is paralleled by heightened competition of leading states for supporters and that this condition offers individual states a variety of opportunities for *independent action*. Of course, this increased latitude of states resulting from the principal "contestants'" competition for supporters is plausible only if it is assumed that (1) states may move freely from one pole to another in the process of fixing alignments (a condition that may exist only where allies resist the transformation of alliance systems into empires) and that (2) states may expect a welcome in the opposing bloc after defection. This argument is illustrated by certain stages of the Spartan and Athenian alliance systems written about by Thucydides. Individual city-states were able to exercise considerable choice in forming alignments, and defecting actors could confidently expect a welcome from the opposing alliance. Notwithstanding the rigidity of bipolar policy and the seemingly difficult task of thwarting the two leading actors, several city-states were temporarily able to exploit the situation by playing off the two giants against each other.

The greater permanence of bipolar alignment also strengthens the position of the leading states. Recognizing the greater difficulty of shifting alignments, each state is more apt to conform to the dictates of an alliance leader than is the case in multipolar systems. The resultant condition of leading states is a comparatively preeminent one that is especially favorable (given the aforestated assumptions about "sympathy" to collective security) to overcoming the tragedy of the commons.

Moreover, as already has been noted, the shift from multipolarity to bipolarity involves a shift of the protective "wall" that previously surrounded single territorial units from individual states to the entire rim of the polar region. Accompanying this shift are certain structural changes that are considerably more far-reaching than those that characterize multipolar systems. While multipolar alliances typically leave individual states unimpaired as separate units of power, bipolar arrangements are apt to involve procedures for integrated defense, bases, stationing of troops, and related matters undertaken by leading states and their respective "rim" countries. A principal consequence of this "hard shell" system is a more powerful position for the leading

196

states—a position especially important to the success of collective security.

A final reason for arguing the preeminent position of leading states in bipolar systems centers on their increased penetration of intrastate processes of decision making. Given their wide range of concern in the integrated bipolar world, the leading states are especially apt to intervene in the realm of intrastate affairs. This is extremely favorable to "harmonizing" the diversity of discrete state preferences so that security will be preferred as a "collective" rather than "private" good.

Taken by itself, however, the preeminent power position of two major states in bipolar systems is insufficient to assure improved changes for collective security success. Such success requires not only greater superpower control over individual states but the further assumptions that (1) each leading state favors the success of collective security, and (2) each leading state is willing to act accordingly. Unless *these* assumptions can be accepted, there is no reason to believe that the preeminent power position of the two major states in bipolar systems will be especially conducive to collective security success.

The plausibility of these *additional* assumptions may depend significantly upon the intensity of interbloc rivalry. Where this rivalry is particularly intense, these assumptions may be too much for the prudent scholar to accept because the high level of fear and mistrust makes it especially difficult for leading states to embark upon a different kind of security course that no longer depends entirely upon their own relative power positions in world politics. Where it is not particularly intense or where it is clearly on the wane, however, their reasonableness may be enhanced. At the same time, the lessening of interbloc rivalry may have the effect of weakening the preeminence of the leading states within each bloc, thereby *aggravating* the tragedy of the commons by multiplying the number of effectively independent states. (This derives from the argument that the preeminently powerful position of the leading states is based upon the peculiarly intense character of interbloc rivalry in bipolar systems.) Hence, it may be that neither intensifying nor weakening the intensity of interbloc rivalry is wholly satisfactory to overcoming the tragedy of the commons within bipolar systems.

Another factor that influences the attitude of leading states toward the success of collective security is the ratio of power between blocs. For both leading states to favor the success of collective security, it is important that they perceive an approximate equilibrium of power to exist between them. An unequal relationship between the two poles may "tempt" the one that perceives itself as more powerful to value "private" efforts over collective security. Judging itself to have an advantage, it may consider traditional modes of preference-maximizing to be more gainful than collective ones. What really matters here is not inequality per se, but perceptions thereof. Erroneous perceptions of inequality will be no less real in their consequences than well-founded ones.

Some More Complex Conceptualizations of Bipolarity

To this point our conception of bipolar world systems has been limited to what is ordinarily termed "pure" or "tight" bipolarity. No distinction between this form and "loose" bipolarity has been introduced. In the "loose" bipolar system, of course, a more or less sizable number of states exists *apart from* the membership of the two blocs. It follows that so long as the ratio of power between blocs is held constant, loose bipolarity is less favorable to surmounting the tragedy of the commons than the tight form.

Why is this the case? The answer centers on the diminished power position of the two leading states. *Whatever* the attitudes of these states toward collective security, their ability to assure the cooperation of certain lesser states will now be inhibited because the increased number of peripheries that accompanies the shift from tight to loose bipolarity yields a number of states that exist *outside* the two major blocs. These states may find it much easier to act privately in pursuit of security needs. Moreover, the fixing of alignments is no longer restricted to two fixed points in the loose bipolar system. Alignments may now shift around points located apart from the system's two poles, and states may now move from one pole to another in the shifting of alignments. It follows that there exists a greater number of interaction opportunities. As with multipolar systems, this means a greater likelihood of alignment shifts accompanied by a diminution of power by leading states. Assuming that the leading states favor collective security and that they are willing to act accordingly, such diminution is *counterproductive* to undermining the tragedy of the commons.

As has been shown, even the "loose" bipolar universe may be divided

198

into two subcategories for comparison in terms of this problem. With the introduction of *ratio of power between blocs* as an intervening variable, loose bipolarity may be characterized as either *equal* or *unequal.*

In comparison with the "pure" bipolar system in which the ratio of power between blocs is equal, both forms of loose bipolarity fare badly. The existence of "extrabloc" states in these systems renders them less suitable for overcoming the tragedy of the commons than the "symmetrical" pure bipolar one.

When compared to the pure bipolar system in which the ratio of power between blocs is unequal, the loose bipolar system with an equal ratio is more favorable to overcoming the tragedy of the commons in that there is an increased likelihood that each *leading* state will judge compliance with collective security more gainful than private strivings. It is less favorable, however, in that the ordinary states are apt to be *less susceptible* to leading state claims. When compared to the pure bipolar model in which the ratio of power between blocs is unequal, the loose bipolar system with an *unequal* ratio is less desirable because of its extrabloc features.

In a comparison of the two forms of loose bipolarity with each other, the system with an equal ratio of power between blocs is certainly apt to be more conducive to overcoming the tragedy of the commons. While both systems are characterized by the presence of states that exist apart from the two blocs, the system with the unequal ratio has the additional disadvantage of a power inequality between poles. Such inequality is likely to be unfavorable to the success of collective security. It offers an added incentive to the more powerful bloc to favor private over collective security.

Just as the bipolar universe of cases could be subdivided to create more complex conceptualizations of the world system in terms of structure, so can the multipolar universe. Apart from the large number of logically possible multipolar variants that might be investigated in terms of the tragedy of the commons, the literature already contains one of its own. As we know, this is the "multibloc" system created by Roger Masters.

In its most basic form, the multibloc system is merely a multiplicity of blocs: a multipolar configuration with five or more regional blocs as actors. For purposes of illustration, it is suggested that these blocs might be the Western Hemisphere, Western Europe, the Soviet Union and Eastern Europe, Africa, and an Asian region dominated by China. In terms of collective security how does this system compare to the others that have been examined?

In the first place, its severe reduction in the number of actors is extremely favorable. Other things being equal, the ability of an actor to determine whether or not its own prospective compliance with agencies of collective security will be generally paralleled is apt to vary inversely with the number of actors in the system. In this sense, the multibloc system might be even more favorable than the pure bipolar one.[66]

At the same time, as each bloc actor in a multibloc system is likely to be extremely powerful, a single perceived defection from the dictates of central management will be apt to prompt the remaining actors to abandon the pursuit of security as a collective good. This derives from the assumption that each actor will judge noncompliance with central management to be more gainful than compliance if it perceives that any other actor will not comply. In a system with a larger number of actors (e.g., bipolarity or "orthodox" multipolarity), however, the critical number of complying actors any one actor feels is needed to warrant its own compliance is far more likely to be *less than all*. In this sense, the reduced number of actors in a multibloc system may be counterproductive to overcoming the tragedy of the commons.

Finally, because the multibloc system would have fewer actors than a balance of power or orthodox multipolar one, alliances would be apt to be more reliable. This situation could be favorable to overcoming the tragedy of the commons in that alliance cohesion may reduce the effective number of actors striving for security on a private rather than collective basis. This assumes, however, that alliance leaders are themselves in favor of the latter form of preference maximizing. However, it could be unfavorable in that cohesive alliances yield inequalities of power that offer an added incentive to the more powerful to favor private over collective security.

The concern in this discussion has been with the structural bases of collective security. While the structural configuration of world politics is only one factor that must be examined in connection with overcoming the tragedy of the commons, it is an especially important one. Indeed, it cannot be overstated that understanding the different collective security implications of bipolar and multipolar world systems represents a crucial step toward national transformation and world order reform.

As indicated at the beginning of this investigation, the most propitious structure for circumventing the tragedy of the commons appears to be bipolarity. More specifically, if the bipolar universe of cases is divided into tight and loose subcategories, the former variation *in its strictest form* represents the preferred version of bipolarity. Finally, if *ratio of power between blocs* is introduced as a last intervening variable, the most desirable form of "pure" or "tight" bipolarity is one in which this ratio is *equal.*

In summary, the foregoing analysis has indicated that the most suitable structure for successful collective security is a pure bipolar world system with an equal ratio of power between the two blocs. While this conclusion has been obtained in conformity with the requirements of internal consistency, it must be checked against appropriate historical fact. In the final analysis, this conclusion must be supported or contradicted by observable phenomena. The level of confidence we ultimately express in its predictive implications is tied very closely to the outcome of the *correspondence* operation.

STRUCTURE AND RECENT HISTORY: THE AMERICAN INITIATIVE

Whatever the theoretic advantages of different forms of global structure, the prevailing drift in international relations has been a steady shift from bipolarity to multipolarity.[67] This drift has taken place not only in the political sphere, but in the military one as well. Moreover, as the proliferation of nuclear weapons continues, military multipolarism could become permanent and irreversible.

What are the implications of this important structural development for national transformation and world order reform? Answering this question requires exploring the structural premises of recent American foreign policy. As will be shown, these premises are rooted in the Nixon-Ford-Kissinger foreign policy doctrine favoring a pentagonal constellation of world powers and in the Carter agenda for continuing global cooperation with allies, with the Soviet Union, and with China. The product of these premises, therefore, has been a basic acceptance of multipolarism.

There are many potential problems with such acceptance. One of the most serious of these problems is the alleged connection between multipolarism and the prevention of "hegemonism" or dominance by another power. Even though the primary objective of American strategy toward the "new" multipolarism is peace and not the prevention of hegemony as such, there is still no reason to believe that the prevention of hegemony actually produces peace.

There is no historical evidence to support the basic contention of this strategy—that the only time that there have been extended periods of peace has been when there has been a balance of power.[68] And there is no persuasive logical argument that points to the general conclusion that it is when one state becomes more powerful in relation to its potential competitor that the danger of war arises.[69] Indeed, the first of these statements is entirely inaccurate while the second ignores some of the most serious dangers that inhere in today's nuclear system. From the standpoint of history, periods of balance have inevitably yielded periods of war. From the standpoint of logic, perceptions of balance in power relations need have no effect on the likelihood of warfare, whatever its form and whatever the nature of its participants.[70]

There is also no reason to believe that the "new" multipolarism is even capable of thwarting hegemony. In the first place, there is an apparent contradiction between this objective and the continuing American commitment to "strength." While this commitment need not require actual American domination of other present and prospective powers, it very definitely presupposes a condition of asymmetrical balance, a relationship of *primus inter pares*. At a minimum, it presupposes this condition together with the Soviet Union, creating, in effect, a narrowly limited bipolar configuration within a broader multipolar context. Such a configuration would have a certain built-in tendency to transform itself into a full-fledged bipolar world, thereby ending the multipolar balance system altogether.

In the second place, there is no reason to believe that even a truly symmetrical balance (which neither the United States nor the Soviet Union would ever encourage) would prevent hegemony. The prevailing doctrine necessarily rests upon the erroneous assumption that all of the major powers share a *preeminent* concern for preventing disproportionalities of power that lead to dominance and that each major actor will act accordingly. The assumption that states always rank the prevention of hegemony at the apex of their particular preference orderings is erroneous because it suggests that such prevention is always believed by each state to be in its own best interests. In fact, there is certainly *no* reason to believe that states will consistently value the avoidance of hegemony more highly than alternative preferences. Any of the leading state actors in a symmetrical multipower balance system may, on occasion, calculate that the benefits expected to accrue from hegemony by any one state are great enough to warrant the probable costs.

But there is really no reason to dwell on the antihegemony implications of a symmetrical balance situation since such a situation is remarkably implausible. The principal members of the favored balance arrangement are patently asymmetrical. The United States and the Soviet Union are not well-matched along the economic dimension, while Japan and Western Europe are military peers of neither superpower. And China's developing military power is still unparalleled on the economic front. It follows that a realistic analysis of the multipolar system must take as its starting point the idea of an asymmetrical balance—an idea that might very well be a glaring contradiction in terms.

A third reason for doubting that current multipolarism will be capable of preventing hegemony centers on the absence of a "swing" state or "balancer." Ironically, this feature of the new balance system touted as "proof" of departure from classical balance dynamics is actually a drawback from the standpoint of thwarting heady ideas by major powers. A major power strongly committed to the balancer role and perceived as such by every other major power might magnify the anticipated costs of hegemony to the point where they would exceed prospective gains. Assuming that national decision makers choose rationally between alternative courses of action, this means that perceptions of a powerful and committed balancer might signal a crucial or even necessary input into the decisional calculi of states contemplating hegemony.

The multipolar balance system favored by the U.S. also contains an inherent contradiction between its commitment to more durable and strengthened alliances and its encouragement of multipolar tendencies.

In effect, these are competing values. Alliance reliability is apt to be greater in bipolar world systems than in multipolar ones. The trend back toward the flexible alignments of the classical balance system that is signaled by the loosening of hierarchic ties within a major coalition represents a trend back toward mercurial forms of collaboration.

The feasibility of multipolarism is also undercut by its essential reliance upon diplomacy and by its increased measure of decisional uncertainty. As a result of the expanded number of major actors and probable axes of conflict, would-be aggressor states would find it increasingly difficult to anticipate the retaliatory consequences of their actions, including the probable source and the substance of reciprocity. Although this increased measure of uncertainty might inhibit a state's willingness to engage in aggressive activity in certain instances, it very likely provides a less effective deterrent than that offered by the high probability of punishment associated with bipolar systems.

This discussion points to the conclusion that the approach to structural design reflected by today's American foreign policy is wholly ill-founded. The essential logic of peaceful global relations in a decentralized world system is thoroughly subverted by the operational dynamics of multipolarism. It follows that the current architects of U.S. foreign policy have failed to investigate the theoretical underpinnings of their structural preference with sufficient care. Such care is indispensable to the productive use of the structure dimension in the essential task of world order reform.

CONTEXT

In one of her greatest and most prophetic novels, *Re: Colonised Planet 5: Shikasta*, Doris Lessing offers a retrospective and extraplanetary view of the future. Her description of the final days of our planet (Shikasta) during the twentieth century ("The Century of Destruction") is frighteningly plausible. Pointing to war, chaos, corruption, murder, torture, exploitation, and oppression as the dominant motifs of the 1960s and 1970s, Lessing speaks of the current period as the time of the epidemics and diseases, of famine and mass deaths:

> On the main land mass two great Powers were in mortal combat. The Dictatorship that had come into being at the end of World War I, in the

204

centre, and the Dictatorship that had taken hold of the eastern areas now drew into their conflict most of Shikasta, directly or indirectly . . . .

The war began in error. A mechanism went wrong, and major cities were blasted into deathgiving dusts. That something of this kind was bound to happen had been plentifully forecast by technicians of all countries . . . .

In a short time, nearly the whole of the northern hemisphere was in ruins. Very different, these, from the ruins of the second war, cities which were rapidly rebuilt. No, these ruins were uninhabitable, the earth around them poisoned.

Weapons that had been kept secret now filled the skies, and the dying survivors, staggering and weeping and vomitting in their ruins, lifted their eyes to watch titanic battles being fought, and with their last breaths muttered of "Gods" and "Devils" and "Angels" and "Hell.". . .

The inhabitants of Shikasta, restored to themselves, looked about, could not believe what they saw—and wondered why they had been mad.[71]

Why *had* they been mad? Why are we *presently* mad? Why do we continue to cultivate the illusion that security springs from a condition of extended and extending nuclear terror?

To answer such questions and to continue the search for more secure world forms, it is necessary to look closely at the weapons technology *context* of international relations. If states are to transform their search for peace and well-being from a competitive to a cooperative mode, they will first have to undertake far-reaching steps to curtail the nuclearization of armaments. In the absence of such curtailment, the prospects for world order reform will inevitably yield to the horrors anticipated by Doris Lessing.

This is not to suggest, however, that apocalyptic presentiments are the exclusive province of fiction writers. Quite the contrary! The continuing failure to identify realistic options in the urgent search for alternatives to nuclear war has already been recognized by our finest scientists and scholars. Since 1955, eminent scientists from all over the world have functioned, through the *Pugwash* Movement, to heed the voices of reason, to work toward stopping a seemingly unstoppable nuclear arms race. While general publics throughout the world remain lulled, distracted, and confused by repressive or unreasoning leaderships, publications like *The Bulletin of the Atomic Scientists* fight the militarization of the planet with careful studies that support the portentious omens of the fiction writers. Indeed, in January 1980, as the

205

Bulletin began its thirty-fifth year, it decided to move the hands of the *Bulletin's* clock—symbol of the world's approach to a nuclear doomsday—forward from 9 to 7 minutes before midnight.[72]

Nor is there any shortage of information about the consequences of nuclear war. In an article written for *The Bulletin of the Atomic Scientists,* Bernard T. Feld, a distinguished Professor of Physics at MIT, calculates that even if SALT-II ceilings prevail, the amount of explosive power deployed in strategic nuclear weapons by the superpowers will amount to more than 15 billion tons of TNT (approximately 3,000 megatons in 15,000 warheads for the United States, and about 10,000 to 15,000 megatons in 8,000 to 10,000 warheads for the Soviet Union). According to Dr. Feld:

> An exchange involving some substantial fraction of these could promptly destroy some 75 and 60 percent, respectively, of the populations (the urban fractions) of the United States and the Soviet Union, and upwards of 50 percent of the remaining rural inhabitants through the subsequent fallout.[73]

Regarding the effects of fallout, he states:

> Fallout is, of course, not confined by national boundaries. Nations bordering on the antagonists would be profoundly damaged as well, although they might escape the total annihilation that would be the lot of the superpowers in the case of a full-scale strategic nuclear exchange. But the rest of the world would not escape either. There would be worldwide contamination of the atmosphere in the event of such an exchange, as a consequence of the fission products and induced radioactivity that would be distributed both in the elemental form and on dust carried aloft in the expanding fireball and which would be widely dispersed by normal atmospheric circulation.[74]

In one of the earliest authoritative treatments of the consequences of nuclear war, biologist Tom Stonier asked the question, "What would happen if a 20 megaton thermonuclear weapon were exploded on New York City?" His answer is summarized as follows:

> As mass fires raze the destroyed city below, fallout begins to descend from above, poisoning the surrounding countryside. One bomb might endanger the lives of people in a 4,000 square-mile area. Such a larger thermonuclear device exploded in midtown Manhattan, for example,

would probably kill 6,000,000 out of New York City's 8,000,000 inhabitants and produce an additional 1,000,000 or more deaths beyond the city limits.[75]

Concerned about the probable effects of a full-scale nuclear attack on the nation as a whole, Dr. Stonier forecast the following scenario:

Even before the threat of fallout radiation completely subsided, the country could be thrown into a state of economic and social chaos—including serious outbreaks of famine and disease—and the ensuing shock, loss of morale, and weakened leadership would further hamper relief operations and impede rehabilitation. The effects of this disruption could persist for decades, just as would the somatic damage inflicted on people exposed to radiation. Even individuals who escape the hazards of the explosion and who are themselves uninjured by radiation might carry a legacy of genetic damage, which they would then pass from generation to generation. Perhaps most uncertain, and potentially most disastrous, are the ecological consequences, the imbalances in nature itself, which might well create the preconditions for the disappearance of American civilization as we know it.[76]

Fortunately, much of the uncertainty lamented by Stonier in 1964 has now been dispelled in a 1975 study entitled *Long-Term Worldwide Effects of Multiple Nuclear-Weapons Detonations*. This report, prepared by a special committee of the National Research Council, National Academy of Sciences, was undertaken in response to a request by Dr. Fred C. Iklé, former director of the U.S. Arms Control and Disarmament Agency. Its point of departure, according to Dr. Philip Handler, president of the National Academy of Sciences, is:

. . . a horrendous calamity: a hypothetical exchange involving the detonation of many nuclear weapons. In the worst case considered, about one half of all nuclear weapons in current strategic arsenals, viz., 500 to 1,000 weapons of yield 10 to 20 megatons each and 4,000 to 5,000 lesser (sic!) weapons with yields of 1 or 2 megatons each, i.e., a total of 10^4 megatons (10,000,000,000 tons) of TNT-equivalent are exchanged among the participants. No report can portray the enormity, the utter horror which must befall the targeted areas and adjoining territories. Nor does this report so attempt.[77]

The report attempts to portray the long-term, worldwide effects following the exchange of 10,000 megatons of explosive power in the northern hemisphere in a plausible mix of low- and high-yield weapons at a variety of altitudes of detonation. Merely acknowledging the "unimaginable holocaust" that would occur in the primarily afflicted nations, the report confines its attention to possible long-term effects on more distant populations and ecosystems, with special reference to the atmosphere and climate, natural terrestrial ecosystems, agriculture and animal husbandry, the aquatic environment, and both somatic and genetic effects upon humans.[78]

Although the report concludes that the biosphere and the species, *Homo sapiens,* would survive the hypothetical strategic exchange, civilization might not. This conclusion has nothing to do with probable social, political, or economic consequences of the hypothesized nuclear exchange (the report deliberately does not address these consequences, which it characterizes as "entirely unpredictable effects of worldwide terror"), but only with the interrelated physical and biological aspects of this calamity. These possible consequences include major global climatic changes; contamination of foods by radionuclides; possible worldwide disease epidemics in crops and domesticated animals because of ionizing radiation; possible shortening of the length of growing seasons in certain areas; possible irreversible injury to sensitive aquatic species; possible long-term carcinogenesis due to inhalation of plutonium particles; some radiation-induced developmental anomalies in persons *in utero* at the time of detonations; possible increase in skin cancer incidence of about 10 percent, which could increase by as much as a factor of 3 if the ozone depletion were to rise from 50 to 70 percent; and severe sunburn in temperate zones and snow blindness in northern regions in the short-term.

Of course, accurate prediction of the worldwide consequences of all-out nuclear war between the superpowers is fraught with uncertainty. With this in mind, the participants in the six separate committees who produced the NAS report caution their readers about the limitations of the data upon which their conclusions rest. It would be prudent, therefore, to recognize that the devastating effects expected by the NAS scholars might be only the "tip of the iceberg," that other—perhaps even more significant effects—would result. The plausibility of such recognition is underscored by the fact that the magnitude of the war postulated in *Long-Term Worldwide Effects of Multiple Nuclear-Weapons Detonations* may be much too low. Were the superpowers to exchange between 50,000 and 100,000 megatons of nuclear explosives, rather than the 10,000 megatons assumed by the report, global climatological changes would imperil the very survival of humankind. Moreover, according to Bernard Feld:

> It is becoming frighteningly plausible to consider the level of nuclear war that would represent the end of humankind: the detonation of one million megatons of nuclear explosives would result in a global irradiation of around 500 rad. It is very difficult, in the present anarchic world, to be sanguine about the fact that we are now about one-tenth of the way toward the possibility of this ultimate insult (used also in its medical sense) that would certainly spell the end of humankind on planet Earth.[79]

There is a second reason for recognizing that the predictions of the effects of nuclear war between the superpowers represent the minimum level of destruction. This reason lies in interactions between individual effects. A skillful summary of this point can be found in a publication of the U.S. Arms Control and Disarmament Agency, *Worldwide Effects of Nuclear War . . . . Some Perspectives:*

> In attempting to project the after-effects of a major nuclear war, we have considered separately the various kinds of damage that could occur. It is also quite possible, however, that interactions might take place among these effects, so that one type of damage would couple with another to produce new and unexpected hazards. For example, we can assess individually the consequences of heavy worldwide radiation fallout and increased solar ultraviolet, but we do not know whether the two acting together might significantly increase human, animal, or plant susceptibility to disease. We can conclude that massive dust injection into the stratosphere, even greater in scale than Krakatoa, is unlikely by itself to produce significant climatic and environmental change, but we cannot rule out interactions with other phenomena, such as ozone depletion, which might produce utterly unexpected results. We have come to realize that nuclear weapons can be as unpredictable as they are deadly in their effects. Despite some 30 years of development and study, there is still much that we do not know. This is particularly true when we consider the global effects of a large-scale nuclear war.[80]

In March 1979, a study entitled *Economic and Social Consequences of Nuclear Attcks on the United States* was published by the Committee on Banking, Housing, and Urban Affairs of the United States Senate.[81] Going beyond the usual and often crude physical measures of destruction, such as human fatalities and casualties, number of cities destroyed, and damage to overall economic capacity, this study identifies and explores the so-called "interactive effects" of nuclear attacks. As a result, it concludes as follows:

> A closer look at the "interactive" effects of various nuclear attacks leads to the conclusion that many studies of nuclear war in the open literature, which have been used to support policymaking have underestimated the aggregate impact of a nuclear exchange on industrial States; particularly their ability to survive and recover their preattack position in a reasonable period of time. This understatement of the consequences results from concentration on simple quantitative indicators while ignoring interactive effects . . . . Similarly, casualty figures often include only victims of immediate blast or radiation effects, neglecting deaths traceable to the severe loss of medical facilities and personnel, which are heavily concentrated in the likely target areas. In a like manner, the ability of fallout or other shelters to save and preserve lives in urban areas has been overrated, as a result of an almost exclusive focus on initial blast or radiation hazards. This perspective understates the importance of side-effects (fire storms, exploding gas mains, lack of water supply, etc.) or longer-term effects (loss of adequate food supplies through production, processing or distribution failures, for example). In trying to establish minimum thresholds for national survival and recovery or criteria for nuclear attack acceptability, the adverse consequences of understating nuclear attack effects should be readily apparent.[82]

In May 1979, the Office of Technology Assessment of the Congress of the United States released its study, *The Effects of Nuclear War.*[83] An assessment made in response to a request from the Senate Committee on Foreign Relations to examine the effects of nuclear war on the populations and economies of the United States and the Soviet Union, *The Effects of Nuclear War* explores the full range of effects that nuclear war would have on civilians. These effects include blast and radiation as well as indirect consequences from social, economic, and political disruption. Two of the study's major findings are that conditions would worsen over time after a nuclear war "ended" and that the effects of nuclear war that cannot be calculated in advance are at least as significant as those that can be calculated in advance. According to the introduction to the executive summary of the study:

> Nuclear war is not a comfortable subject. Throughout all the variations,

210

possibilities, and uncertainties that this study describes, one theme is constant—a nuclear war would be a catastrophe. A militarily plausible nuclear attack, even "limited," could be expected to kill people and to inflict economic damage on a scale unprecedented in American experience; a large-scale nuclear exchange would be a calamity unprecedented in human history. The mind recoils from the effort to foresee the details of such a calamity, and from the careful explanation of the unavoidable uncertainties as to whether people would die from blast damage, from fallout radiation, or from starvation during the following winter. But the fact remains that nuclear war is possible, and the possibility of nuclear war has formed part of the foundation of international politics, and of U.S. policy, ever since nuclear weapons were used in 1945.[84]

Building upon some of the work found in *Economic and Social Consequences of Nuclear Attacks on the United States* and *The Effects of Nuclear War,* Kevin N. Lewis, in an article entitled "The Prompt and Delayed Effects of Nuclear War," further underscores the conclusion that "nuclear war remains an unmitigated mutual disaster, and that no conceivable civil-defense preparations could materially change the prospect."[85] Challenging the view that both of the superpowers need to be concerned about the integrity of their strategic retaliatory capabilities, Lewis demonstrates that all-out war remains a losing proposition for both sides. In this connection, his conclusion is worth noting:

In sum, the cumulative effects of an all-out nuclear war would be so catastrophic that they render any notion of "victory" meaningless. The formal methodologies of the assured-destruction scenarios do not reveal the full extent of these effects. Moreover, arguments that throw doubt on the sufficiency of the deterrent capability of the U.S. exclude some of the most profound and long-lasting of these effects. When the delayed effects of all-out war are taken into consideration, it should become clear that no countermeasure would significantly lessen the degree of devastation that would surely occur. Even if a highly efficient program for the evacuation of cities could substantially reduce prompt fatalities, it could not prevent the delayed social consequences of industrial and economic devastation. The magnitude of either the prompt disaster or the delayed one would be so great that neither disaster could ever be considered tolerable.[86]

Yet, such studies notwithstanding, the government of the United States continues to counsel its citizens that nuclear war can be survived and tolerated. This position is articulated in an information booklet

211

prepared by the Defense Civil Preparedness Agency of the Department of Defense, *Protection in the Nuclear Age* (February 1977). Available in post offices and government bureaus across the country, this publication concedes that a nuclear attack upon the United States "remains a distinct possibility" and recognizes that millions of Americans would undoubtedly die in such an attack. On the more optimistic side, however, it contends that tens of millions who would survive the initial effects of blast and heat could be saved through the erection of fallout shelters or by relocation to less vulnerable areas before an attack. Indeed, in reading from the introduction, one gets the reassuring impression that things might really not be all that bad, that good old-fashioned American know-how combined with neighborly cooperation would set things right within a tolerable time frame. According to the booklet:

> Much has been done to prepare for a possible nuclear attack. Public fallout shelter space has been located for millions. Civil defense systems also include warnings and communications networks, preparations to measure fallout radiation, emergency operating centers to direct lifesaving and recovery operations, emergency broadcasting stations, local governments organized for emergency operations, and large number of citizens trained in emergency skills.
>
> If an enemy should threaten to attack the United States, you would not be alone. The entire Nation would be mobilizing to repulse the attack, destroy the enemy, and hold down our own loss of life. Much assistance would be available to you—from local, State, and Federal governments, from the U.S. armed forces units in your area, and from your neighbors and fellow-Americans. If an attack should come, many lives would be saved through effective emergency preparations and actions.[87]

The fallout danger could reportedly be dealt with by good pre-attack planning and preparation. To protect themselves from these particles of pulverized earth and other debris that have been sucked into the nuclear cloud and contaminated by the radioactive gasses produced by the explosion, Americans are urged to retreat to a fallout shelter. Detailed plans for building such a shelter are offered, as is advice for "shelter living."

A later chapter deals with what is described as "The Relocation Option," i.e., the temporary relocation of people from high-risk areas to safer-areas during periods of international crisis. High-risk areas are

Figure 4-2. Department of Defense Preparedness Directions

WHAT TO DO BEFORE YOU LEAVE A HIGH-RISK AREA

1. Get ample supply of any prescription medicines and special foods.
2. Collect all your important papers and package them preferably in plastic wrappers in metal container (tool box, fishing-tackle box, etc.).
3. Check home for security; see that all locks are secure; store valuables being left behind (silverware, etc.) in a safe place.
4. Close all window blinds, shades, and drapes to help prevent fires from the heat wave of a nuclear explosion.
5. If you use your car, be sure you have enough gasoline, and prepare to take shovels, picks, hammers, and work gloves—all will be needed to help improvise fallout shelter.
6. Stay tuned to your local TV or radio station for instructions on relocating if so directed by government officials.
7. Go over all instructions with your family so that all will understand what to do.

WHAT TO TAKE WITH YOU IN RELOCATING TO A SAFER AREA
(Take all these items if using your car. If using public transportation, take those marked "X.")

Clothing and Bedding
☐ X work gloves
☐ X work clothes
☐ X extra underclothing
☐ X outerwear (depending on season)
☐ X rain garments
☐ X extra pair of shoes
☐ X extra pair of socks or stockings
☐ sleeping bags and/or blankets and sheets

Food and Utensils
☐ Take all the food you can carry (particularly canned or dried food requiring little preparation.)
☐ water
☐ thermos jug or plastic bottles
☐ bottle and can opener
☐ eating utensils
☐ plastic or paper plates, cups, and napkins.
☐ plastic and paper bags.
☐ X candles and matches
☐ plastic drop cloth

Personal, Safety, Sanitation, and Medical Supplies
☐ X Battery operated (transistor) radios, extra batteries
☐ X flashlight, extra batteries
☐ X soap
☐ X shaving articles
☐ X sanitary napkins
☐ X detergent
☐ X towels and washcloths
☐ toilet paper
☐ emergency toilet
☐ garbage can
☐ newspapers
☐ first aid kit
☐ X special medication (insulin, heart tablets, or other)
☐ X toothbrush and toothpaste

Baby Supplies
☐ X diapers
☐ X bottles and nipples
☐ X milk or formula
☐ X powder
☐ X rubber sheeting. etc.

Tools for Constructing a Fallout Shelter
☐ pick ax
☐ shovel
☐ saw
☐ hammer
☐ broom
☐ ax
☐ crowbar
☐ nails and screws
☐ screw driver
☐ wrench

Important Papers
☐ X Social Security Card
☐ X Deeds
☐ X Insurance Policies
☐ X Stocks and Bonds
☐ X Will
☐ X Saving Accounts Books
☐ X Credit Cards and Currency

WHAT NOT TO TAKE WITH YOU IN RELOCATING TO SAFER AREA

Do not Take
☐ FIREARMS—(guns of any kind)
☐ NARCOTICS
☐ ALCOHOL BEVERAGES

Source: Department of Defense, *Protection in the Nuclear Age* (February 1977).

213

defined as metropolitan areas of 50,000 or more population or areas near major military installations. The safer areas, which would become the "host areas" during emergency relocation, are defined as the surrounding small-town or rural areas. According to *Protection in the Nuclear Age:*

> Your Federal Government and many State and local governments are currently planning for the orderly relocation of people in time of an international crisis. These plans call for (1) allocating people from high-risk areas to go to appropriate low-risk host areas for reception and care, and for (2) developing and improvising fallout protection in the host areas.[88]

Moreover, citizens can take heart that a detailed set of instructions and a checklist for supplies is provided.[89] And in what is perhaps the most pathetically humorous prescription ever offered by a government to its citizens, the booklet cautions:

> If you get caught in a traffic jam, turn off your engine, remain in your car, listen for official instructions, and be patient. Do not get out of the line to find an alternate route. All routes will be crowded.[90]

But why is it so important to understand the consequences of nuclear war? Shouldn't the only real concern be *prevention?* What possible connection can there be between an awareness of the effects of nuclear war and a fruitful strategy for nuclear war avoidance?

The answer is simple. Without an awareness of the effects of nuclear war, students of world affairs stand outside the arena of mortality, unable to picture themselves as victims. We are already lost, as another fiction writer, Kurt Vonnegut, tells us, in our own "gibberish." The growing number of formulations of livable post-apocalypse worlds are not only nonsense, but dangerous. They interfere with the essential task of cultivating the kind of "end-of-the-world" imagery that must precede a durable peace.

Pursued by a terrorless evil, contemporary men and women must spark a confrontation with those who substitute gobbledygook for truth. Only then can there be an expectation of holocaust that puts an end to a world dominated by numbing false hopes and hopelessly empty promises. Our nurturance of such an expectation can benefit from the

214

visual experience of art, especially those examples that denote the agony of multitudes through the desolation of individuals. Art, Picasso rightly observed, is a lie that makes us realize the truth. The staggering visual antiwar polemics of the Mexican mural painter, David Alfaro Siqueiros, and the graphic representations of the same subject included in Francisco Goya's collection, *The Disasters of War*, present compelling central images of the holocaust: wastelands of twisted metal and broken bodies, haunted by apparitions of a struggling and unreasoning humanity; such would be the probable habitat of the next and final generation of survivors.

In their art, Siqueiros and Goya record, like a seismograph, the deepest rumblings of a world whose tremors are always presentiments of ultimate catastrophe. As prophetic visions of a dead universe, their scenes of horror can serve us as models of what lies ahead, on a worldwide basis, if nuclear arms racing continues unabated. With such models in mind, humankind could begin to take the first feeble but critical steps back to life, steps based not on illusions of immortality but on a calling-forth and mastery of visions of total annihilation.

But what steps can be taken? What specific strategies can truly heighten the prospects for denuclearization and world order reform? Indeed, are there *any* strategies that can still be taken, or has time effectively run out for humankind?

Chapter 1 explored the role of international law in preventing nuclear war. It considered the bilateral and multilateral agreements, statutes, and safeguards that comprise the nonproliferation regime and discussed the probable benefits of such steps as a return to strategies of "minimum deterrence"; a comprehensive nuclear test ban; a renunciation of the right to first use of nuclear weapons; the extension of nuclear weapon-free zones to other parts of the planet; and the widespread control of nuclear exports. These steps must be augmented with even more far-reaching ideas for reform.

Ultimately, the chances for a successful detachment from strategic arms competition will depend upon concrete steps taken to underscore the total disutility of a nuclear threat system. And these steps will depend upon a prior understanding, by the superpowers, that their own security interests are congruent with the security interests of the world as a whole. The balance of power between the Soviet Union and the United

States can never be more stable than the balance of power in the whole of international society. By recognizing this fact and by subordinating the maintenance of the existing hierarchy of military power to the requirements of more universalized interests, the superpowers can significantly improve the context of world politics.

To survive into the future the superpowers will have to step into the unknown, taking chances that the risks of arms control and disarmament measures will be offset by the benefits of increased global security. This will require a degree of courage for which there is no meaningful precedent in world affairs. Imagination, the outreaching of national "minds," the casting off of nuclear mooring ropes—these are the qualities that must be displayed by Soviet and American leaders in the years ahead. Only by daring to call forth, and live among, new visions can they enlarge the potentiality for peace.

Such visions will also need to be extended to every other state in world politics. To accomplish such an extension, thereby enlarging the scope of an effective nonproliferation regime, will require a cooperative effort by the superpowers to control limited aspects of their respective alliance systems. Indeed, such an effort will even require extending the reach of these alliance systems to all prospective proliferators that fall within the orbit of superpower influence. Although such a recommendation seems to smack of a new elitism, its effect would be to bolster not primacy, but world order. Rather than reassert an earlier form of joint hegemony, a selective tightening of bipolarity in world power processes could provide the structure within which the nonproliferation regime would function successfully.

Why should this be true? As already has been noted earlier, it is because a tightening of superpower control over allies and other states would limit the freedom of action these states have to "go nuclear." Hence, the "tighter" the dualism of power, the greater the ability of the superpowers to assure broad compliance with nonproliferation objectives.

Of course, taken by itself, the tightening of Soviet and American ·control over other states is not enough to ensure the success of nonproliferation. Such success would require not only greater superpower control over individual states, but also requires the additional assumptions that (1) each superpower favors the success of the

216

nonproliferation regime, and (2) each superpower is willing to act accordingly. Unless these assumptions can be accepted, there is no reason to believe that the expanded leverage of the superpowers would be conducive to nonproliferation.

How plausible are these additional assumptions? At first glance, considering the commonality of interest between the superpowers in halting nuclear spread, they seem eminently plausible. However, this optimistic view is contingent on the absence of renewed tensions or intense crises between Russia and the United States. This is because a heightened level of fear and mistrust would make it especially difficult for the superpowers to embark upon a security course based upon cooperative rather than competitive definitions of self-interest.

Similarly, the optimistic view that the superpowers would act in concert to further nonproliferation goals is contingent upon an approximate equilibrium of power between them. A dramatically unequal ratio of power between the Soviet Union and the United States might tempt one or the other to value the traditional modalities of *realpolitik* over collective efforts to assure security. Hence, if the effectiveness of the nonproliferation regime is to depend upon a cooperative tightening of control by the superpowers, it is essential that both the Soviet Union and the United States perceive a condition of rough parity between them.

Summing up, the prospects for nonproliferation would be improved to the extent that the superpowers could assert limited control over other states in the system, so long as (1) the superpowers both favor nonproliferation; (2) the superpowers operate within a peaceful and crisis-free environment; and (3) the superpowers perceive a roughly equal ratio of power between themselves. Where these conditions are satisfied, the tightening of bipolarity improves the prospects for broad compliance on nonproliferation measures. The general point, therefore, is that a reduction in the effective number of decision makers on any issue improves the chances for cooperation.

So long as the number of effectively independent states is low, the prospects for cooperative action are high. However, where this number is increased, the chances for successful cooperation diminish accordingly. Understood in terms of the problem of nonproliferation, this suggests that a tightening of control over individual national decisions must be

217

exerted to prevent additional states from "going nuclear" and that increased superpower control is the best means to this end.

A major part of the nonproliferation problem, then, is not simply the implementation of new procedures, agreements, and treaties, but the control of too many independent national wills. And such control is an instance of the more general problem of decision that arises when the benefits of common action are dependent upon the expectation that all parties will cooperate—the "tragedy of the commons." Nonproliferation efforts will always be in doubt as long as they depend upon voluntary compliance by states that expect reciprocal compliance by all other states. To remove this dependency, the United States and the Soviet Union must move deliberately and cooperatively to ensure the compliance of other states with all elements of the nonproliferation regime.

TRANSFORMING STATES: THE DISAPPEARANCE OF NATIONAL INTEREST

This chapter has been based upon the idea that states must learn to identify their own interests with the interests of the entire state system in advancing world order reform. For this reason, three design dimensions for creating more secure world forms have been described and explored: (1) the kinds of nonstate actors in world politics; (2) the structure of world politics; and (3) the weapons technology context of world politics. It has been assumed that by identifying alternative systems of world politics with which states could harmonize their national interests, a behaviorally transformed world might be "blueprinted."

In response to the bankruptcy of a private and competitive style of international interaction, however, states might also learn to act in the interest of systemic well-being *for its own sake*. Here, the self-interested character of state behavior would be eliminated altogether. Rather than create a condition wherein states believe that what is best for the system as a whole is also best for themselves, this path to world order reform would render the very idea of national "self-interest" meaningless. It would do so by a perfect and complete fusion of private and collective interests. The poet Alexander Pope hints interestingly at this idea in his *An Essay On Man:*

Thus God and Nature link'd the gen'ral frame,
And bade Self-love and Social be the same.

The first sort of behavioral transformation of states would require judgments of self-interest to be realigned rather than eliminated. Transformed states would act in conformity with the best interests of the entire world system, but only because these interests would be judged congenial to their own private national interests. Self-interest would be defined in terms of systemic well being.

Ambitious and fanciful as this particular behavioral route to world order reform might appear, the second sort of behavioral transformation of states is even more ambitious. States would act in behalf of systemic interests, but in this case they would value these interests *for their own sake.* Their actions would not derive from a presumed congruence between community and national interests. Rather, the very idea of national self-interest would be rendered inappropriate. As with the "rational beings" of Marcus Aurelius' *Meditations,* acting in the interests of the entire system would "delight for its own sake."

States in such a world system would resemble global analogues of what has sometimes been called "the new generation." By passing through a series of sublimations of national consciousness, states might overcome their characteristically egoistic behavior and achieve a condition wherein all are perpetually in pursuit of genuine relationships of mutual concern. This condition would follow upon a succession of self-changes directed toward a new vision of human community.

Of course, this particular kind of behavioral change must appear monumentally impracticable. Could any other recommendation of philosopher or scientist more richly deserve Oswald Spengler's remark that "Men of theory commit a huge mistake in believing that their place is at the head of and not in the train of great events"? Can students of world affairs seriously entertain the prospect of international relations without individual states clamoring and scrambling *for themselves?* Do the present and historic forces of fragmentation and disunity portend anything else but a *renewal* of competitive world politics? And don't these forces remain inevitably ahead of the tide of cooperation and unity?

Even if the prospects for this kind of transformation seem remarkably dim, the poet Goethe's dictum should not be forgotten entirely: a perfect

219

creation must transcend itself and go on to become something unique. Applied to states, this means an advance of national consciousness toward a condition whereby each state achieves its noblest expression in its collective existence. A wondrous key to more worthwhile international life, such an advance would represent—in Chardin's remarkable system of thought—the "ultra-hominisation" of world politics.

The beginning of such a transformation would come when significantly large numbers of individual people in positions of national leadership learn to push their mental powers toward more distant human boundaries. Only with the progressive perfection of their mental energies can such a far-reaching change of national behavior take place.

Such a change is also likely to require states to extend the radius of their affinity with other states to global proportions. Undoubtedly, the satisfaction of this requirement would be contrary to the ongoing tide of conflict and revulsion and to the enduring inability to extend national "affection" to more than a few. The reasonable proponent of this kind of behavioral transformation, therefore, would be hard-pressed to argue convincingly that the universe of states may soon personify itself, creating an atmosphere wherein an elemental attraction of international harmony and selflessness will appear.

In any event, this particular kind of behavioral transformation is certainly not apt to spring full-blown from the present system of international relations. Rather, it would very likely require prior behavioral transformations of the two sorts already discussed. This means that directly or indirectly the behavioral route to world order reform always comes back to individual human beings and to the need for their cumulative improvement.

This idea was already hinted at by Francis Bacon's theory of man as microcosmos, a theory that judged man as a model of the entire world "as if there were to be found in man's body certain correspondences and parallels which should have respect to all varieties of things . . . which are extant in the great world." Where this theory is deemed fruitful, it is up to the student of world order to focus once again on the directions and prospects of individual human transformation. Since the elements that combine to form the world system as a whole derive from the composition of individual people, an alteration of the latter inevitably affects the character of the former. Indeed, the person is a "little world," a conception that signals almost unimaginably potent consequences for survival on this endangered planet.

Hence, if this form of behavioral transformation is to lead to a new world order, it must take as its starting point the reformation of the idea that the human being is a poor creature of mundane limits. In conformity with the preeminent theme of medieval civilization, this reformation must emphasize complete harmony between individual and society. And in keeping with the inestimable debt we owe to the spirit of Romanticism, this reformation must take full advantage of the enormous possibilities resident in human nature as it generates a growing awareness of the outer world of *other* people.

In a system of world politics founded upon the erroneous principles of a *Pax Atomica*, an atomic peace, a "system-directed" pattern of national behavior appears remarkably distant. The ideal of sovereign states acting in behalf of their narrowly competitive judgments of self-interest remains as firmly entrenched today as it was back in the difficult times of the breakup of medieval Christendom. Indeed, the nineteenth and twentieth centuries have consecrated ever-increasing measures of commitment to certain principles of Machiavelli and Grotius.

At the same time, the cosmopolitan spirit of the eighteenth century has not disappeared altogether. Evidence of this spirit, nurtured by the visions of Marcus Aurelius, Dante, Crucé, Samuel Johnson, Lessing, Goethe, Veblen, and de Chardin, can be found in various current forms of internationalism. Whether or not these forms can ever take hold of the prevailing drift of world politics and steer it in the holistic direction of systemic concern is apt to depend significantly upon the perceived urgency of the developing planetary crisis. Where this perception approaches the outermost limits of tolerance and where the futility of competitive strategies becomes perfectly obvious, states may pass quickly through the prior sort of national transformation and ultimately become susceptible to the kind of behavioral change now under discussion. Ironically, the prospects for such successive transformation would require a near-fatal proximity to the brink of global despair.

Admittedly, in principle at least, the evolution of a state system comprised of "selfless" actors needn't necessarily presume the imminence of worldwide calamity. In his own way, Goethe lifted

221

himself above all prejudices of national identification without an apocalyptic leap, remarking that others might also strive for this stage where "one stands in a certain measure above all nations, and feels the happiness or the woe of a neighboring people as though it were his own."

Goethe, however, offers an unlikely prototype for a new national consciousness. Presently, any realistic hope for transforming states in a manner that would render them "citizens of the world" would have to be based upon widespread perceptions of irretrievable disaster. Only then could we even begin to foresee the distant abandonment of the idea that ties state behavior to the most narrowly conceived judgments of self-interest. With such perceptions individual states might begin to reassess their purposes from a systemic vantage point and ultimately learn to consecrate their efforts for the well-being of all states taken as a whole.

The last two chapters have offered a number of behavioral strategies of world order reform. Although they have been presented separately, their interrelatedness is marked and warrants emphasis. Indeed, it may even be useful to think of the essential possibilities for behavioral transformation as successive phases of a single process of change—a process that represents a substantial and promising enlargement of the prevailing institutional view of world order scholars.

Moreover, if we are interested in transforming behaviors within the arena of world politics, it may be worth noting that the fulfillment of the final phase might signify the disappearance of states altogether. In a world system wherein the behavior of state actors is dictated only by the perceived interests of the system as a whole, the very rationale of "international politics" is removed. Here, political compartmentalization might be broken down with far-reaching effects for a new "personalization" of planetary interaction. These effects might include a new spirit of worldwide organic community stressing an unprecedented measure of mutual awareness, complementary commitment, and collective concern.

To the extent that such a scenario of behavioral reform ever does transpire, world order scholars will be reminded of the overarching importance of *individual human behavior* to their inquiry. At all stages of behavioral transformation, the individual human roots of world order reform figure most prominently. Above all else, these bases of an alternative world future require continuing study and careful cultivation. To heed this plea is to reorient the present direction of world order studies in a most promising manner and to take a genuinely decisive step toward creative planetary renewal.

NOTES

1. It should be pointed out, however, that this conception of institutional change is still far broader than the prevailing one. In effect, what has been described earlier as the "institutional strategy" is almost always limited to recommending changes in the distribution of force and sovereign authority.

2. See Richard N. Cooper, Karl Kaiser, and Masataka Kosaka, *Towards a Renovated International System* (New York: The Trilateral Commission, The Triangle Papers no. 14, 1977), p. vii. The Trilateral Commission is a private North American-European-Japanese initiative on matters of common concern.

3. Cooper, Kaiser, and Kosaka, *Towards a Renovated International System,* pp. 11-15.

4. Cooper, Kaiser, and Kosaka, *Towards a Renovated International System,* pp. 32-34.

5. See C. Fred Bergsten, Georges Berthoin, and Kinhide Mushakoji, *The Reform of International Institutions* (New York: The Trilateral Commission, The Triangle Papers, no. 11, 1976), p. 5.

6. Cooper, Kaiser, and Kosaka, *Towards a Renovated International System,* p. 32.

7. See third edition, Cambridge, Mass., Harvard University Press, 1966.

8. Clark and Sohn, *World Peace Through World Law,* p. xv.

9. Clark and Sohn, *World Peace Through World Law,* p. xxiii.

10. The World Federalists, USA, are located at 2029 K Street, N.W., Washington, D.C.

11. Clark and Sohn, *World Peace Through World Law,* p. xlii.

12. This plan is described in a series of mailed advertisements designed to "present a constructive alternative to impending worldwide catastrophe." The association's address is 1480 Hoyt Street, Suite 31, Lakewood, Colorado 80215.

13. The term was popularized by Garrett Hardin, "The Tragedy of the Commons," *Science,* 162, December 1968, 1243-1248. As Hardin and others have used the term, it refers to any category of "actor," usually individual human beings. The definition used here is an adaptation that treats states as actors.

14. A. LeRoy Bennett, *International Organizations,* 2d edition (Englewood Cliffs, N.J.: Prentice-Hall, 1980), pp. 366-404.

15. Wolfgang Friedmann, Oliver J. Lissitzyn, and Richard Crawford Pugh, *International Law: Cases and Materials* (St. Paul, Minn.: West Publishing Co., 1969), Chapter 11, "International Law of Cooperation," pp. 1008-1154.

16. Bennett, *International Organizations,* p. 378.

17. Bennett, *International Organizations,* p. 383.

18. Arnold Wolfers, "Collective Defense versus Collective Security," in *Discord and Collaboration* (Baltimore: Johns Hopkins University Press, 1962), p. 183.

19. See "Remarks on the History of England," *The Works of Lord Bolingbroke* (1967), Vol. I, p. 386; 4 vols. (London: Cass & Co., 1844).

20. See Hansard, *Parliamentary History*, XII, pp. 168-169; cited in Edward Vose Gulick, *Europe's Classical Balance of Power* (Ithaca, New York, Cornell University Press, 1955), p. 61.

21. Emmerich de Vattel, *The Law of Nations*, Book III, Chapter III, sec. 46, in Joseph Chitty, ed. (Philadelphia, T & J.W. Johnson, 1861), pp. 310-311.

22. Sir Thomas More, *Utopia*, edited by Edward Surtz, S.J. (New Haven: Yale University Press, 1964), Book II, p. 116.

23. Francis Bacon, "The Wisdom of the Ancients," in A. Spiers, ed., *Bacon's Essays and Wisdom of the Ancients* (Boston: Little Brown, 1884), p. 331.

24. Edmund Burke, "Three Letters to a Member of Parliament on the Proposals for Peace with the Regicide Directory of France," Letter 1, in *The Works of the Right Honorable Edmund Burke*, 5th ed., 12 vols. (Boston: Little Brown, 1877), Vol. V, p. 317.

25. See Thomas Paine, "Prospects on the Rubicon," in Moncure Daniel Conway, ed., *The Writings of Thomas Paine* (New York and London: G.P. Putnam's Sons, 1906), Vol. 2, p. 196.

26. *The Federalist*, No. 15.

27. The members of EFTA are known commonly as the "Outer Seven," in contrast to the "Inner Six" of the EEC.

28. Friedmann, Lissitzyn, and Pugh, *International Law*, p. 1105.

29. *Nuclear Weapons Proliferation and the International Atomic Energy Agency*, An Analytical Report, Prepared for the Committee on Government Operations, United States Senate, by the Congressional Research Service, Library of Congress (Washington, D.C.: U.S. Government Printing Office, March 1976), p. CRS-56.

30. Warren H. Donnelly, "Selected Excerpts from 'Commercial Nuclear Power in Europe: The Interaction of American Diplomacy with a New Technology,'" in *Nuclear Weapons Proliferation and the International Atomic Energy Agency*, Appendix 2, p. 6.

31. Triangle Paper no. 13, A Report of the Trilateral Task Force on Constructive Trilateral-Communist Cooperation on Global Problems (New York/Tokyo/Paris: The Trilateral Commission, 1977), p. vi.

32. Triangle Paper no. 13, pp. vii-viii.

33. Bennett, *International Organizations*, pp. 398-399.

34. Clyde H. Farnsworth, "How The World Bank Manages Its Money," *The New York Times*, December 2, 1979, p. F3.

35. *International Development Strategy*, a Report on the Fourteenth Conference on the United Nations of the Next Decade, Porvoo, Finland, June 24-29, 1979, sponsored by The Stanley Foundation, Muscatine, Iowa, p. 27.

36. C. Fred Bergsten, Georges Berthoin, and Kinhide Mushakoji, *The Reform of International Institutions,* Triangle Paper no. 11 (New York: The Trilateral Commission, 1976), p. v.

37. Bennett, *International Organizations,* p. 401.

38. Abstract of Rand Paper, P-5261, "International Terrorism: A New Kind of Warfare," June 1974, 13 pp., cited in *A Bibliography of Selected Rand Publications* (January 1977), p. 2.

39. Brian Jenkins, "International Terrorism: A New Mode of Conflict," Research Paper no. 48, California Seminar on Arms Control and Foreign Policy (Los Angeles: Crescent Publications, 1975), p. 21.

40. Research Study, *International and Transnational Terrorism: Diagnosis and Prognosis,* U.S. Central Intelligence Agency, p. 29.

41. Report by Cdr. R.E. Bigney, USN, *et al.,* Defense Documentation Center, Defense Supply Agency, June 3, 1974, p. 41.

42. This is the title of a book by Abdul A. Said and Luiz R. Simmons, eds., *The New Sovereigns: Multinational Corporations as World Powers* (Englewood Cliffs, N.J.: Prentice-Hall, 1975).

43. See Richard J. Barnet and Ronald E. Muller, *Global Reach: The Power of the Multinational Corporations* (New York: Simon and Schuster, 1974).

44. Barnet and Muller, *Global Reach,* p. 15.

45. United Nations, "Multinational Corporations in World Development," in George Modelski, ed., *Transnational Corporations and World Order* (San Francisco: W.H. Freeman and Company, 1979), p. 15.

46. George T. Brown, Jr., "Multinational Corporations: Their Impact on the Future of the Nation-System System," Paper prepared for the 1976 Annual Meeting of the Southern Political Science Association, November 4-6, 1976, Atlanta, Georgia, pp. 3-4.

47. For a comprehensive treatment of these instruments, see Karl P. Sauvant, "Controlling Transnational Enterprises: A Review and Some Further Thoughts," in Karl P. Sauvant and Hajo Hasenpflug, eds., *The New International Economic Order: Confrontation or Cooperation Between North and South?* (Boulder, Colorado: Westview Press, 1977), pp. 404-19.

48. Ervin Laszlo, Robert Baker, Jr., Elliot Eisenberg, and Venkata Raman, *The Objectives of the New International Economic Order* (New York: Pergamon Press, 1978), pp. 134-35.

49. Laszlo, Baker, and Eisenberg, *Objectives of the New International Economic Order,* p. 135.

50. See "Multinational Corporations," *GIST,* Bureau of Public Affairs, Department of State, Washington, D.C., August 1977.

51. "Multinational Corporations."

52. Ervin Laszlo, Baker and Eisenberg, *Goals for Mankind: A Report to the Club of Rome on the New Horizons of Global Community* (New York: Signet, 1977), p. 178.

53. These arguments may be considered in Kenneth N. Waltz, "The Stability

of a Bipolar World," *Daedalus* 93 (Summer 1964): 881-907; and Karl Deutsch and J. David Singer, "Multipolar Power Systems and International Stability," *World Politics* 16 (April 1964): 390-406.

54. See especially Hans Morgenthau, *Politics Among Nations*, New York, 4th ed., Knopf and Morton Kaplan, *System and Process in International Politics* (New York, Wiley, 1957).

55. As an alliance grows more permanent, states are more likely to feel less and less affected by the relative strength of the other partners because the likelihood decreases that today's partner will be tomorrow's foe.

56. States are also less likely to fault alliance obligations in the bipolar system because there are fewer places to which defecting allies can turn to create new arrangements. In the bipolar world, not only is there only one other principal point around which defecting allies must look for new arrangements, but the peculiarly intense and antagonistic nature of interbloc antagonism characteristic of bipolarity makes it especially difficult to find a welcome around that point. This is all the more so where the polar antagonism is reinforced by an ideological cleavage.

57. Such "tying" characterizes the definition adopted by Karl Deutsch and J. David Singer, "Multipolar Power Systems and International Stability," *World Politics* XVI (April 1964): 390-406. By using this definition and applying the standard formula for possible pairs,

$$\frac{n(n-1)}{2},$$

they were able to demonstrate the extent to which an increase in the number of independent states increases the number of possible dyads or bilateral interaction opportunities in the world system.

And although Deutsch and Singer do not point this out, it can also be demonstrated that an increase in the number of states not only increases the number of possible interaction opportunities, but it also decreases the ratio of the alliances to which any given state may belong to the total number of possible alliances between states. Where this ratio is found to be

$$\frac{2^{n-1}-2}{2^n-2},$$

it can readily be seen that as n increases, this ratio decreases.

Thus, in terms of the Deutsch and Singer definition, which ties "poles" to the number of "independent actors," the shift from bipolarity to multipolarity, while increasing the number of possible interaction opportunities, *decreases* the ratio of the number of alliances to which any given state may belong to the total number of possible alliances. In this sense, an increase in the number of independent states may be judged to decrease the ability of alliances to assist states in projecting the image of a credible deterrence posture.

58. Assuming that states seek to fix alignments around principal points of power in the system, it is likely that alignment shifting will increase as one moves

from bipolarity to multipolarity because of the increase in the number of points around which states seek to generate alignments. Thus, the shift from bipolarity to multipolarity may be associated with an increased number of *desirable* interaction opportunities even where one does not accept the idea that movement between poles for the purpose of fixing alignments is far more restricted in the bipolar system.

59. By credible deterrence posture, of course, is meant the ability (in terms of physical instruments and delivery skill) and the resolve (willingness) to deliver an unacceptably destructive or annihilating response. The point at which the initiation of the use of force is contemplated against a state believed to possess a credible deterrence posture is the point at which the prospect of cost and risk outweighs prospective gains.

60. John H. Herz, *International Politics in the Atomic Age* (New York, Columbia University Press, 1959), pp. 115-16.

61. While there is, of course, no logical reason why multipolar alliance agreements might not involve the same far-reaching structural changes as bipolar agreements, and while the crux of this argument seems to rest on the historically tutored conception of bipolarity vis-à-vis multipolarity, there are strong logical reasons suggesting that such changes are *more likely* to accompany the bipolar type of arrangement. Some of these reasons derive from the greater permanence associated with bipolar alliances as well as from the unique position (in terms of power, resources, and breadth of interest) of the leading states that form the two "poles" of such a system. Moreover, bipolar alliances are more apt to be characterized by widespread functional integration of facilities than multipolar alliances because the peculiarly antagonistic stance that prevails between blocs in the bipolar system enhances the likelihood that states will be able to equate their own interests with those of their alliance partners.

62. Herz, *International Politics in the Atomic Age*, p. 121.

63. Wolfam F. Hanrieder, "The International System: Bipolar or Multibloc," *The Journal of Conflict Resolution* IX (September 1965): 299-308.

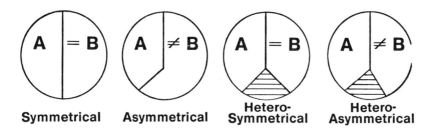

| Symmetrical | Asymmetrical | Hetero-Symmetrical | Hetero-Asymmetrical |

64. Roger Masters, "A Multi-Bloc Model of the International System," *American Political Science Review* LV (December 1961): 780-98.

65. Richard N. Rosecrance, "Bipolarity, Multipolarity, and the Future," *JCR* X (September 1966): 314-27; and Oran R. Young, "Political Discontinuities in the International System," *World Politics* XX (April 1968): 369-92.

66. This is the case, of course, so long as nonleading actors in the pure bipolar model retain some measure of decisional autonomy. Where the hardening dualism of power reduces all allies to satellites, however, then there is an even smaller number of *effective* actors in the pure bipolar world than in the multibloc one.

67. The actual time of the shift, however, is a matter of continuing disagreement among statesmen and scholars. Former President Nixon identified the shift away from bipolarity as a phenomenon of the 1970s ("United States Foreign Policy for the 1970s: The Emerging Structure of Peace," a Report to the Congress, February 9, 1972); John Herz speaks of the passing of bipolarity in the late 1950s *(International Politics in the Atomic Age*, New York, Columbia University Press, 1959, p. 34); Zbigniew Brzezinski notes that the decline of bipolarity was completed by 1968 ("How the Cold War Was Played," *Foreign Affairs*, 51 [October 1972]: p. 207); Michael J. Brenner reinforces the Nixon view of a contemporary shift ("The Problem of Innovation and the Nixon-Kissinger Foreign Policy," *International Studies Quarterly* 17 [September 1973]: 255-94); and Kenneth Waltz predicts the continuation of bipolarity until the end of the century ("The Stability of a Bipolar World," *Daedalus* 93 [Summer 1964]: pp. 898-99).

68. While the balance of power appears to have offered two relatively peaceful periods in history, the ones beginning with the Peace of Westphalia and the Congress of Vienna, the hundred-year interval between the Napoleonic Wars and World War I was actually a period of frequent wars in Europe. The fact that the balance of power has been disastrously ineffective in producing peace during our own century hardly warrants mention.

69. Contrariwise, it has been argued persuasively that equilibrium heightens the danger of war by giving all parties the impression of possible victory, whereas disequilibrium deters the weaker sides while the stronger ones lack incentive. For the best examples of this position, see A.F.K. Organski, *World Politics* (New York: Knopf, 1958), p. 292; and John H. Herz, *International Politics in the Atomic Age* (New York, Columbia University Press, 1959), pp. 316-338.

70. This is because there is nothing about the new multipolarism that is able to ensure the credibility of particular deterrence postures. In its mistaken orientation to notions of selective equilibrium and the prevention of hegemony, multipolarism thus ignores the truly essential basis of peaceful international relations in a world system that lacks government. It goes almost without saying that multipolarism also ignores a number of other grievously dangerous risks to security, some of which are unrelated to the "deadly logic" of deterrence. These risks are in the form of accidental nuclear war, nuclear war that is precipitated by unauthorized individuals, nuclear war which results from incorrect

calculations concerning reciprocity, and nuclear war that is initiated by those actors in world politics who are insensitive to traditional threats of retaliatory destruction, i.e., irrational national leaders or guerrilla/terrorist groups.

71. *Re: Colonised Planet 5: Shikasta* (New York: Alfred A. Knopf, 1979), pp. 92-93. This is the first in a series of three novels known collectively as *Canopus in Argus: Archives.*

72. *The Bulletin of the Atomic Scientists,* 36, no. 1 (January 1980): 1-3.

73. Bernard T. Feld, "The Consequences of Nuclear War," *The Bulletin of the Atomic Scientists* 32, no. 6 (June 1976): 12.

74. Feld, "Consequences of Nuclear War."

75. Tom Stonier, *Nuclear Disaster* (New York: Meridian, 1964), p. 24.

76. Stonier, *Nuclear Disaster.*

77. See Dr. Handler's letter of transmittal, which is contained at the beginning of the report, *Long-Term Worldwide Effects of Multiple Nuclear-Weapons Detonations.*

78. Handler, in *Long-Term Effects of Multiple Nuclear-Weapons Detonations.*

79. Feld, "The Consequences of Nuclear War," p. 13.

80. *Worldwide Effects of Nuclear War . . . Some Perspectives,* A Report of the U.S. Arms Control and Disarmament Agency (no date, but produced after the 1975 NAS report), pp. 23-24.

81. *Economic and Social Consequences of Nuclear Attacks on the United States,* Congress of the United States (Washington, D.C.: U.S. Government Printing Office, March 1979).

82. Executive Summary, *Economic and Social Consequences of Nuclear Attacks on the United States,* pp. 1-2.

83. U.S. Congress, Office of Technology Assessment, *The Effects of Nuclear War,* No. OTA-NS-89, Washington, D.C.

84. OTA, *Effects of Nuclear War,* p. 3.

85. *Scientific American* 241, no. 1 (July 1979): 35.

86. *Scientific American* (July 1979), p. 47.

87. See *Protection in the Nuclear Age,* Defense Civil Preparedness Agency, Department of Defense, H-20, February 1977, p. iii (Introduction).

88. *Protection in the Nuclear Age,* p. 49.

89. *Protection in the Nuclear Age,* pp. 50-51.

90. *Protection in the Nuclear Age,* p. 54.

Index

THE BOOK MANUFACTURE

People, States, and World Order was typeset at Meridian Graphics, Chicago, Illinois. Printing and binding was at R. R. Donnelley & Sons Company, Crawfordsville, Indiana. Cover design was by John Firestone & Associates, Canal Winchester, Ohio. Internal design was by F. E. Peacock Publishers art department. The typeface is Caledonia.